The Girl Who Just Wanted to be Loved

The Girl Who Just Wanted to be Loved

A damaged little girl
and a foster carer who wouldn't give up

ANGELA HART

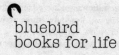

bluebird
books for life

First published 2016 by Bluebird
an imprint of Pan Macmillan
20 New Wharf Road, London N1 9RR
Associated companies throughout the world
www.panmacmillan.com

ISBN 978-1-5098-0711-6

1 3 5 7 9 8 6 4 2

A CIP catalogue record for this book is available from the British Library.

Typeset by Ellipsis Digital Limited, Glasgow
Printed and bound by CPI Group (UK) Ltd, Croydon, CR0 4YY

Visit **www.panmacmillan.com** to read more about all our books
and to buy them. You will also find features, author interviews and
news of any author events, and you can sign up for e-newsletters
so that you're always first to hear about our new releases.

1

'I'm never lucky!'

The first time we ever saw Keeley was in a Pizza Hut. She was having lunch with her social worker, and it had been arranged that my husband, Jonathan, and I would turn up casually, as if by chance.

'Unfortunately Keeley's current placement is breaking down,' our support social worker, Sandy, had explained over the phone. 'We'd like to move her as soon as possible, but she doesn't know yet. Do you think you could go and meet her, see what you think?'

It's uncommon but not unheard of for Social Services to set up a meeting like this: supposedly bumping into a social worker and a child in a relaxed setting like Pizza Hut means there is no pressure or expectation on either side.

I felt optimistic when I agreed to the plan. In the seventeen years we'd been fostering, Jonathan and I had only ever met one child we didn't think we could look after – a teenage girl who instantly gave us both the same uncomfortable feeling that we simply weren't right for her. Neither of us could put our finger on exactly why this was the case, but we decided it was wise to follow our gut instinct. We were completely honest with the social workers and the placement went no further. I'm sure it was the right thing to do, as you need to feel positive and confident, for everybody's sake, when you take a new child into your home.

'What can you tell me about Keeley?' I asked Sandy enthusiastically.

This was my typical reaction whenever a potential new foster child was mentioned. It was 2004 now, and Jonathan and I were in our late forties. We'd looked after more than thirty youngsters over the years, yet I never failed to feel a surge of excitement at the prospect of caring for another one.

Sandy began by explaining that Keeley was eight years old, an only child and had been in and out of foster care since she was five. In that time she had stayed with four sets of carers on short-term placements, to give her mother occasional breaks, and over the past twelve months she had been in full-time care with two different families.

'Why have the full-time placements not worked out?' I asked. 'What seems to be the problem?'

'Keeley's bad behaviour. Both foster carers tell similar stories. Keeley's behaviour got worse instead of better as time went on, and both carers reached breaking point after several months, saying they simply couldn't manage with her any longer. That's why we're keen for you to take her on, Angela. I'm sure you'll do a brilliant job.'

I appreciated the compliment. Sandy was in her fifties

and had a very no-nonsense attitude that seemed to entirely fit with her smart and sensible appearance. I respected her, and receiving praise from Sandy meant a great deal. Knowing that our efforts were appreciated never failed to give me a lift. Even though Jonathan and I always work as a team, fostering can be an isolated job as you are working independently in your own home, typically keeping in contact with social workers on the phone rather than seeing them in person.

After starting out as foster carers in the late eighties, for many years Jonathan and I had also been providing specialist care for children whose placements in mainstream foster homes had broken down, and who needed some extra help. We heard about the need for specialist carers through an advert on the local radio in the nineties and, after putting ourselves forward, Jonathan and I underwent extensive training in looking after teenagers with complex needs. The training was ongoing and we still do it to this day, to sharpen our fostering skills and keep up to date with new research and methods of caring for difficult children.

Even though the training courses and workshops are designed to help us deal specifically with teenagers, Social Services often call on us to help when a younger child like Keeley has nowhere else to go, because mainstream fostering is not working and they might otherwise end up in a special unit. Foster children of all ages who come to us for specialist care are generally expected to stay between three and six months before being returned to mainstream care or going back to live with family, although there are no hard and fast rules. Over the years some youngsters have stayed with us for many years after ostensibly arriving for a brief respite stay.

I arranged a time for Jonathan and I to arrive at Pizza Hut on the coming Saturday afternoon, having organised for our part-time assistant to cover us over the busy lunch-time in the florists. Once the meeting had been confirmed, Sandy called me back and gave me some more background information on Keeley.

'She was on the Child Protection Register under the category of "emotional abuse" before she came into care,' Sandy said, reading from a file. 'Keeley's mother, Tina, has been unable to bond properly with her daughter since birth. Tina has a long history of mental illness, which has resulted in her being sectioned on a number of occasions. There are reports that Keeley was smacked regularly with a slipper and locked in an empty box room when she was naughty. Her birth father has never been on the scene, but her maternal grandfather, Eric, lives next door and is a regular visitor to the family home. On a number of occasions Tina has accused Eric of sexually abusing her when she herself was a child, but nothing has ever been proven and Tina has always refused to take this further or press charges. Unfortunately, there are concerns that Keeley may have also been sexually abused by Eric, and possibly also by her mother.'

'I see,' I said quietly, disturbed by the detail, and particularly the suspicion of sexual abuse within the family and from mother to child.

'Again, nothing has been proven with regard to the suspicions about Tina,' Sandy continued. 'The concluding note in the file states: "It appears the lack of early years bonding and the negative attitude of Keeley's mother towards her child has affected Keeley's ability to interact and function socially, resulting in her sustained bad behaviour."'

'There they are,' I whispered to Jonathan as we walked into Pizza Hut. He followed my gaze to a large booth in the centre of the busy restaurant, where Keeley's social worker, Joan, was installed behind a large bowl of salad. We'd know Joan for many years and were very fond of her. She looked more like an ebullient grandmother than an extremely professional and efficient social worker of some thirty years' experience, and she had a wonderful rapport with children and foster carers alike.

Settling into the seat beside her was a striking-looking young girl with an olive complexion, deep brown eyes and a mass of long black curly hair that was held back from her face with a bright red hairband. My first thought was that Keeley looked more Spanish than English, and to add to this image she was wearing a red and white polka-dot dress with a wide, red silk ribbon tied around her waist.

'Here goes,' I muttered to Jonathan as we casually approached the booth. I was just about to feign surprise in bumping into Joan when she threw out her arms.

'Angela! Jonathan!' she exclaimed brightly. 'How lovely to see you both! How are you? Why don't you join us?'

'Oh hi, Joan,' I smiled. 'It's good to see you too, and that would be lovely. Is there space for us?'

'Of course. We can shuffle up a bit, can't we, Keeley? Angela and Jonathan, this is Keeley.'

'Pleased to meet you,' we both said, smiling at Keeley.

'Hello,' she replied, shooting us a rather unfriendly look as she moved in closer to Joan, sliding her fizzy drink swiftly across the table as she did so. Unfortunately, the next moment the large glass hit a groove in the table top and toppled over, splashing lemonade onto Keeley's pretty dress.

'Fuck!' Keeley shouted.

'Keeley,' Joan reprimanded, giving her a stern look. 'Please don't use language like that.'

A group of teenagers on the next table looked over and started sniggering.

'Well what d'you fucking expect?' Keeley ranted. 'Look at the state of me!'

She threw Jonathan and me an accusing look, but we didn't react. Joan was in charge of this situation and we had to let her deal with it.

'I'm very sorry,' Joan said to us, as she mopped up the spillage with paper napkins. 'Now, Keeley, let's start again shall we? You can go and refill your drink. It was just an accident so let's not allow it to spoil our lunch.'

Keeley scowled and then stomped off to refill her drink at the self-service machine. I felt a pang of pity for her. To hear bad language from any young child always upsets me, and not just because I find the words offensive. It usually shows that the child has been exposed to an unsuitable environment, and that some of their childhood innocence has been taken from them too soon. The fact Keeley was such an appealing-looking girl and dressed in such a pretty outfit somehow made her foul language all the more shocking; it was completely at odds with her sweet appearance.

Jonathan and I ordered a coffee and chatted to Joan about what the weather would be like the following day, when there was a popular country fair taking place in the region.

'Can I go?' Keeley asked, her ears pricking up. 'Is it like a fairground?'

'It's more like a country show, with animals on display and a farmers' market and stalls,' Joan explained. 'I don't know if your foster carer is planning to go, you'll have to ask her.'

'There's no chance,' Keeley snorted, tossing her hair back and rolling her eyes. 'She won't take me!'

'You don't know until you ask,' Joan said. 'It's a big event and a lot of people go. You never know, you may just be lucky.'

'No, I already know what the answer will be. I'm never lucky! I fucking hate her!'

'Keeley!' Joan hushed. 'What have I said about your language?'

'Urgh? What language?'

'Your bad language. Now, come on, let's not have any more of it. Let's get on with our lunch. I'm starving.'

Jonathan and I drank our coffee and tried to make conversation, but Keeley was far more interested in when her pizza was arriving and what was on the desert menu than chatting with a couple of strangers like us. That was perfectly understandable, and Jonathan and I politely finished our drinks and said our goodbyes. The meeting must have lasted less than fifteen minutes, but it was long enough for us to make up our minds.

'We'd love to have Keeley,' I told Sandy on the phone later. 'Please let me know when she can come and stay. I'm looking forward to it already.'

Keeley was undoubtedly going to be a challenge. The bad language and petulant behaviour did her no favours, but I was optimistic nonetheless. She had spirit and character, and I wanted to help her.

2

'I've hurt myself'

'Angela! Come quick!'

It was Sue, who's a good friend and neighbour, shouting and hammering on my door.

'What is it?' I gasped. 'Is everything all right?'

'No. It's Keeley. She's hurt one of the Morris boys.'

There was a recreation area behind our house where lots of the local children played. It was safe and overlooked by houses on all sides. Parents were generally very happy to let their little ones out to play on their own as most of the neighbours could see onto the 'rec', as it was known, from their home. I could have easily kept an eye on Keeley from our lounge window, which was on the middle floor of our three-storey town house. This gave me a very clear view across the football fields and play area, but I had decided to stay out with Keeley, to make sure she settled in with the other children and played nicely. She seemed to be joining in perfectly well, and so when I eventually needed to use

9

the bathroom I was happy to ask Sue to watch her for me for a few minutes.

'I'll be as quick as I can,' I said to Sue, after first explaining to Keeley that I had to nip inside.

'Take your time, Angela,' Sue smiled. 'She's absolutely fine and I'll stay right here. Don't rush.'

Having Sue running to fetch me like this, just minutes later, was therefore very unexpected, and alarming.

Following the meeting in Pizza Hut, Keeley was now staying with us for a weekend trial visit, with a view to moving in full time at the end of the month. She had been in a pleasant and receptive mood from the moment we'd collected her from her full-time foster carer, meeting as we did in a retail park halfway between our two homes. I'd had a good feeling about Keeley's stay. Her eyes were shining and she climbed into our car very willingly, bubbling with excitement and telling us she was really looking forward to the visit.

Keeley was chatty and pleasant throughout the car journey and showed none of the surliness or rude behaviour we'd seen at Pizza Hut. As soon as we arrived back I showed Keeley around our home and florist shop, which we'd owned and run for many years and was incorporated into the front of the ground floor of our house. I also explained to her that we had two teenage boys also staying with us, and that she would meet them later, when they came home for dinner.

'Wow!' she giggled when I showed her to her large bedroom, which was along the landing from the boys' bed-rooms and the bathroom they would all share, on the top floor of the house.

'I like it!' Keeley smiled, deep dimples appearing in her golden cheeks. 'It's nicer than at *her* house.'

I let this remark go, not wanting to enter into a discussion about Keeley's current foster carer. As soon as the guided tour was over Keeley had asked if she could play out, telling me she wanted to show her ragdoll, Jinty, to the other children she had seen outside.

'Of course you can,' I said, pleased she had the confidence to put herself out there so soon after arriving. 'Just make sure you look after Jinty!'

'I will,' she replied sweetly, looking at me with her big brown eyes. 'I promise.'

I took her outside and introduced her to some of the children I knew and then for a good twenty minutes I sat on a bench with Sue and watched Keeley tearing around the field, playing tag and taking turns pushing her doll around in a toy buggy belonging to another little girl. It was lovely to see Keeley looking so happy and carefree, running around in the fresh air with her mass of shiny black curls tumbling down her back.

This was to be the first of two weekend visits. As far as Keeley was concerned she was simply coming to us for respite, in the same way she used to go on short breaks with foster carers when she was still living with her mum. However, if all went well, her social worker would explain to

Keeley that she could move in with us full time, if she was happy to.

I had been thinking about whether this would happen while watching Keeley play, and hoping that it would. When Sue banged on my door I had two thoughts in quick succession: how had she hurt the Morris boy, and would this incident spoil the plans for Keeley's move?

'What do you mean, she's hurt one of the Morris boys,' I said, running back to the rec. I normally used the gate that leads onto a passageway to the rear, left-hand side of our house, but there was also a gate at the bottom of our garden that opened directly onto the back of the rec. It was fractionally quicker to go that way, and so I tore across the back lawn, with Sue dashing behind me.

'I'm not sure what went on,' Sue confessed. 'I'm really sorry, Angela, it must have all happened in the blink of an eye. I didn't see anything until it was too late.'

To my dismay, I saw Ben Morris, who was about six or seven years old, sitting on the grass and sobbing uncontrollably. He was clutching his arm and his older sister was crouched beside him holding a tissue spotted with blood. She turned to me and scowled.

'That brat pinched him really hard,' she accused, pointing at Keeley.

'Liar!' Keeley spat.

'You're the liar!' Ben's sister retorted.

'What on earth has happened?' I asked. 'Ben, are you all right, love? Can you tell me what happened?'

The boy ignored me and continued to cry, hiding his face on his sister's shoulder.

'They were playing tag,' Ben's sister stated. 'And *she* just pinched him for no reason.'

I looked at Sue who shook her head. 'I'm sorry, Angela,' she repeated, 'I just didn't see what happened . . .'

Keeley was standing a few feet away from all of the other children who had gathered around Ben. She was clutching Jinty the ragdoll defensively to her chest, and her lip was curled angrily.

'Liar!' she said again, scowling at Ben's sister.

'You're the liar,' Ben's sister repeated.

'Keeley, I want you to tell me what happened,' I said calmly. 'Did you pinch Ben's arm or is there some other explanation?'

'Dunno,' she shrugged insolently, jutting her chin up and arching her dark eyebrows. The expression on her face said, 'What do I care? Prove it!'

'How can she just say "dunno"?' Ben's sister shouted. 'She pinched him so hard he's bleeding, look! I saw her do it!'

The girl held up the bloodied tissue and pointed out that there were indents still visible on the inside of Ben's forearm. It certainly looked feasible that he had been pinched, and pinched very hard indeed. Several of the other children backed up the account Ben's sister had given, but Keeley refused point blank to admit she had done anything wrong.

'Perhaps it was an accident?' I offered. 'Is that possible, Keeley? Did you snatch Ben's arm too hard without meaning to, during the game of tag? Perhaps you caught him with your nails, by mistake?'

'No, I told you. I didn't even touch him!' she yelled, eyes narrowed into a steely stare.

'You did!' chorused several of the other children. 'We saw you!'

'Liars! I was nowhere near him. He said he would steal Jinty off me and so I was keeping away from him, if you must know!'

Ben looked up and gave her a withering look. 'Why would I want your stupid doll?' he sniffed. 'You're lying, liar!'

I ended up bringing Keeley in and advising Ben's sister to take him home to his mum. Later on, when Jonathan was home after closing the shop, I popped round to see Ben's mother. Most of the neighbours knew we were foster carers and thankfully Ben's mum was very understanding and told me not to worry; Ben was fine and no lasting harm had been done.

'What did you say to Ben's mum?' Jonathan asked afterwards.

'I apologised profusely and said I would have words with Keeley again, when perhaps she had had time to reflect and might tell the truth. I also said it wouldn't happen again.'

It was Jonathan's turn to raise an eyebrow now, and I knew exactly what he was thinking.

'It could happen again, couldn't it?' I said, stating the obvious.

we were always very vigilant about keeping any sharp objects out of sight and reach, including tweezers, razors and kitchen knives. It had become second nature to us, to the point where even Jonathan's tool shed had appropriate locks on the door and every drawer of his tool chest.

'I used my scissors, because I didn't like the way it looked,' Keeley said, staring at me with unblinking eyes.

'Your scissors? I didn't know you had scissors.'

'Yes. They're only small ones and they are not very good. I keep them in my pencil case, for cutting at school.'

I took some comfort from the fact that the scissors Keeley had used were most probably those semi-blunt, round-ended safety ones, meant only for paper cutting in the classroom. This would explain the rough, stubby cut; at least, thank God, she hadn't been manoeuvring a large pair of sharp scissors in front of her face.

'I think your hair is beautiful, sweetheart. It always looks absolutely lovely. I can't understand why you would want to change it in any way. When I was your age my hair was short and straight. I'd have done anything for a head of pretty curls like yours. You're a lucky girl.'

'I'm not. I hate my hair. I don't like the colour, or the curls.'

'I'm sorry to hear that's how you feel,' I soothed, realising I wasn't going to convince Keeley to change her mind. 'But the thing is, you won't make it look better by cutting it yourself. Please don't do that again, Keeley. If you want to change the style, then it's something we can talk about.'

'OK,' she nodded. 'Sorry.'

'I'd also like you to give me the scissors from your pencil case. From now on I will look after them. If you want to use them at home you need to ask me, and I will sit with you while you do your cutting. There's no need to carry them to school, they have plenty you can use in the classroom.'

'OK. Sorry, Angela.'

She gazed at Jonathan and me with puppy-dog eyes, as if she wanted us to offer more sympathy and more attention. I didn't think this would be helpful, as she clearly wanted to wallow. Instead, I swiftly turned my attention back to her arm, cleaning her little cut with a splash of warm water and applying a dab of antiseptic cream.

'There we are!' I said brightly. 'Now then, we thought we'd go to the cinema this evening. Would you like that?'

Keeley looked bemused.

'Aren't you going to tell me off?'

'What for?'

'Er, hurting my arm, and cutting my hair?'

'Well, you don't know how you hurt your arm, so how can I tell you off for that? And we've talked about your hair. I understand you didn't do it to be naughty. You did it because you'd like to change your hair, didn't you?'

Keeley nodded half-heartedly.

'And now you know that you can talk about changing your hair, if that is what you want to do, but that you can't cut it yourself. You agree with that, don't you?'

Keeley nodded again, but still appeared perplexed that her mischief had not created a bigger drama.

18

I went on to explain that I was not allowed to arrange for Keeley to have a haircut without permission from her mother or social worker, but I told her that if she came to stay with us again this was something we might be able to look into arranging, if her mum agreed.

'I'm not that bothered, really,' she replied, looking slightly exasperated at my response. 'My hair's not that bad.'

'Oh well, that's good,' I replied chirpily. 'Now then, *Scooby Doo 2: Monsters Unleashed* has just come out. Do you fancy that?'

'Yes!' Keeley said. 'I love Scooby Doo!'

'That's great, so do I. I'll book the tickets.'

Later, when Keeley was out of earshot, Jonathan whispered that he was glad I hadn't mentioned what else was showing at the cinema.

'Why?' I asked.

'Look,' he smirked, pointing to a listing in the local paper for the film *Confessions of a Teenage Drama Queen*. 'That one might have been a bit too close to home!'

The two of us hadn't actually discussed Keeley's evident penchant for drama at this point, but we didn't have to. It had been clear to see and, in any case, more often than not Jonathan and I have quite a telepathic understanding of what the other is thinking.

'So you've worked that out too?' I smiled. 'She's a bit of an attention seeker, isn't she?'

'Well, it's not exactly rocket science,' Jonathan replied,

giving me a smile. 'I guess we'll have to keep an eye on that, won't we? I think we could be in for a few more amateur dramatics, don't you?'

3

'Can I come and stay again?'

The cinema trip was a great success. The two boys we had staying with us, Carl, who was fifteen, and Phillip, thirteen, chose to stay at home, which Keeley seemed very pleased about.

'So it's just me and you watching the film, Angela?' she had asked excitedly.

'You, me and Jonathan,' I replied.

'You're both taking me?' she asked, furrowing her brow.

'Of course. We both love going to the cinema and we love all types of films.'

'Really? That's good.'

My mum, Thelma, had been vetted and passed by Social Services to babysit for any foster children we had staying with us, which was an arrangement that worked very well. Mum was in her seventies now and had suffered from rheumatoid arthritis for a long time. She was not as active as she used to be, but her mind was as sharp as ever and all the foster children we had staying with us over the years seemed to really appreciate her company. Carl and Phillip were no exception. The three of them often had a game of cards or watched snooker on TV together, which Mum thoroughly enjoyed. Also, I think the boys felt they had a bit more free reign in the house when Jonathan and I were off the scene, though this was not actually true, as Mum never missed a trick.

Anyhow, Keeley was delighted with the early evening arrangements and chatted excitedly all the way to the cinema.

'Can I sit in the middle?' she asked as we all took our seats in the auditorium, and of course Jonathan and I both said that she could.

'Can I hold the popcorn too?'

'Yes, sweetheart,' I said. 'As long as you don't eat it all!'

'No, I won't, I promise! You can have as much as you like.'

Keeley giggled and munched her way through the film and it was a pleasure to be in her company. Driving home, she discussed all the characters and decided that she liked bespectacled Velma better than the more glamorous, flame-haired Daphne.

'Velma's very clever, isn't she?' I said. 'Is that why you like her the best?'

'No,' Keeley said thoughtfully. 'I just don't like Daphne. She's too pretty. She's probably a bitch.'

'Keeley!' I gasped, shocked at how easily the word tripped off her tongue. 'You can't use language like that, it's not nice.'

'Sorry. Pretty girls are always bitches though. I don't like the pretty girls at school.'

'But you are a very pretty girl, Keeley. How would you like it if people said nasty things about you, just because of the way you look, and perhaps even before they got to know you?'

'Well they wouldn't, because I'm not pretty.'

'That's not true, sweetheart. You are a very pretty girl indeed.'

'You're only saying that,' she huffed. 'I know I'm not.'

Just like when we'd discussed her hairstyle, it was clear Keeley wasn't going to budge on this. This time I could see this was more than an attention-seeking ploy; Keeley really did seem to have a genuinely low opinion of her appearance, and that was something I would need to keep an eye on too.

The next day Keeley asked if she could play out again and I reluctantly agreed, telling her that I was going to sit out on the bench and watch, to make sure there was not a repeat of any trouble at the rec.

'It wasn't my fault,' she said defensively.

'I never said it was. We don't want any more trouble though, do we? I'll be there, to make sure you're all right.'

'OK,' she said, narrowing her eyes. 'Can you go on that bench over there though?'

She pointed to the bench furthest from the area where all the children played.

'Fine,' I said, realizing she was worried I might cramp her style.

Keeley had brought a skipping rope with her and she told me she was practising for a sponsored skip that was taking place in her school the following week.

'I'll sponsor you,' I said, hoping the encouragement would make her focus on the practice rather than winding up the other kids, as I feared she might try to do.

I sat myself down and then watched as Keeley entered the play area. I was relieved to see her go straight up to two girls and start talking. They looked about the same age as Keeley, and moments later the girls both sat down on the grass and watched Keeley skip. After a few minutes Keeley let one of the other girls have a turn skipping while she sat down next to her friend. They all seemed to be getting along fine, but then the girls suddenly ran off together, leaving Keeley alone.

As soon as they had gone I saw Keeley turn around and glance over at me. I smiled back and gave her a little wave. The next minute Keeley ran out of the play area, taking herself onto the patch of field furthest from me. Then she began skipping very quickly and rather recklessly along one of the concrete paths surrounding the grassy park area. Seconds later she tripped herself up – apparently on purpose, though I couldn't be certain – and then she dropped to her knees and stayed on the ground, looking quite helpless.

Once again, I found myself running across the rec. From what I had seen I didn't think Keeley could have really hurt herself, at least not badly, but of course I wanted to make sure she was OK.

'Are you all right, sweetheart?' I shouted over, but she was crying now and covering her face with her hands, and she didn't reply.

When I reached Keeley's side I was shocked to see that both her knees were badly grazed and bleeding.

'I fell over,' she said. 'It was an accident, sorry.'

'There's no need to say sorry, love. Come on, let's get you inside.'

'I'm useless at skipping.'

'No, you're not. I saw you skipping beautifully, and sharing nicely with those two girls.'

Keeley smiled through her tears as she walked tentatively back to the house, and once she was sitting at the kitchen table, her knees cleaned and dressed with two large plasters, she seemed to be not just all right, but in her element.

'I like you looking after me, Angela,' she beamed, as I quickly noted down the details on an accident sheet. 'Can I come and stay again?'

I was required to keep detailed notes and diaries for Social Services, and on the sheet I made a note of exactly what I'd observed on the rec, the time Keeley's accident took place and how I had responded and treated her.

It was time-consuming filling in so much paperwork but I was always happy to do it, and still am. When Jonathan and I had started out as foster carers in 1987 there were no such formalities and even the scant paperwork that was generated within Social Services sometimes went astray. Thankfully, when records were computerised during the nineties this problem went away, and nowadays the system is even better. I think the notes and records that carers are required to keep not only help Social Services provide the best, safest and most consistent care for a child – not to mention an accurate report in case an incident leads to a court case – but they can also help foster carers to take stock and move forwards. In my experience, being obliged to sit down and write a precise summary of what has happened in a daily log can be therapeutic. On many occasions putting pen to paper has helped me make sense of a situation, or made me see it from another angle, which I think can only be a good thing.

Just as Keeley was asking me if she could come and stay again, Jonathan walked into the kitchen.

'Oh dear, Keeley, have you been in the wars again?' he asked kindly, but she looked straight through him and turned to me once more.

'Can I, Angela?' she implored very seriously. 'Can I come and stay with you again?'

'I'll talk to your social worker,' I said, not wanting to make any promises I may not be able to keep. 'Leave it with me, sweetheart. I'd like that too.'

4

'We can't keep any secrets'

Keeley came for a second visit two weeks later, and this time she turned up with her head full of hundreds of lice and a bruise on her cheek.

'My foster carer pushed me against a wall, Angela,' she said, as she climbed into our car at the retail park where we picked her up. As she spoke Keeley looked at me with her now familiar doe eyes, and she batted her eyelashes in an exaggerated way, making herself look forlorn and vulnerable.

'She pushed you against a wall?' I replied, buckling my seatbelt and turning to check she was fastening hers in the back of the car.

When you employ this mirroring technique, repeating back what a child has said, the hope is that they will carry on talking without the risk of being influenced by a leading question. Unfortunately, often the conversation dries up, because without a direct prompt the child doesn't know what to say next, or simply finds it easier to say nothing. This was not the case at all with Keeley.

'Yes, she pushed me out the way, and that's how I got the bruise,' she said before launching into a breathless account of how her foster carer had told her off for something, and then shoved her into the kitchen wall, apparently while trying to get past her to leave the room.

I was upset to hear this and encouraged Keeley to give me more details, though I also had to explain to her that I would need to pass this information to Social Services.

'Do you have to tell them everything?' she asked.

'Yes, I do.'

'Why?'

'Because that is the rule. We can't keep any secrets, and so it's important you tell me things exactly as they happened.'

Keeley then admitted she had done 'something' wrong – though she couldn't remember what – immediately beforehand. From her explanation it sounded like the foster carer might have inadvertently pushed her into the wall as she tried to get away, maybe to stop the situation escalating. I didn't imagine for one minute that the foster carer had pushed Keeley deliberately, or intended to hurt her, but of course I wasn't there and so this was clearly just my opinion.

The view I formed may have been completely inaccurate and when it came to reporting this to Social Services, as I would have to do, in this situation my opinion didn't count in any case. I would have to pass on Keeley's verbatim account without adding any of my own views, and then it would be over to the social workers to investigate.

Many years earlier, we'd had an incident in the park involving Jonathan and a teenage boy we had staying with us. They were happily playing with a Frisbee when the boy, who had a very unpredictable temper, suddenly and very deliberately flung the Frisbee directly in Jonathan's face, knocking his sunglasses off. Jonathan was furious and, in the heat of the moment, he lost his temper and swore at the boy. Jonathan apologised as soon as he'd calmed down, but he had no choice but to phone Social Services and report himself for what he had said and how he reacted. The call was logged and followed up by a social worker, who praised Jonathan for owning up straight away and giving a truthful account of what happened. She also talked to the boy very fairly about what he had done wrong, and no further action had been taken.

We felt the social worker handled the situation really well. Jonathan had never been involved in anything like that before, and nothing of that nature has ever occurred since. We discussed how you need to be extremely patient to be a foster carer, and the social worker acknowledged that of course it's impossible to never be impatient, or to never lose your temper.

'I couldn't do your job,' she said, which is something many social workers have said to us over the years.

I was reminded of this conversation when I came across a 'thought of the day' recently, on the website of The Post

Institute, which is an American organisation offering advice and support for carers of children with challenging behaviour. The thought of the day pointed out that we cannot be patient all of the time, commenting wryly that it would help if you lived in a monastery and 'didn't have a child demanding of you each moment, as you also have the demands of life pulling at you'. The article went on to say that you should of course apologise to the child when you lose patience, but added that you should also apologise to yourself, because you have upset and offended yourself. This was certainly true in Jonathan's case. He felt terrible for what he had done, and he regretted the incident personally, as well as on behalf of the teenager.

Ultimately, that experience has always stayed with us, reminding us how life can very easily turn on a sixpence, and how very careful and professional we need to be in our daily lives. Everybody does lose his or her patience. When you are a foster carer you are often pushed to the limits and you have to work very hard to keep yourself in check, because there is a tremendous amount at stake.

This is just one of the many disciplines we have learned over the years. We have also been trained never to pass judgement on another carer, or any child's parent or relative, whatever the story we may have heard, or whatever unsavoury facts we are party to. An extreme example of this is when we once had a child staying with us who had been sexually abused by her father. She still adored her dad despite what he had done to her, and we had to take her to supervised contact sessions with him and sit quietly outside, keeping our feelings about this man completely to ourselves while he played happily with his daughter.

Similarly, we are also trained never to judge or question a child when they make a disclosure. I'm sure some people might have questioned whether Keeley had exaggerated or even made up the story about how she got the bruise. After all, we'd had the suspicious injury to Ben's arm, her own arm and the apparent accident with her skipping rope, but my instinct was not to openly doubt Keeley in any way, as that would also go against everything I've been taught over the years.

Asking a child 'are you sure this really happened?' or 'are you sure it happened that way?' are phrases that should not be in the vocabulary of any foster carer. You never know when a child might be on the brink of telling you something very important, and so you must always be ready and willing to listen, and to make the child feel they are being heard and believed in every scenario you come across. Some youngsters take years and years to find the courage to talk about what has taken place in their life, and being doubted by a carer after they have made a disclosure of any sort can be very damaging indeed. In the worst-case scenario it can make the child clam up completely, with devastating effects on their long-term recovery.

I knew that when we got home and I put the call in to Social Services, giving them Keeley's account of how she got the bruise, it would mean that her former foster carer could be suspended from looking after any kids until the case had been fully investigated. Keeley was her only foster child at the time, but even so this would inevitably cause a great deal of distress and disruption to the carer's life. I was worried about this, but once again it was not something I had any choice or control over.

I've learned that to succeed in fostering you also need to be very pragmatic and actually quite tough – the sort of person who can diligently follow rules and guidelines, but also has the guts to challenge the authorities when they feel a child isn't getting what they need.

As new foster carers, Jonathan and I were concerned that if we spoke out Social Services may disagree with our views, and we were worried about being dropped as carers if we stuck our heads above the parapet. Nowadays it's very different, and this is down to the excellent training we've received ever since becoming specialist carers. From that point on, in the nineties, it was made clear to us that it was our duty to be there for the child and to fight for their rights if need be. Our support social worker would be there to back us up, and if they didn't agree with our views we could discuss the situation together and work out a plan going forward.

Since then Jonathan and I have had the confidence to always speak our mind to social workers and their managers, because our main concern is the child, and we will always fight their corner, even if it doesn't make us popular. I'm not worried anymore, because I've learned that if you follow Social Services protocol, make the necessary reports in the correct manner and behave with integrity, with the child's interests at heart, you cannot be unfairly judged or penalised. Sometimes this means stepping outside of Social Services to fight for a child's rights, and I have done this many times after first discussing it with our support social worker and gaining their approval.

An example of this is when Jonathan and I had a very frustrating problem getting a child in our care into school locally. She had special needs and came to us from a different county, many miles away, and both her social worker and ours had pulled out all the stops to try to make her transfer swift and smooth. The girl was in her GCSE year and so it was important she didn't miss any lessons. A school place was available on our doorstep but at the eleventh hour red tape held everything up. The problem was that the girl had ADHD and needed extra support. She had been statemented to this effect while still living at her former address, but the extra funding required to educate her had been allocated to her home county, as that was the way the system worked. Her allocated funding had to be passed on to our county so she could take up her school place, but for some unknown reason this didn't happen when it should have done.

The girl ended up sitting at home or coming into the shop with me when she should have been in the classroom, which was an outrageous situation. After exhausting all the regular channels of communication with Social Services I told my social worker I was going to contact our local education authority directly, to discuss the situation and potentially take up the case with the Special Educational Needs and Disability Tribunal, which I had researched. The social worker supported me, and fortunately the situation was resolved very soon after I wrote a strong letter to the LEA. The child finally went to school, having missed a month of lessons completely unnecessarily.

Soon after we arrived home from the retail park, I did what was needed and put the call in to Social Services about Keeley's bruise, passing on everything Keeley had told me, word for word, to a duty social worker. I also wrote notes in my daily diary about the state of Keeley's hair with all the lice, for the social worker to read at her next visit. However badly this reflected on her previous foster carer, it wasn't right that Keeley had such a bad case of head lice, and I had a duty to flag it up.

'Can I play out?' Keeley had asked as we pulled up at our house.

'You can later,' I said. 'But I've noticed your hair needs a good wash first. Will you let me do it for you?'

'Why? I normally wash it in the shower by myself.'

'I think you may have head lice, Keeley. Has your head been itching?'

'Yes.'

'I thought so. I think we'll wash your hair over the bath and I can comb it through with conditioner to get the lice out. Then I'll put some special lotion on that should clear the problem up. I've got some in the cupboard.'

'Have you got nits?'

'No, but lots of children get them and so it's something

I keep in the house. It's very common, Keeley. Don't worry about it, we'll soon have you sorted out.'

She didn't argue, and for the next hour or so I painstakingly combed through her long, thick curls with a fine metal nit comb, watching scores of live lice of different sizes fall from her hair as she held her head over the bath. Afterwards I dried and plaited her hair, which really suited her, and she finally went out to play, taking her ragdoll, Jinty, with her once more. I reminded her to play nicely with the other children and told her that this time I would be watching from the house. She assured me very sweetly that she would, and I felt a surge of love for her. It must have been awful having all those lice in her hair, and having to sit there for so long while I tried to tease them out. Keeley didn't complain though. I admired her for that, and it made me want to care for her and protect her even more. She deserved to be loved and cherished, and I wanted to make her life as happy and comfortable as I possibly could.

'How's she doing?' Jonathan asked, coming to stand next to me at the window.

'She seems very chirpy,' I replied. 'She's a lovely little thing, really. Mind you, I've noticed she's usually good when she's getting one-to-one attention from me. I suppose that figures, given her mother's issues.'

I'd gleaned a little bit more information about Keeley's mother in my last telephone conversation with our support social worker.

'Can you tell me anything more about the emotional

abuse Keeley suffered?' I asked Sandy. 'Only I've been thinking about how her mother failed to bond properly with her.'

Sandy explained that Keeley had a therapy session once a month, principally to help her deal with the emotional neglect she had suffered from birth.

'I can't disclose the details of the therapy because of patient confidentiality, of course, but what I can tell you, Angela, is that Keeley's mother has the mental age of a young adolescent. She wasn't equipped to care for her daughter properly. A note in the file says: "Tina is not a loving and consistent mother figure to Keeley. She is emotionally absent, neglectful, unpredictable and occasionally violent." That is why Keeley was eventually placed on the Child Protection Register.'

'I see,' I replied thoughtfully.

'Unfortunately,' Sandy went on, 'by that point Keeley was six years old and damage had already been done, not least because it appears the only regular help Tina received was from Keeley's grandfather, Eric, whose character was, and still is, in question.'

After I'd plaited Keeley's hair and she'd gone out to play I stood by the back gate, watching her approach a large group of children gathered in the small play area in the far corner of the rec. Keeley went straight up to a girl on the swings, and almost immediately began hitting her on the legs with Jinty, the ragdoll.

I ran across the field calling Keeley's name, but by the

time I arrived at the swings she was out of control, shouting and swearing and lashing out at several children.

'She's just tried to kick me between the legs!' one young boy blurted out.

'She's crazy,' the girl on the swing shouted.

'I'm sorry about all this,' I said, taking hold of Keeley's arm. 'What do you have to say, Keeley? I think you have some apologising to do.'

'What for?' she said, fluttering her eyelashes and cuddling Jinty, as if butter wouldn't melt in her mouth. 'They started it! She wouldn't let me go on the swing!'

'Did you ask nicely for a turn?'

'Yes!' Keeley said indignantly.

'No she didn't!' several of the kids testified.

'Come on, Keeley, I'm taking you in. I'm sorry, kids. I'll sort this out at home.'

The words hung in the air. How was I going to sort this out? I wasn't sure yet, but I vowed to myself that I was going to, somehow. It wasn't Keeley's fault that she was like this. She had been dealt a very difficult hand in her early life, and I was going to give her all the help and support I possibly could to help her grow into a happy, decent and kind young person.

5

'You're a total bastard!'

Keeley finally moved in with us full time in the spring, about five weeks after we'd first met her. Shortly after her last weekend visit, we'd had what is known as a 'core meeting' to discuss the arrangements, which was held at an old and rather run down Social Services building close to Keeley's two previous foster homes and her mother's flat, some thirty miles away from where we lived. Jonathan and I were technically 'out of area' for Keeley, but this was not a problem. We often took in children from even further afield, either because of child protection issues which meant it was safer for a child to live away from their old neighbourhood, or more typically because there were no other specialist carers available closer to home. This was the case with Keeley.

She had been in respite care since her weekend stay with us, as the allegations she made about her foster carer giving her the bruise on her cheek meant she could no longer stay in that placement. The carer was under investigation for the time being, so it was not feasible for Keeley to stay and emergency cover was hastily found. Unfortunately, Keeley couldn't move in with us until her transfer to our local primary school and other practicalities were dealt with, and the core meeting had been held to agree all of these arrangements. This was attended by our social worker, Sandy, plus Sandy's manager, Sheila Briggs, and Keeley's social worker, Joan.

The first thing we learned after Jonathan and I took a seat around the large wooden table in the Social Services office was that Keeley wasn't happy in respite care and couldn't wait to move in with us. Joan had found this out after speaking to Keeley in advance of the meeting, which of course we were pleased to hear.

'I asked Keeley if she minded moving to a new area and a new school when she moved in with Mr and Mrs Hart,' Joan reported. 'Keeley said that no, she didn't mind at all and in fact she couldn't wait. She doesn't like her respite carer and wants to move as quickly as possible. She said she would miss her friends when she moved out of the area, but she wasn't worried about this and knew she would make new friends, and might still be able to see her old ones if she went to her old neighbourhood to visit her mother in the future.'

It can take up to twenty-eight days for a child to transfer between carers, as this is the notice period a carer must give if they want a child removed. Keeley's previous full-time carer had already given her notice, but of course with the investigation now taking place this was irrelevant in any case. We were ready to take Keeley in as soon as she was able to come, and it was agreed at the meeting that her transfer to us would be prioritised and put in place as quickly as possible.

As well as setting up a new school place, the child needs to be registered with our local doctor, dentist and optician, and we need to organise contact visits with the parent or parents, where appropriate. In Keeley's case it was decided that her mother would be allowed weekly, supervised contact in a small Social Services office near her home. Jonathan and I agreed we would take Keeley there on a Friday for 4.30 p.m. My mum would come over to our house to be in for Carl and Phillip coming in from school and our assistant would close up the shop for us. If ever we couldn't manage the round trip to the contact session, which could take up to an hour and three-quarters, we were told we could make arrangements in advance for a social worker to take Keeley there and back.

Keeley's monthly therapy session took place on a Monday afternoon at 4 p.m., also in her old neighbourhood, and so we would therefore need to ask for permission to take her out of school early that day in order to get her there on time, as well as making the same arrangements for Carl, Phillip and the shop to be taken care of.

These arrangements were necessary because of the so-called 'safe caring policy' we had been taught to follow, which recommended we travel in twos wherever possible. This policy is designed to reduce the risk of a child making a false accusation against their foster carer, and as Keeley had already made various allegations in her past, many of which were not proven, we would try to stick to this advice as much as possible. Once, years earlier, a social worker had recommended that if only one of us could travel with a child we should record in our daily notes what time we set off and arrived at the destination. Jonathan and I weren't particularly happy with this, as it meant relying on the people at our destination to remember and be able to verify what time we arrived, which didn't seem very feasible. In any case, we nearly always worked as a team, and it was only the school runs that I ever did on my own, which I felt were safe to do as they were very short and of course the child would be registered on arrival.

We were given no further details about Keeley's therapy, so all we knew was that it was to help her deal with the emotional neglect she had suffered in her younger years. I mentioned to the group that Keeley seemed to have problems playing nicely with other children, and that she used bad language at times, and it was suggested by one of the social workers that we could use a star chart to reward good behaviour, and 'time out' in her bedroom if Keeley misbehaved. I agreed to try both, though something told me it might be a little ambitious to think Keeley's complex problems could be tackled with such simple tactics.

'So, is everybody happy?' Sheila asked brightly, as she signed the necessary paperwork and closed the meeting.

'Yes,' all the adults responded, nodding and thanking the manager for her time, and for agreeing to prioritise Keeley's case.

*

Keeley eventually moved in about a week later, on a Friday. She was absolutely delighted when we picked her up and drove her to our house with all her belongings filling the boot of my Volvo. She had brought a *Now That's What I Call Music!* CD with her and asked if she could play it on the journey, which we said was fine. All the way back to our house she sang her heart out to her favourite songs: Beyoncé's 'Crazy in Love', Jamelia's 'Superstar' and 'Sleeping With The Light On' by Busted. She asked for the same tracks to be played over and over again, and Jonathan and I practically knew the lyrics off by heart by the end of the journey. It was a pleasure. Keeley was happy, and her mood was infectious.

She was extremely excited when she looked around her new school later that day, too, and she was thrilled to bits when I took her to the uniform shop in town the next morning and bought her everything she needed.

'Thank you, Angela,' she beamed as the lady behind the counter handed her a bulging bag full of new clothes. 'I love the uniform so much! It's better than my last one.'

'Goodness me, I don't often see children so enthusiastic,' the shop assistant commented. 'I hope you enjoy your new school.'

'I will,' Keeley replied sweetly. 'Thanks for helping.'

Keeley remained in high spirits all the way back to our house, and she revelled in finding a place in her wardrobe for all her new clothes. She had brought a large collection of dolls of all shapes and sizes stuffed into a large black bin bag. Once she'd put away her uniform she arranged the dolls in neat rows under her window, with the big ones at the back, medium-sized dolls in the middle and all her Barbies and Sindys sitting at the front. Jinty, the ragdoll, presided over them all from her prime spot on Keeley's pillow.

'Come and see, Angela!' she called when she'd finished arranging her room.

'Well, I *am* impressed,' I smiled. 'You've done a lovely job, Keeley. It looks great in here. Now, would you like to come down to the kitchen with me? I'm getting the dinner ready.'

'OK. Can I bring my colouring?'

'Of course you can. You can sit at the table with it. I've got plenty of coloured pencils and felt tips if you need them.'

'Wow! Really? Show me!'

Keeley had a great big colouring book full of extremely intricate designs, many of which she'd started but not finished. Her work was really neat, though, and once she was installed at the kitchen table she took great delight in chatting to me about which colour pen she was going to use next, while also keeping an eye on what I was cooking.

'It smells lovely, Angela. I'm really hungry. How long will it be?'

'About fifteen minutes. Carl and Phillip will be in then, and I'm sure they'll be hungry too. They usually are!'

The mention of the boys didn't seem to please Keeley. In

fact she scowled, and when they appeared in the kitchen soon afterwards she resolutely ignored them. She had met them before, of course, but on her weekend visits she hadn't had a lot to do with them and had hardly spent any time with them.

'Aren't you going to say hello to the boys, Keeley?' I chivvied. 'They've been looking forward to you moving in.'

'No. And I bet you are only saying that.'

'I'm not. The boys have both told me it would be nice to see you again, and have you stay for longer this time, haven't you, boys?'

Carl and Phillip both nodded. They were nice lads and had seemed perfectly happy at the news that Keeley was moving in but, like a lot of teenagers, being expressive was not their forte. They didn't convince Keeley, and she stayed in an uncommunicative mood all through the meal while Jonathan gamely encouraged the boys to chat about their day at school.

Carl was in Year 10 and had end of year exams coming up, and so he was working hard on his revision. He was a gentle, diligent boy who had been with us for about six months, and he was no trouble at all. He swam for a local club two or three nights a week and often spent the weekend with his father or one of his older brothers who lived close by.

'I think I might have to cut back on the swimming during the exam period,' he said. 'It's taking up too much time.'

'That sounds sensible,' Jonathan remarked. 'I'm sure the

club will understand. Do you like swimming, Keeley? Perhaps we could take you? The local pool is pretty good.'

'I'll go if you want me to,' Keeley replied reluctantly. 'I'm quite good at swimming. Can you take me, Angela?'

'Of course,' I replied, glancing discreetly at Jonathan. It wasn't difficult to notice that Keeley was favouring me over Jonathan, but we both knew that when we did take her swimming, the two of us would accompany her. Jonathan and I were a team, and Keeley was going to have to accept this.

Phillip said he's had a boring day at school with nothing to report, other than repeating a familiar mantra: 'I really hate Mrs Harvey.' Phillip suffered from dyslexia and his English lessons with Mrs Harvey were an ongoing trial for him, even though he had extra help from a support teacher. I think it's fair to say he endured school; he rarely said anything positive about it. Most of Phillip's free time was spent playing football with his friends, and he also loved being in the garage with Jonathan, tinkering with the car, the lawn mower or in fact anything mechanical or covered in grease and oil.

'Do you like English, Keeley?' Jonathan asked, trying once more to bring her into the conversation. 'I know Angela used to love English at school, didn't you?'

'I did indeed. It was always my favourite lesson, and I love reading.'

Keeley gave me a shy, sideways glance.

'I like books too, Angela. Will you read with me later?'

'Of course. Have you brought some books with you?'

Keeley seemed to be quite interested in learning generally and she had told me about some of the topics she'd enjoyed in her old school. Studying food eaten in different countries and looking at photographs and art from around the world seemed to be her favourites. I thought that next time she was in the kitchen with me while I was preparing the dinner I'd encourage her to help. Cooking is something I always like to involve the children in, in any case. It teaches them so many practical skills, and it enables you to talk without having to give each other eye contact, which can help a child to open up if they want to.

'Books? Yes, I've got a book about a dancer,' she said. 'I think you'd like it, but *they* wouldn't,' she said rather rudely, nodding towards the boys and Jonathan. 'It's just for girls, really.'

'Oh, I don't know about that,' Jonathan teased. 'I used to be a famous ballet dancer when I was younger, didn't you know?'

Keeley's eyes widened for a moment and then Carl and Phillip groaned in unison, making her realise this was just one of Jonathan's silly jokes, which the boys and I were well used to.

After dinner, the boys went up to their rooms to do their homework while I cleared up. Keeley said she was going to do some more colouring in her bedroom, and she took her book and some pencils and pens from the kitchen table and quietly went upstairs. However, after about ten minutes I heard a commotion coming from the top floor landing.

'Bastard!' I heard Keeley shout. 'You're a total bastard!'

I shot up the stairs to find Phillip red in the face and clearly very angry indeed. Keeley was standing in front of him with her hands on her hips, looking like a proper little madam.

'Leave me alone!' Phillip retorted. 'What did I tell you? Just leave me alone, will you?'

'What on earth is going on?' I demanded.

'It's her!' Phillip shouted. 'She keeps coming in my room and annoying me. I've asked her to stop but she won't listen!'

'Keeley, what have you been doing?'

'Nothing,' she said, in a voice suddenly so soft and gentle I felt sure she was putting it on for effect. 'It's him. I just wanted to borrow a rubber and he was nasty to me.'

'Did you knock before you went into Phillip's room?'

'Yes.'

'No, you didn't! Angela, she's come in three times without knocking, and when I asked her to stop she pinched me and said I made her do it. Look!'

Phillip held out his hand and, sure enough, there was an angry red pinch mark between his thumb and wrist.

'I didn't do that,' Keeley insisted indignantly, batting her eyelashes gently and tilting her head to one side.

Phillip looked like he was about to explode. 'You did! How can you stand there looking all innocent, saying you didn't do it? Oh my God, you are such a little liar!'

'Right,' I said firmly, 'you go back to your room, Phillip, and I will have a chat with Keeley.'

He gladly retreated, slamming his door behind him, while Keeley smiled smugly, apparently seeing it as a victory that Phillip had been sent off on his own while she had my one-to-one attention.

'Now then, Keeley,' I began. 'I want you to think about how Phillip felt when you went into his room uninvited, when he was trying to do his homework quietly.'

'I only wanted a rubber!'

'That may be true, Keeley, but it was annoying for Phillip to be interrupted, and to have you walking into his room. You invaded his privacy. We need to always knock on each other's bedroom door if we want to talk to one another, and we're not allowed in each other's room. It's the rule, and I know I have already explained this to you. I remember saying it more than once, in fact.'

When Jonathan and I started out as carers in the late eighties, foster children were allowed to go into another person's bedroom as long as they knocked first and were invited in, but rules passed down from Social Services had been tightened up over the years. Now we were regularly reminded on training courses that this was not what is known as 'safe care'.

Even as a carer I had to be cautious about when I entered a child's room. Of course, I had to dust and vacuum and fetch laundry, particularly for younger children, and there were occasions when it was appropriate for me to enter a bedroom, such as when Keeley first moved in and then when she showed me her dolls and put her new uniform in the wardrobe. It would not be feasible for me to never go in the room, but I limited my visits to those that were strictly necessary. When Keeley went to bed at night, I hugged her before she went in the room then stood at the door and said goodnight, making sure she was in bed. I never kissed her or tucked her in, as this was not advisable, or 'safe' as Social Services phrase it. It probably sounds hard to anyone not familiar with fostering, but the rules are in place for a good reason. A child like Keeley can be unpredictable, especially at this early stage in a placement. As we had already seen, her words and actions didn't always appear to ring true, and so I had to protect myself and follow the guidelines to the letter. The same was true of Jonathan, of course, and whenever we had a girl in the house he never entered their room for any reason whatsoever, as it simply wasn't worth the risk of putting himself in a situation where he may be wrongly accused of something he hadn't done.

'How would you like it if the boys just walked into your room?' I asked Keeley, still trying to get through to her.

Keeley shrugged. 'It's no big deal.'

'OK, let me put it like this. What if they kept coming in, time and time again, and then you got annoyed and one of them pinched you?'

'I wouldn't like it, but I didn't pinch Phillip!'

'Then why did he say you did, and why did he have that pinch mark on his hand?'

'Dunno. Must have done it himself.'

'Is that really what you are saying? Think carefully, Keeley. You must tell the truth.'

'I'm not lying.'

I sighed. I felt there was no point in pressing her on this as it was clear she was sticking to her story, and so I changed tack, going on to tell Keeley that I wouldn't think she was a bad girl, even if she had pinched Phillip.

'If you admit you have done something wrong it does not mean I will view you as a bad person. I say this to the boys, too, and to all the foster children who stay with me. You are not a bad person if you behave badly, do you understand that? I can help you behave better, that's part of my job, but you have to be truthful. That is the deal.'

Keeley nodded uncertainly but didn't reply.

'Right. I think you need some time out to think about this. Stay in your room for ten minutes, please, Keeley, and try to think about how your behaviour tonight made Phillip feel.'

I walked away quietly, stopping off to see Phillip and assure him that I was dealing with Keeley. He had calmed down by now and was grateful that I believed his version of events, and I told him to let Jonathan or me know immediately should Keeley aggravate him again.

Unfortunately, after ten minutes of 'time out' Keeley bolted down the stairs like a raging bull. She was absolutely furious, had a foul look on her face and began shouting at me to let her out to play.

'No, Keeley, you can't play out while you are in this mood,' I said. 'I don't want you to upset any of the other children, and when you are shouting and being aggressive that is what is likely to happen.'

'I won't! I'm not a bad person!'

I was rather impressed with this swift response. It told me Keeley was a clever girl, but I still wasn't letting her play out when she was in this mood.

'Keeley, you are upsetting me. I don't like being shouted at, and I don't like it when you scowl at me. It's not nice. As I said to you upstairs, you have to think about how you make other people feel.'

'I have,' she said indignantly. 'What do you think I've been doing in my room! Durgh!'

'There is no need to be rude, Keeley. What did you think about Phillip? Have you thought about how your behaviour upset him?'

'I don't care. He was horrible to me.'

It was clear, once again, that it wasn't going to be easy getting through to Keeley.

Later that evening I had a discussion with Jonathan about the best way forward, and we agreed that 'time out' was perhaps not the answer, as Keeley was a child who responded well to attention, and particularly one-to-one attention. Being sent to her room was probably only going to antagonise her, rather than encourage her to reflect and calm down.

'Perhaps we should start the reward chart in the morning, see if that works?' Jonathan said, as this was the other method one of the social workers at Keeley's core meeting had suggested might help with improving behaviour.

'It's worth a try,' I replied, though I couldn't help

thinking there had to be a more imaginative way of helping a girl like Keeley. 'I'll set it up tomorrow. What have we got to lose?'

6

'Let's hope it keeps her out of mischief'

When Keeley came down for breakfast I explained that we were going to put a star chart on the wall, and that when her behaviour was particularly good she would get a gold star. Once she had earned ten stars she could choose a treat.

'What are the treats?' she asked cautiously, clearly wondering if this was going to be worth her while.

'Well, I was thinking you could choose a new outfit or accessory for one of your dolls. How does that sound?'

She smiled and asked if she could have a new set of pens too.

'OK then. When you've got ten stars you can choose which treat you want first.'

'Can't I have both?'

'Yes, if you get twenty stars.'

'Twenty? You said ten.'

'It's ten per treat.'

'Oh,' she said, 'that's easy. I can do that.'

*

After dropping Keeley at school I came straight home to do some housework for an hour or so before taking over from Jonathan in the shop, as he needed to go to the wholesalers. Although we had a part-time helper and employed a relief manager to cover holidays, generally speaking Jonathan and I juggled the shop between us. It was a very well-established and successful business when we took it over from my parents in the mid-eighties. Profits had dropped off over the years as supermarkets sprang up on the outskirts of town, all of which sold flowers at competitive prices, but we'd continued to tick over. Thankfully, we had a loyal customer base and a very good reputation supplying wedding flowers. Jonathan and I both enjoyed running the business, and most of the time the work fitted around our fostering commitments really well.

On this particular morning, I decided to start the housework on the top floor of the house where the children slept, and the first thing I did was go into their bathroom. The boys usually kept it in a fairly decent condition, but with Keeley now sharing with them I was making a point of checking and cleaning it more frequently than normal.

I was dismayed by what I saw. The toilet roll holder was empty and when I looked down the loo I saw that the cardboard roll was shredded and floating in the water. Not only that but lumps of wet toilet paper were stuck up the sides of the washbasin, and splattered all around the shower cubicle. I cleaned the mess up with a heavy heart. The boys had never done anything like this, and I felt sure it had to be Keeley's work. Unfortunately, I also had a good idea how she would react when I brought it up after school. If her past performances were anything to go by, no doubt she would deny all knowledge, blame someone else, or simply say 'dunno' and scowl.

When I'd cleaned up the bathroom I went into Keeley's bedroom to fetch her washing, which was something I'd told her I would be doing that morning, so she had some warning that I would be entering her personal space. My heart sank a little more. Keeley had chopped the long hair off one of her dolls and scattered the black tresses all over the floor. I fetched the vacuum cleaner and began clearing up, and as I did so I found two pairs of wet knickers, wrapped in layers of toilet roll and stuffed behind her dolls. Then, as I lifted the rug to shake out the doll's hair, I found several of Phillip's football cards stashed underneath it.

I wasn't too concerned about the wet underwear. It isn't uncommon for a child of primary school age who has an accident to try to cover it up, particularly in the early stages of a placement. I wondered if perhaps this had something to do with the mess that had been made in the bathroom with the toilet roll, and I imagined it might well be. I would have to talk to Keeley and explain that it was not a problem if she had an accident, but that she must tell me, so I could wash her clothes and keep her room fresh. It was also important that she kept herself clean too, of course, which I'd noticed she wasn't particularly good at. Even after taking a shower, in my experience Keeley didn't seem to smell very fresh and perhaps this was the reason, if she had a problem keeping her knickers dry. The shower issue was something I'd have to keep my eye on, in case she simply wasn't washing properly. I'd seen this with countless other foster children, too many of whom had never been taught how to shower properly and take care of their personal hygiene, and just didn't know how.

However, the hidden football cards were a different matter. I recognised them immediately as being part of a collection Phillip had been painstakingly putting in an album for months on end, throughout the football season. Every weekend he spent some of his pocket money buying several new packets of cards. He was always delighted if he was lucky enough to get one or two that he was missing, or a special shiny one, and he enjoyed swapping any duplicates with his friends, who were all competing to be the first to complete the set.

There did not seem to be any other explanation but that Keeley had taken the cards from Phillip's room without him knowing. This was more than an invasion of privacy; she had effectively stolen from him, and I'd have to have some serious words with her about this.

'How did Keeley react to the star chart?' Jonathan asked when I went to take over from him in the shop. 'Only I was just looking in the wholesalers' catalogue at some of the trimmings on sale. I spotted some glitter stars, little plastic sticky ones that sparkle and come in all colours. They're meant for decorating cards, but I was wondering whether to get some for Keeley's chart?'

'Well, she's quite delighted at the prospect of treats,' I

replied, thinking how thoughtful this was of Jonathan. 'But I have to say, I'm wondering if it's a bit ambitious to be thinking about rewarding her for good behaviour.'

'Why do you say that?'

'Because I'm not really seeing any good behaviour.'

I told Jonathan about what I'd just found upstairs in the bathroom and in Keeley's bedroom and he nodded sagely. 'I see what you are saying. A few sticky stars are perhaps not going to do the trick with Keeley, are they?'

'Exactly. It was a lovely idea to get some special ones, but I think we'd be clutching at straws to imagine they'd do much good. Perhaps we need a completely different plan.'

It was a fairly quiet morning in the shop and I had time to take stock as I busied myself with tidying up the drawers where we kept the floristry ribbon and gift cards.

I thought about how much Keeley enjoyed colouring in, and I started to wonder whether engaging her in a creative project might be a better way of keeping her in check. 'Time in' rather than 'time out' is how I would describe it today, although back then I don't think I knew that phrase and I was simply following my instincts.

Keeley clearly enjoyed having my attention and, as the morning wore on, amongst other things I wondered whether there was some kind of artistic project we could do together. My eyes fell on a stack of leaflets one of the neighbours had left on the counter that morning. There was a carnival coming up in the town, which was an event I was involved in every year. It was a big fundraiser for the community and all the local business owners helped out.

Jonathan and I always donated flowers to decorate the parade floats, and this year I had volunteered to make paper mache bonnets decked with spring flowers for a group of young singers who were putting on a performance. I'd already made a start, and I thought Keeley would love to help me make them.

'That's it!' I said to myself. 'Keeley can help me make them!'

'I beg your pardon?' Jonathan asked.

I'd been so deep in thought I'd barely registered that he was back from the wholesalers and was now lifting boxes into the storeroom at the back of the shop.

'Keeley!' I said. 'She can help me make those bonnets, the paper mache ones I've been working on.'

'What a good idea,' he called through. 'She'd love that. Let's hope it keeps her out of mischief.'

'That's exactly what I'm thinking. Did you get plenty of pink ribbon?'

'I did indeed,' Jonathan replied, and with that he stuck his head around the door of the storeroom and added, 'what d'you think?'

I burst out laughing. Jonathan had looped a length of baby pink ribbon around his neck and tied it in an elaborate bow.

'Perfect!' I said. 'Though I'm not sure you'll get a place on a carnival float. I think the image needs a bit of work!'

'Spoilsport!'

Jonathan has a knack of lightening the atmosphere at just the right moment, which I'm very grateful for. It's easy to feel burdened by the pressure of dealing with a child's difficult behaviour, and having a sense of humour and a playful nature is crucial in helping to put things in perspective, and to keep you feeling optimistic.

While Jonathan had been out I'd also been thinking about our summer holiday, and once the two of us were behind the counter, enjoying a cup of tea, I told him I'd been having a few ideas, as I thought this would help keep our spirits up.

'Now that doesn't surprise me!' he teased. 'You, Angela? Thinking about a holiday? Well I never!'

I'm typically the one who does the research and drives the booking through, as I'm more patient and determined than Jonathan when it comes to trawling through brochures and filling in booking forms and so on. However, the truth is we both love our weekend breaks and trips away, and we always try to have one or two things in the diary to look forward to.

Caring for children means we have to be very organised around school holidays, and often there are long-winded processes to go through to obtain permission from parents or legal guardians, so forward planning is essential. With this in mind, we had already asked Carl and Phillip's families if we could potentially take them away for a fortnight in the school summer holidays, and they had agreed. On top of this, we had a weekend in Wales booked in June, after Carl's exams, when we would take our touring caravan, stay on a campsite and do some walking, sightseeing and fishing, which was something Jonathan and the two boys were particularly interested in.

All we had to do now was decide where we wanted to go in the school summer holidays, and see if we could take Keeley with us too. It wasn't set in stone that she would still be living with us in August, when we were planning to go, but it was looking likely and so we had to plan for the possibility. We'd learned from experience that you couldn't wait and see when it comes to taking kids on holiday. Bookings have to be made, even if they subsequently have to be altered or even cancelled, or otherwise you might never get away. In the past we've lost hundreds of pounds in cancellation and amendment fees because kids have moved out between the time of booking and the actual trip, or because their parents have changed their mind and decided to withdraw their permission. Sadly, this is typically for no other good reason than that they don't want us to give their kids something that they can't.

Jonathan and I had already talked about the possibility of driving to the south coast with Carl and Phillip. Both boys would have been happy to chill out on a rural campsite, but with Keeley now involved I'd had a good idea.

'I've been thinking, what about splitting the trip between a theme park break and staying on a campsite?' I said. 'Then we'd have the best of both worlds. Could suit everybody?'

Jonathan nodded approvingly. 'As usual, you've come up with a perfect plan,' he smiled. 'It sounds ideal. Let's look into it and get it booked. Hopefully it will be a good incentive for Keeley, to encourage her to improve her behaviour.'

'Quite. I'll get on to it today.'

7

'Mum went mad lots of times'

When Keeley was home from school I told her all about the carnival bonnets I wanted her to help me with.

'I'd love to do that!' she said excitedly. 'What do we have to do?'

I explained that I had already experimented with the paper mache, sticking it on balloons of different shapes and sizes to get the shape and structure of the hats right, and now I was ready to go into production. We needed eight bonnets, and once they were dry we'd have to paint them in bright colours before adding ribbons and bows and finally the fresh flowers, which might have to be laced or tied on with more ribbon, or floristry tape.

'They sound lovely!' Keeley enthused. 'Can I have one?'

'I tell you what, why don't we see how we get on? If it goes well I'm sure we could make one for you too. What do you say?'

Keeley was thrilled, and she behaved impeccably as she helped me cover the dining table with an old cloth to set up our little bonnet-making factory. I asked her to take off her school uniform to keep it clean, and she happily obliged, returning in a long-sleeved top and jeans, over which she put on an apron.

It was fun sticking the glue-smothered newspaper strips onto the balloons I'd lined up. Keeley was engrossed, and out of the blue she suddenly started talking about her mother.

'My mum was horrible,' she said thoughtfully.

'I'm sorry to hear your mum was horrible, Keeley.'

'She was, but she still let me do stuff like this though!'

'You did paper mache with your mum?'

'Well, not exactly. I used to make stuff in my room, sticking and colouring and that. Sometimes I made a mess. One time a pen leaked all over my quilt cover, but Mum didn't go mad like I thought she would. She didn't shout or anything. It was weird.'

'You thought she would go mad?'

'Yes. Mum went mad lots of times. She used to hit me for no reason, but then when I thought I'd been bad she didn't do anything.'

'I'm sorry to hear you say your mum hit you for no reason, Keeley.'

She shrugged. 'That's just the way she is. You never know what she's going to do. I still love her though. She's still my mum. It's not her fault, that's what she said sometimes. Granddad hit her, she told me that. I think it's Granddad's fault.'

Keeley had been absent-mindedly massaging the same

piece of newspaper into the bowl of glue, and before I could reply she suddenly looked down and noticed her cuffs were covered in the sticky paste.

'Urgh!' she said, pushing her sleeves up to her elbows. 'Look, I'm all sticky. Urgh! That feels horrible, and it smells!'

Not only had the moment been lost for Keeley to say any more about her background, but also, when she pushed her sleeves up, I noticed that both of her arms were dotted with lots of tiny purple bruises.

'Keeley! Whatever has happened to your arms?'

'What?'

'The bruises. Where did they come from?'

'Dunno.'

'Keeley, please have a think. Do you know how you got them?'

'No. How would I know?'

I asked her if she had bruises anywhere else on her body and she told me she didn't. I recorded all of these details in my diary and vowed to keep a close eye on this. Keeley herself didn't seem in the slightest bit concerned, and moments later she turned her focus back to the paper mache as if this conversation, and the disclosures about her family, had never happened.

'When can we go swimming?' she asked shortly afterwards.

'Funny you should mention that. I was talking to Jonathan about it. How would you fancy going on Saturday early evening, after we shut the shop?'

'Yippee!' she said, punching the air. 'Will it be me and you?'

'I'm sure Jonathan will come too, but the boys will both be out. Does that sound all right?'

'You bet!'

The next morning I had terrible trouble getting Keeley ready for school. She seemed to invent dramas out of thin air, and appeared hell bent on making herself late.

'I can't put my shoes on,' she complained, making a terrible fuss as she tried to prise her feet into her patent leather shoes without unfastening the buckle across on the top.

'I think the problem is you need to unbuckle them, Keeley, like you normally do.'

She did this, but then went through a charade of making it look as if the shoes were too small for her, which wasn't the case. She slammed her narrow feet awkwardly into them, catching her toes on the sides and complaining repeatedly about the 'stupid shoes'.

'Can't do it!' she said, before hurling both shoes at the front door in a fit of temper.

'Keeley, please don't do that,' I said. 'Just do what you normally do to put your shoes on, and let's not have so much fuss. We need to hurry up. I'm worried you're going to be late.'

As soon as I'd said this she gave me a smug look, and I realised I'd made a mistake and played right into her hands. I had reacted to her button pressing and had let her know I was feeling under pressure of time because of her, which was exactly what she wanted. Then, predictably, she started being even more difficult, spilling the contents of her book bag as she lifted it upside down from the bottom stair, and refusing to wear a coat even though showers were forecast.

Don't react! I was telling myself, but it was difficult not to as the clock was ticking and I really didn't want her to be late.

In the end we missed the bell but, after a stressful drive through rush hour traffic, I managed to get Keeley to the school office before the end of registration.

'We really need to leave the house a bit earlier tomorrow,' I told her, finding it difficult to hide my irritation.

Keeley didn't apologise or seem in the slightest bit bothered by the consequences of her behaviour. If anything I think she quite enjoyed the little drama she had created unnecessarily. The fact I'd got a little hot under the collar worked like a dream. It had meant Keeley received extra attention from me, and, as I'd started to understand more and more, that was precisely what she wanted. This wasn't necessarily malicious or spiteful, I reasoned. This was probably a default position Keeley found herself in as a result of her upbringing. Though nobody had officially spelled this out to me, it seemed that the lack of bonding with her mother had very seriously affected how Keeley interacted with people. She wanted my attention, which is perfectly natural in an eight-year-old girl living in a new foster home, but she didn't know how to get in in a positive way. It was the same with the kids on the rec. Every time she played out Keeley found it impossible to just go outside and join in with the other children without putting herself at the centre of some kind of scene.

The next day she pulled all the same stunts, but I was better prepared this time. The shoes were thrown at the door again, her packed lunch was 'accidentally' tipped out of her bag and she argued about taking a coat. Then, when we finally headed to the car, she claimed she could only walk very slowly, as she had a sore leg that was making her limp.

'That's a shame,' I said very calmly, 'but never mind. What can we do? If you've got a sore leg, you've got a sore leg.'

'But won't we be late?'

'Quite possibly, which is a shame. If the main gate is shut you will have to go to the office and then tell the teachers why you missed the bell again.'

'I can't do that again! I'm not supposed to be late. You'll get into trouble!'

'Me? No, Keeley, I won't get into trouble. I have been ready and waiting for ten minutes. I was on time this morning, but you weren't and I had to wait for you. If the teachers ask me, I'll have to tell them that, because that is the truth.'

Keeley smouldered all the way to school.

'Shall I park up and come with you to the office?' I asked cheerfully when we pulled up outside the school. 'I don't mind. I've got time, if you think it would help you. I can tell them what the problems were this morning.'

'No, thank you,' she snapped. 'I can do it by myself.'

The next day Keeley got herself ready on time and was

well mannered and extremely polite. I praised her and gave her a gold star sticker on her chart, which we'd decided to persevere with for the time being, despite our reservations about how useful this incentive might be. I also made a point of being extra attentive all the way to school, in the hope that she would realise that such good behaviour would earn her much more attention from me than the bad.

On Saturday Keeley was very excited about going swimming. We had a very good leisure centre nearby which had a kid's pool and some slides, as well as a large fitness training pool with diving boards of varying heights.

'So you're quite a good swimmer, are you, Keeley?' Jonathan asked.

'Not bad. I love swimming. I've been with school and had lots of lessons. I was the best in the class, my old teacher said.'

'Great!' Jonathan replied. 'Maybe I'll give you a race!'

I took Keeley into the female changing area and we arranged to meet Jonathan at the poolside. She got changed by herself without a problem and met me outside the lockers as I'd asked her to, with her bag and towel. I took the belongings off her and placed them in the locker, but as I did so I noticed yet more bruises on Keeley's body. They were all down her legs as well as her arms, and there must have been about twenty of the tiny black and blue marks on each limb.

'Keeley,' I said as discreetly as possible, though I was

really very alarmed. 'Look at all those bruises. Where did they come from?'

'I don't know,' she said. 'They're all right though, they don't hurt.'

I shoved my bag and towel hastily into the locker.

'Let me have a proper look,' I said, panic rising as I stared at the marks.

'Can't you look later? I'm fine. I want to go and swim now.'

'We can go in a minute ...' I began, but before I'd finished my sentence Keeley had given me the slip, and was darting through the door that led to the fitness pool.

I rushed after her, pacing as rapidly as I could without actually running, but when I went through the swinging door to the poolside I couldn't see Keeley anywhere. My eyes darted around every square inch of the water and across every single step and the seating area at the far end of the pool before I spotted her. To my dismay, Keeley was charging up the steps leading to the diving boards.

'Keeley!' I called. 'Wait for me! Stop there!'

I had no idea if she had ever dived or jumped off a board before, or how strong a swimmer she was, and I wanted to stop her and at least talk to her before allowing her to launch herself from such a height. Keeley completely ignored me, though, and continued dashing up the steps, not to the first level or to the second, but to the highest board, which was five metres off the ground.

'What the ... ?' Jonathan exclaimed. He had heard me shouting and come dashing over to my side. Then we both gaped in horror as Keeley flung herself head first off the top board. It felt like time stood still as we watched her slender little body, dressed in a vibrant yellow halter-neck swimsuit, dropping through the air. Then, all of a sudden, Keeley landed with an ear-splitting, belly-flopping splash in the deep water below.

Jonathan instinctively jumped in the pool and swam to her side, which was just as well because when Keeley surfaced she was gasping for breath and floundering around. He managed to lead her safely to the steps – thankfully Jonathan is a very strong swimmer, and had done a bit of lifesaving in his youth – and Keeley climbed out of the pool with her legs shaking and promptly burst into tears.

'Keeley, love, are you all right?' I soothed. 'Here, shall we go and fetch your towel and you can sit quietly for a few minutes?'

Keeley nodded and sniffed. Once she was wrapped up warm she stopped crying and gave me a brave smile.

'I'm sorry I scared you, Angela.'

'I'm sorry you scared yourself, sweetheart.'

'I didn't,' she said, which wasn't what I expected her to say at all. 'I've done that loads of time. It wasn't scary! I just did a belly flop by accident, and it hurt. That's why I cried.'

From what I'd seen I was quite sure this wasn't true, but I didn't let her know I doubted her word in any way. As ever, I was aware that keeping a dialogue open and encouraging Keeley to talk was very important. If I argued or accused her of telling fibs it could stop her telling me about other, more serious, issues. Safety was very important too, of course, and so I had a word about the dangers of deep water. I think she took this in; the experience had certainly shocked her, and I was sure she wouldn't want to repeat it or take any more chances any time soon.

'I tell you what, shall we go into the kid's pool and we can have a go on the slides instead?' I suggested.

Keeley nodded, and as we trouped through to the adjacent pool, with Keeley leading the way, Jonathan and I snatched a whispered conversation.

'We can't let her out of our sight for a second,' I hissed.

'I know,' agreed Jonathan. 'I'll stay by her side, don't worry, and we'll stay in the shallow end. My nerves are jangling, Angela, I don't know about yours.'

'Mine too. Come on; let's do our best to have some fun. We can talk to her again later, to reiterate the safety side of things.'

We did indeed have fun in the pool. There were all shapes of inflatables and floats in the water, a huge sprinkler and even a wave machine. Keeley seemed very happy to stay in the shallow end, or on the slides, and Jonathan made her laugh her head off by chasing her with a giant blow-up dolphin.

Afterwards we went to the cafe, where I ordered a large cream cake and a mug of coffee. Jonathan, who just had a cup of tea, took the mickey when he saw the size of my cake.

'Comfort food,' I said, giving him a smile. 'I think I deserve it after the shock I've had,' I added quietly, out of Keeley's earshot.

Keeley tucked into a glass of orange squash and a big

slice of chocolate cake, looking completely unperturbed by her experience. Her face was shining, her hair was drying into an amazing set of glossy ringlets and she looked as happy as Larry.

'Would you like to have some extra swimming lessons?' I asked. 'Only I can see you like swimming, and maybe you would like to learn more?'

'Yes!' she said. 'I'd love that. I don't need them, but I'd like to have them.'

'OK, sweetheart, I'll ask at reception on the way out. They usually do courses in the school holidays. We'll just have to check with Joan and make sure everybody is happy about that, but let's hope we can fix something up.'

On the way home my mind was on two things. Firstly, we'd have to find the right moment to talk to her again more thoroughly about safety and the dangers of deep water, and certainly before the next time we took her swimming. Her safety came first, and we had to be sure she understood that she needed to treat the water with more respect and not take any risks. It seemed like she had learned a lesson, but I had to be one hundred per cent sure. Secondly, and more worryingly, I'd have to do something about the bruises on Keeley's body. There were so many of them, and I'd never seen anything like it before.

Oh my God, I suddenly thought to myself as Jonathan drove the car. *Leukaemia. What if she's got leukaemia?*

8

'I'm worried about those bruises'

'Leukaemia?' Jonathan said, frowning and instantly losing the colour from his face when I shared this terrible thought.

'Yes, it hit me when we were on our way back from the swimming baths. I've read about how the symptoms first show themselves. There was an article on one of my magazines a few months back. A mother described how she first noticed something was wrong with her son. It was when she spotted tiny bruises, like pinpoints of blood, scattered around his body. Her description came back to me when I was thinking about Keeley's bruises in the car, as that's exactly what her bruises look like.'

Jonathan scratched the back of his head and I saw tears prick his eyes. Neither of us wanted to say it, but it was impossible not to mention leukaemia without thinking of our nephew, Aiden. He died in 1989, shortly before his seventh birthday. The illness had taken him rapidly, and we still felt his loss acutely; only recently, in fact, Jonathan's brother had mentioned that Aiden should have been turning twenty-one this year.

'My God, my first thoughts were that she had been pinching herself, you know, in an attention-seeking or self-harming kind of way,' Jonathan said. 'I feel absolutely terrible now. It never even occurred to me that she might have some kind of illness, and certainly not something as serious as leukaemia. Surely we can't be facing that again?'

I made a doctor's appointment immediately and explained to Keeley in a roundabout way why I was taking her to the GP.

'I'm worried about those bruises,' I told her.

'I told you, Angela. They don't hurt. I'm fine.'

'However you feel, Keeley, it isn't right to be covered in bruises like that. We need to get you checked over, make sure you are in good health.'

She shrugged and didn't argue anymore, and when we went to the doctors a few days later she didn't kick up a fuss at all.

'What seems to be the problem?' the rather intense, newly qualified GP asked.

I explained that Keeley had bruises all over her body. He asked if he could take a closer look and Keeley stripped down to her knickers without complaint, while I tried to hide my alarm and fear. I saw that there were now more bruises than ever; about thirty to forty on each limb, including what looked like new ones down her sides, around the edges of her back and all around her stomach.

'What do you think might be causing this, Keeley?' the GP asked kindly.

'Dunno,' she said. 'They don't hurt though. I don't really mind.'

I had not mentioned the word leukaemia to the doctor or to Keeley, and I soon became very relieved that I hadn't, as the GP looked at me conspiratorially before speaking again to Keeley.

'This really is quite a curious case of mysterious bruises,' he said, furrowing his brow. 'You see, if they were caused by an illness I don't think they would appear in these patterns. What's puzzling me is that the bruises are on your arms and legs, and your tummy, but you don't have them all over your back.'

'Don't I?' Keeley asked.

'No. It's this part, in the middle of the back, where there are no bruises at all.'

He tapped the centre of Keeley's back gently with his fingertips and then asked her to turn around, so that I could see the pattern on her back too.

'Do you think you could touch this part of your back, where my finger is now?' the GP asked.

Keeley stretched one arm up her back and tried to touch the spot he was pointing at but couldn't quite reach. Then, using her other arm, she attempted to stretch over one shoulder, but still couldn't touch the central point in her back. While Keeley was still facing away from us the doctor caught my eye and gave me a look as if to say: 'Do you see what I'm getting at?'

I nodded discreetly, realising what the doctor was showing me. The bruises only appeared on parts of Keeley's body that she could reach, and it seemed very obvious now that she must have been making these marks herself, which is exactly what Jonathan's gut reaction had been.

'Maybe you could have another think about how you got the bruises?' the doctor suggested gently. 'In the meantime, I will arrange for a blood test, just to be on the safe side, but I really don't think they are caused by any nasty illness.'

The GP suggested he would phone me after his morning surgery the next day, 'to see how things are going'. In fact, the purpose of his call was to check if Keeley was still attending therapy to help her deal with the emotional abuse she had suffered, as this was recorded on her medical records. I confirmed that she was still going for monthly sessions and was due to attend one shortly, as she hadn't been for one since moving in with us.

'Good,' he replied. 'I believe self-harm is not uncommon in children like Keeley, but I am no expert in that field. I think this is a job for her therapist. He or she should be best placed to help her deal with it, and I'm pleased she is still having counselling. If she wasn't I would have referred her.'

I filled in the necessary paperwork and passed this on to Social Services and to Keeley's school, but I have no idea what impact this had on her treatment, if any, as Jonathan and I were never given any information at all about Keeley's therapy sessions.

*

The blood test, predictably, returned a negative result, which I used in a positive way, to help encourage Keeley to stop pinching herself.

'Great news,' I told her. 'The doctor was right. You aren't ill.'

'Told you!'

'Yes. Now, let's see if you can go for a whole week without getting a new bruise, shall we?'

'OK. Will I get a star on the chart?'

'I'll do better than that. I'll count the bruises in a week and if there are less than before you can have a new doll. How about that?'

After that I counted the bruises each week and always bought Keeley a treat if the number had reduced. Sadly, though, Keeley was rarely bruise-free and she never, ever admitted to self-harm, even when I asked her gently, and when she was in a responsive mood, if she might possibly have made the bruises herself, perhaps without meaning to.

'What?' she always said, looking either insulted or confused if I tried to get her to open up. 'I don't know where they came from. I must have fallen over and I can't remember.'

'You know you can tell me if something else has happened,' I always said.

'I know, but there's nothing to tell!'

One time she added: 'I used to get bruises more when I was living with my mum.'

'Did you? You used to get bruises more when you were at home with your mum?'

'Yes. She hit me with her slipper when she was mad. She threw me in a room and locked me up too.'

'I remember you told me before that your mum hit you. She hit you with a slipper, did she, and threw you in a room and locked you up?'

'Yes. The box room. It had no carpet and no furniture and the floor was hard and cold. She hit me with a walking stick too sometimes, when she was really mad. It was Eric's walking stick.'

'Eric's walking stick?'

I knew from when I was first given her background history that Eric was Keeley's maternal grandfather, but I didn't want to be the one to mention this, so I left a pause. Keeley thought long and hard before she spoke again.

'Eric's walking stick, yes. He was my granddad. I hated him. He was weird, and he was horrible to me.'

Of course, I also knew that Eric was suspected of sexually abusing both his daughter and granddaughter, but that nothing had ever been proven and that Keeley's mum had never seen through a formal complaint to police or even Social Services. Whatever Keeley said on the matter could be extremely important. I tried to keep the conversation going by repeating back what she had said in a gentle, questioning tone, but Keeley clammed up and started staring into space.

It hadn't escaped me that Keeley had spoken about her grandfather in the past tense, even though he was still alive.

I made a note of this in my diary, and also when I passed on all the details of these latest disclosures to Social Services, being careful to quote Keeley word for word.

Afterwards, I thought back over precisely what I had been told by Sandy at the start of the placement, because I was searching for anything that might help me deal with Keeley. However, 'suspected sexual abuse' was all Sandy had said, both in relation to Eric and to Keeley's mother. That was all I knew, and it was very little. I had no idea of the level of abuse or the exact nature of Tina's accusations against her father. Nor did I know why Tina was suspected of sexually abusing her own daughter. What was the evidence, if any? Had Eric or Tina been falsely accused, or had they got away with serious crimes? I wanted to know, but then again I didn't. I couldn't bear thinking about what Keeley may have been through.

9

'I'm afraid there's been an incident'

On the Friday, after school, Jonathan and I took Keeley to the first of her supervised sessions with her mother since she had been in our care, and I for one was dreading it.

'You don't seem yourself,' Jonathan commented when we nipped home to change after handing over to our assistant in the shop. My mum had arrived and was now installed with a cup of tea and a crossword book to keep her occupied until the boys returned from school. Then she would help them get dinner, which I'd prepared in advance and just needed heating up, before the boys went off to their separate Friday night activities.

'It's a bit of a rush all this, on a Friday afternoon. You look a bit harassed, Angela. Are you all right?'

'It's not that,' I replied flatly. 'I'm not sure how I'm going to react to Tina, or how she is going to react to us. More importantly, I am not sure how Keeley will deal with it.'

Because of the hastily arranged move to her last respite carers, and her move to us, Keeley's routine had been disrupted and she hadn't actually seen her mum for a month, which was the longest the two of them had ever gone without contact. However, when I'd mentioned the visit earlier in the week Keeley seemed quite indifferent, and the only comment she made was to quip, 'I'll put on a dress then.'

As we were collecting her from school I'd assumed that Keeley would go to the session in her uniform. I didn't question her though when she mentioned getting changed, as it seemed a positive thing to do, to make an effort and wear a dress for her mum.

'Do you want me to help you choose a dress?' I asked.

'No, it's OK. I know which dress she likes me in. She bought it for my birthday.'

'OK. You'll probably have to get changed before you leave school, can you do that? We need to head off straight from there you see, as we've never been to this contact centre before and we need to give ourselves plenty of time to get there.'

Keeley wrinkled her nose. 'No, I'll just get changed in the car,' she said. 'I'll give you the dress to bring.'

'OK, if you're sure that's what you want to do.'

'It is. It's fine.'

When she moved in, Keeley had arrived with two suitcases full of clothes, ranging from the jeans and leggings and pretty tops that she generally favoured to a large collection of dresses. Her favourite was the red and white polkadot one she was wearing when we first met her, which really suited her, and she also had a denim tunic that she loved to wear, although she preferred trousers most of the time. To my surprise the dress she wanted to wear, which her mum had bought for her birthday, was a strappy, vibrant pink number that was shimmering with sequins and would not have looked out of place in a junior ballroom dancing competition.

'Gosh, that's posh!' I exclaimed, trying to say something positive but probably not sounding very genuine, as the outfit didn't seem suitable for the occasion at all.

Keeley shrugged. 'It's all right. My mum likes it better than I do.'

'Well, perhaps you'd be more comfortable in something else?' I tentatively suggested. 'I'm sure your mum would understand if you just went in your uniform, if you wanted to.'

'No, she might go mad. And she'll only kick off if I turn up in trousers. It's OK, I'll put this on, it's fine.'

Keeley waited until the very last minute to put on the dress, asking Jonathan to park in the quietest corner of the car park outside the contact centre, so she could change discreetly. It was a warm evening and I was relieved that in the event she didn't look too out of place; thankfully, eight-year-old girls tend to be able to pull off most outfits.

The social worker in charge of the contact session met us just inside the entrance of the building. He was a shy-looking man in his late twenties we'd never met before, and he took us directly to the large room where the session was taking place. The usual routine for such visits is that Jonathan and I are briefly introduced to the parent or parents and then we wait outside while the social worker supervises the session.

Tina had not yet arrived. Keeley was very quiet and said nothing as the social worker made polite small talk and invited us all to sit at a table at the back of the room and make ourselves comfortable. Jonathan and I sat down but Keeley chose to stay standing near the door, where she stared into space and played with her hair, twirling it absent-mindedly around her fingers. She had worn it plaited for school that day, but she'd taken the plaits out in the car and her hair was flowing down her back, which I was actually quite glad about, as at least it covered her bare shoulders.

Tina arrived ten minutes late. Her long hair was platinum blonde; she was chewing gum loudly and dressed in extremely tight white trousers, platform sandals, a crop top and large, gold-hooped earrings. I knew she'd had Keeley when she was young, but I hadn't expected her to be this young. She looked like a teenager, though I later found out she was twenty-three and had had Keeley when she was fifteen.

As soon as Tina entered the room she swooped on her daughter and completely ignored the rest of us. She didn't offer any apology for being late either, which we would have appreciated. I tried to tell myself this was understandable, as after all Tina had not seen Keeley in several weeks, but nevertheless I still felt quite put out. I don't like bad manners under any circumstances, and Jonathan and I had got to our feet when Tina came in. We both smiled at her and the social worker even walked towards her and held out his hand, preparing to make the introductions, but Tina didn't acknowledge any of this at all.

Jonathan and I were left feeling slightly embarrassed, not knowing if we should now leave the room or wait for Tina to say hello. We decided to wait, as we didn't want to be rude and simply walk out. The social worker crossed the room and went and hovered by Tina and Keeley, presumably deciding that he would give Tina a few minutes to be reacquainted with her daughter before attempting to make the introductions again.

After she'd fussed over Keeley for a minute or two we all watched as Tina lifted her daughter in the air and spun her around excitedly.

'It's so good to see you, babe!' Tina shrieked, planting a big kiss on Keeley's lips.

I glanced at Jonathan and knew he was thinking exactly the same thing as me: that kiss seemed a little inappropriate. It was clear that Keeley didn't enjoy it either, as she was now wiping her mother's bright red lipstick off her mouth with the back of her hand.

The social worker looked on with a rather worried expression on his face, and he then stepped forward once more and had a quiet word with Tina.

'I'll say hello to them people in a minute!' she said loudly, curling her lip in a way that reminded me of Keeley.

'Shall Mummy give you a lovely big cuddle?' Tina then giggled, gazing at Keeley and using a tone of voice that would have been more appropriate with a toddler than an eight-year-old. 'I've missed you, babe. Come here, come and have a cuddle!'

Keeley gave her mum a half-hearted smile, and with that Tina lifted her daughter in the air again, this time encouraging Keeley to hold on tight by wrapping her legs around her waist. First Tina hugged her daughter in this position, and then she started to spin her around. It was only then that I noticed that Tina's hands had disappeared up the back of Keeley's sparkly dress. She wasn't moving her hands or anything like that, and she was in full view of the social worker, Jonathan and myself, but nevertheless it was uncomfortable to witness, not least because Tina clearly didn't think this behaviour was inappropriate at all. Fortunately, Keeley didn't seem worried, or at least she didn't struggle or ask her mum to stop.

After that Tina finally put Keeley down and clomped over in her high heels to say hello to Jonathan and me.

'Nice to meet you, Jeremy and Angela,' she said, chewing her gum loudly as she spoke.

'It's Jonathan and Angela,' I replied brightly, 'and we're very pleased to meet you too.'

'Cool,' she muttered, immediately turning her attention back to Keeley.

I indicated to the social worker that Jonathan and I would now step out of the room, though Tina clearly wasn't bothered if we were present or not, and started chatting loudly to Keeley while we were making our way to the door.

'Granddad's been round,' she said excitedly. 'He says to send his love.'

'That's nice,' Keeley smiled sweetly. 'Send mine back, won't you?'

This of course was completely at odds with Keeley's reaction last time her grandfather's name was mentioned, which worried me somewhat. Jonathan's expression betrayed his concern too, and we locked eyes as we left the room. Something wasn't right about this, but of course we weren't in a position to interfere at this moment in time.

Once we were in the waiting room I made a mental note to log this in my diary. I felt something so inconsistent might be important information for the social workers and Keeley's therapist, and so I would make a point of writing it down and telling Sandy about it. I was very concerned about why Keeley appeared to pretend to her mother that she liked her grandfather. Was she worried about upsetting her mum if she told her what she had told us, which was that Eric was 'weird', and 'horrible to me'? Or was she frightened that her mother might be angry and fly off the handle if Keeley said anything against Eric? It was impossible to know, given that Eric was suspected of sexually abusing both Tina and Keeley, and that Tina had physically abused Keeley and may have also sexually abused her.

Foster carers are not encouraged to express personal opinions and we have to keep our own points of view to ourselves in our written notes and calls to Social Services, but I felt this amounted to more than mere suspicion on my part. Keeley's words were in total contrast to those she'd used before about her grandfather, and I couldn't let this go. Besides, I had learned from experience that it's best to write down most things, even if you are not sure how significant they may be. On several occasions an event that hadn't seemed important turned out to be very relevant, and I was glad I'd erred on the side of caution and written it down on the day.

Three days after seeing her mother, Keeley had her first therapy session during her time with us. As planned we arranged cover in the shop and my mum came over to help with the boys so that Jonathan and I could collect Keeley from school early and take her on the thirty-mile drive.

Jonathan waited in the car while I went into the school. We were a little early and imagined I would have to sit and wait in reception for a few minutes until Keeley was brought from her classroom, but to my surprise she was already sitting in the front office with her jacket on, and her school bag in hand.

'You're keen!' I smiled, but Keeley just looked at the floor.

'I'm afraid there's been an incident,' the deputy head, Mrs Tiller, said, appearing from her office door adjacent to the reception area.

'Oh,' I said, crestfallen. 'I'm sorry to hear that. What happened?'

'Do you have five minutes, Mrs Hart?'

I said that I did, and the deputy head told Keeley to continue waiting in the receptionist's office while Mrs Tiller and I had a 'little chat' in the privacy of her office.

'I'm sorry to say that Keeley has let herself down very

badly indeed,' Mrs Tiller began, looking disappointed. 'During her last lesson she stabbed another pupil in the back with the sharp end of a compass. The boy in question had to be taken to the nurse's office as he was bleeding. The nurse is still dealing with him now, and we have had to phone the boy's parents and make them aware of the situation.'

'I'm very sorry to hear this,' I said, feeling my heart sinking. 'Keeley seemed to be in a fine mood this morning. In fact, as I recall she came to school with a spring in her step. I don't know what can have gone wrong.'

'Perhaps it is the fact she has her appointment?' Mrs Tiller offered generously, and I added that Keeley had seen her mum on Friday, too, which might have also affected her.

'Both things could impact on her mood and behaviour, of course,' Mrs Tiller agreed. 'Nevertheless I will have to discipline her in school. I have taken five minutes off her playtime for the rest of the week, and she is being moved to the desk in front of the teacher in all of her classes until further notice.'

'OK, I'll support you in those moves, of course. I'll also talk to Keeley and ask her to think about how she made this boy feel by hurting him in that way.'

'Thank you, Mrs Hart. I understand you have a difficult job on your hands at times and I appreciate your support. I will deal with the boy's parents and ensure Keeley apologises to him tomorrow, and hopefully that will be the end of the matter.'

'I hope so,' I said as I got to my feet and went to fetch Keeley. 'I'll also make the necessary reports to Social Services.'

'Of course. We will do the same. Thank you for your time.'

Keeley said nothing as we crossed the car park together and she completely blanked Jonathan as she strapped herself in the back seat of the car. However, once we were on our way she began to talk. This is not unusual; often a child feels more comfortable opening up when they are in the car and not having to give you eye contact.

'It wasn't my fault, Angela,' was her opening line.

Jonathan flicked me a glance. Clearly, Keeley was directing this to me and not Jonathan. He gave me a subtle nod, which I understood to mean that he would keep quiet and let me tackle the conversation.

'Tell me what happened,' I replied.

'Gladly!' she chimed, almost triumphantly. 'It was Miss Fraser's stupid fault. Bitch!'

'Keeley! You are already in trouble. Please don't make matters worse by using bad language. That is very rude indeed. Now please tell me, without swearing, why you think that Miss Fraser is responsible for the fact that you stabbed another child in the back so hard that he bled!'

I'd kept a stiff upper lip when talking to the deputy head, but now my emotions were coming to the surface and I was feeling upset and extremely concerned. Keeley must have stabbed her classmate with quite some force, which was very worrying indeed.

'I'll tell you why it's her stupid fault, Angela! Miss Fraser was making me do the stupidest work ever. EVER!'

'What do you mean, the stupidest work? What were you doing.'

'Literacy.'

'And what's wrong with literacy. I thought you enjoyed it. What were you doing, reading or writing?'

'Writing.'

'Well you like writing. What were you writing about?'

There was a long pause and then Keeley blurted out the words 'family trees' as if she was spitting out poison.

'I see,' I said, my mind racing. I knew that this was a topic that regularly appeared on the curriculum for primary school children, and I also knew that teachers and class-room assistants were trained to handle the subject sensitively, particularly when it came to children from broken homes, those who had lost a parent or those who were adopted or in foster care.

'So what did Miss Fraser say to you, when she explained about family trees?'

'She told me, "Do as much as you can, Keeley."'

'And what did she say to the other children?'

'The same, I suppose.'

'So why were you so upset and cross?'

'It was the way she said it. She had a funny look on her face. She was making fun of me, I know it! And that stupid boy started laughing. He deserved what he got!'

'OK, Keeley,' I said, taking this in calmly and slowly. My heart bled for her, and what I really wanted to do was stop the car and give her a great big hug.

'The thing is, I know Miss Fraser, and I am sure the very last thing she would want to do is make fun of you.'

'So how come that dickhead laughed?'

'Keeley,' I sighed. 'What have I said about your language?'

'I don't care what you've said! I don't care what anybody says, including the stinking teachers. And so what if it's just my mum and me on my family tree? So fucking what!'

Keeley now had her arms folded sharply across her chest and was staring defiantly out of the window.

'What about your grandfather?' I ventured. 'Shouldn't he be on the family tree, as he's your mum's dad, isn't he?

Jonathan's eyes widened and he shot me another glance, this time one that told me I might have said too much, or the wrong thing. I had thought about my question, though, and hadn't just blurted it out carelessly. The fact was that Keeley did have a grandfather and, whatever he had done – which remained unproven – he was a member of her small family. In my opinion, erasing him from the family tree was quite a dramatic statement, and not something that should go unchallenged.

Unfortunately, Keeley went red in the face and suddenly made a rather alarming sound that reminded me of my food blender when I've over-packed it, and the blades are fighting to turn.

'Ggrrrrhhhhh! What about my grandfather?' she growled. 'Ggrrrrhhhhh! Wouldn't you like to fucking know! Ggrrrrhhhhh! Well I'm not telling you. You can all get stuffed, fucking nosy parkers!'

Jonathan and I didn't rise to this, though we both desperately wanted to find out more.

'I'm sorry you feel like this,' I said gently, turning to face Keeley and giving her a sympathetic look.

Keeley ignored me and pointedly returned her gaze out of the car window. *I will have to make a note of all this later*, I thought. Jonathan was probably right; it was a question too far. I would quote myself verbatim in my log, and report exactly how this conversation came about.

As our journey continued I had what felt like a hundred questions grinding around my brain. What exactly had Keeley's grandfather done to her? When had he done it, and for how long? What did her mother know, and what else had she done to Keeley that we didn't already know about?'

I wondered if Keeley would ever tell and, more importantly, would she ever be able to move forward in her life? Would she ever grow up into the happy, beautiful girl she surely was deep down?

10

'It's like living with Jekyll and Hyde'

We had no idea what happened in the therapy session. We waited outside the clinic for the forty-five-minute appointment and of course didn't ask any questions afterwards. We understood that what happened in therapy stayed in therapy, and it would have been inappropriate and unprofessional of us to fish in anyway at all about what Keeley or her therapist discussed.

To our surprise and relief, Keeley emerged in a much happier and more responsive mood, behaving as if nothing had happened at school or in the car. She acknowledged Jonathan politely and even thanked him for driving, and then she began chatting about the carnival bonnets and asking me if we were ready to start painting them, which we were. I decided to enjoy her good mood while it lasted, and didn't mention the events of earlier in the day again.

*

When we got home Keeley went up to her bedroom to change out of her uniform. Jonathan and I saw my mum out and then snatched a few minutes together in the kitchen.

'You know you said Keeley was no angel?' I said quietly, giving a slightly world-weary smile, as I felt quite exhausted and mentally drained by this point in the day.

'You can say that again.'

'Well, I've got a better way of describing her.'

'What's that?'

'It's like living with Jekyll and Hyde! That's the conclusion I've come to. It's peaks and troughs, highs and lows, a total roller coaster of a ride with Keeley.'

'You're right,' he said, nodding. 'You've hit the nail on the head, Angela, but let's look on the bright side. I'm sure the dips will lessen as time goes on. That's why we're looking after Keeley, isn't it? It's our job to help her straighten out these moods and lapses and improve her behaviour. I think we're doing OK. We'll get there, I'm sure.'

I hadn't expected him to be quite so optimistic after the afternoon we'd had, but I felt better after talking to Jonathan. He had the right attitude, and I told myself that I had to keep the faith that Keeley's behaviour would get better, because what was the alternative? If I didn't believe we could help her, what was the point of keeping her in our care? We had to continue trying as hard as we could, and I would simply have to keep on reminding myself that she was not a bad girl; it was the hand she had been dealt in life that was bad.

*

It turned out to be a lovely evening. After dinner we got out the paints and did some work on the bonnets. Keeley thoroughly enjoyed herself and did a very good job. She beamed when I praised her, and she very willingly helped me tidy up. The boys were both in a good frame of mind too, and all five of us ended up sitting around the kitchen table, enjoying a really pleasant chat before Keeley went up to bed.

'Not long until our weekend away,' Carl commented, his eyes shining. 'Are you coming, Keeley?'

She looked at me expectantly.

'Do you know, I haven't even got round to telling Keeley about that yet, but the answer is yes. That's if you want to, Keeley?'

She was thrilled to bits when I explained all about the forthcoming weekend break to Wales. I'd cleared it with her social worker, which was actually the reason I hadn't told Keeley sooner because I'd only just got the all clear.

'The boys will go off fishing and you can too, if you want to, or we can go and do some sightseeing instead. There's a lovely castle we could have a look at.'

Her eyes widened like saucers.

'I'm up to the bit in my book where the dancer is hiding in the castle with the mice! Will there be mice?'

'No, I don't think so, but you never know,' I laughed.

Phillip began excitedly quizzing Jonathan about fishing rods and bait and Carl became very animated, talking about organising a stone-skipping competition, which was something the two boys and Jonathan had done before and loved.

It was one of those times when I was reminded why I do this job. To see Keeley, Carl and Phillip all looking carefree and excited, just as kids should, made me count my blessings.

I ran a bath before bed and as I soaked in the bubbles I thought back to 1986, which is when my fostering journey began. That was when I responded to an advert in the local paper for foster carers, and when I enthusiastically talked Jonathan into giving it a go for a little while, or perhaps until we had kids of our own.

We both look back now and laugh at how naive we were at the start. We thought fostering was simply about giving kids a comfortable home and loving care, and we imagined that if we provided both of those things we'd be doing a perfect job, and nothing could go wrong – just as the many people who've passed comment on our job over the years imagine fostering is like. Of course, we'd learned from experience that, just like with parenting, there is a lot more to fostering than that. We hadn't made it particularly easy for ourselves either, I reflected. Deciding to train as specialist carers for challenging teenagers, five years after starting out as foster carers, had certainly added to the demands of the job. Just like Keeley's placement with us, our fostering experience had been a roller-coaster ride, but I didn't regret a thing. Helping children not just survive and develop, but flourish, is a priceless experience, and one I can never imagine tiring of.

As it happens, Jonathan and I never did have children of our own. After years of waiting and wondering, then being told I had a condition affecting my ovaries that lessened but didn't rule out my chances of falling pregnant, I woke up one day in a house full of kids and finally acknowledged that I would never give birth to my own. I can remember the day vividly, because the feeling I experienced was so powerful. The sun was shining when I got out of bed. I'd slept really soundly and felt a great sense of wellbeing. I could hear the sound of youngsters talking and laughing and chasing around upstairs, and it made me smile as I made my way to the bathroom. The mirrored door on the vanity cabinet was slightly ajar when I walked in the room, and the angle of it meant I caught an unexpected look at my reflection. In that moment, I saw myself with real clarity.

I was Angela the foster carer; Angela who looked after other people's kids – those children who needed help and love and understanding. My heart swelled with pride as I let this thought flood me. I felt very lucky to be in this privileged position, having so many children coming into my life. Over the years many of our foster kids have kept in touch after they left us, and that's another myth of fostering that's been well and truly exploded.

'I don't know how you can give them back,' is a remark I've heard countless times.

'I don't, not usually,' I generally smile. 'They never really leave.'

Over the years we've enjoyed some amazing reunions, where dozens of adults of all ages have gathered around Jonathan and I for a photograph, and we have all caught up with each other's news. The weddings we have attended have been as poignant as if the bride and groom were our own flesh and blood, and our foster children's children have become our godchildren and, in several cases, just like grandchildren to us. I cherish each and every one of the special occasions we all shared, because they are my family now.

That memorable, sunny morning, when I stopped and reflected and counted my blessings, took place a few years before Keeley came to stay, when I was heading towards my mid-forties. Jonathan and I had been married for more than twenty years by that time. We had never taken precautions and, until then, I had never stopped wondering if I might conceive. I always told myself that stranger things had happened, and I read stories in magazines and newspapers every once in a while that made me wonder if I would be the lucky one next time; one of those women who surprised everyone by suddenly and unexpectedly falling pregnant. Jonathan and I talked about it less and less as the years rolled by, because we honestly didn't feel the need to as we were so happy with the way things had turned out. We had kids like Carl, Phillip and Keeley in our hearts and in our home, and our lives were full. Fostering was our destiny and we embraced it willingly.

11

'I told you he was weird, didn't I?'

In June we took our touring caravan to Wales for the week-end, and Carl, Phillip and Keeley were all as good as gold on the journey to the campsite. The weather was fine, and as soon as we'd unpacked the car the five of us headed down to the rocky coastline to get our bearings and stretch our legs.

The boys soon started skipping stones, and Keeley and I sat on a rock and watched for a while. Phillip was on particularly good form, and he managed to make his stone 'skip' seven times, which made him punch the air in delight.

'I can beat that!' Jonathan challenged enthusiastically, before making a disastrous throw that resulted in his stone splashing and sinking the second it hit the water.

Phillip and Carl laughed their heads off and Keeley and I had a chuckle too.

'Poor Jonathan!' I said, although I knew he would take it all in good spirit.

The competition inevitably went up a gear after that, and

the boys and Jonathan became engrossed in beating Phillip's top score.

'Can we go to the fairground now?' Keeley asked, having soon lost interest in watching the boys.

We'd spotted a poster for a small travelling fair on our way to the campsite and had all agreed we'd like to visit.

'We thought perhaps we'd go this evening,' I said. 'Let's see what everybody else fancies doing, shall we?'

'Well, we could go now, couldn't we? Just you and me, Angela?'

'We could, but I'd like us all to go together to the fair. It's something that's usually good fun when there's a group, and I know the boys want to go too.'

Keeley didn't look convinced and she put on a sulky face and sighed.

'I tell you what, why don't you and me have a paddle?'

'OK!' she said, brightening up.

We both took off our sandals and edged tentatively into the water, which felt icy cold despite the warm weather.

Keeley began shrieking and giggling.

'It's too cold!' she yelled. 'Argh! I hate it!'

She didn't really hate it though, as she paddled around for ages, stopping from time to time to pick up interesting looking bits of rock and shell. At one point a tiny crab crawled sideways over her foot, which made her explode with a mixture of fright and delight.

'This is brilliant!' she said. 'I didn't think the holiday was going to be this good!'

Keeley had never been to the coast before and I felt

honoured to witness her first experience of walking bare-foot into the sea. She looked happy and relaxed, and when the five of us eventually started heading back to the caravan for lunch I experienced that same feeling of satisfaction I'd felt when we had sat around the kitchen table together, chatting and discussing the trip. *This is what life is all about*, I thought, and I felt really good.

'I want to go on the roller coaster!' Keeley announced, having turned the conversation back to the fairground once more.

'Me too,' Phillip said. 'I like the dodgems best though. Do you think they'll have dodgems?'

'I expect so,' I said. 'We'll find out later. How about we have a fish and chip supper for tea later on, and then we'll go to the fair after that?'

Everybody was in agreement, but I noticed Carl had been more quiet than usual and was walking slightly apart from the rest of us.

'What's your favourite ride, Carl?' I asked.

He thought about this for a moment and then said that he wasn't sure.

'Not the dodgems, like Phillip?'

'No, not really. They're OK, I suppose.'

'What about the roller coaster?'

'Er, not really. I've never been on one before, I don't think. I'll probably give that a miss.'

'Scaredy cat!' Keeley teased. 'You're scared aren't you, Carl?'

'No, I'm not,' he said. 'I've just told you, I've never even been on a roller coaster so how can I even know if I'm scared of one?'

Keeley had a mocking, triumphant look on her face and I gave her a gentle warning.

'Not everybody is the same,' I said. 'If Carl doesn't want to go on some of the rides, then that is up to him. Don't start teasing him or criticising, please, Keeley. You'll spoil the fun for everybody, and we all want to enjoy the break.'

Keeley looked slightly put out to have been spoken to like this and stomped off in front, while Phillip and Carl decided to race each other back to the caravan.

'Quite fitting that it was the mention of the word "roller coaster" that turned the mood, don't you think?' Jonathan winked, once all three of the kids were out of earshot.

'What do you mean?'

'Well what is it we say about looking after Keeley? It's like a roller-coaster ride. We might have had a lovely morning, but hold on tight for the next twist and turn! The afternoon could be an entirely different kettle of fish.'

I laughed but, unfortunately, Jonathan's slightly tongue-in-cheek prediction turned out to be uncannily accurate.

About twenty minutes later, once we were all back in the caravan, Keeley managed to 'accidentally' tread on Phillip's bare foot with the wooden heel of her sandal. Understandably it made him yelp in pain, but she could scarcely bring herself to say sorry, and Phillip's cheeks flushed red with anger. Next, Keeley complained about the picnic lunch I set out, saying she wanted chips instead. The fact we were having fish and chips for tea didn't seem to make any difference and she grumbled non-stop.

'Keeley, if you don't stop complaining about the food I'm not sure I'll be taking you to the chip shop tonight, or the fairground,' I said, exasperated.

'I don't believe you! That would spoil things for you too! What would we do instead?'

'What do you mean, what would we do?'

'You'd have to stay with me, wouldn't you, Angela?'

'Jonathan and I could both stay and the boys could go on their own. We don't mind, and I don't see why the boys should miss out on the fun of the fair just because of your behaviour.'

Keeley huffed and smouldered for a while, but thankfully had no answer to this. Unfortunately, she wasn't done yet, as when Carl started talking about the next day's fishing trip that was being planned along with Phillip and Jonathan, Keeley rudely told Carl he was 'like a boring old man'.

Jonathan and I desperately wanted to keep the peace, and we told Keeley she was being unkind and rude, and asked her to stop as her behaviour was making other people feel sad and cross.

'You can't put me in time out here, can you?' she teased, giving me a rather menacing smile. 'Because you can't send me to my bedroom!'

This was true, as Keeley would be sleeping on the bed that would be pulled out once the dining table we were gathered around was folded away.

'No, but I could do better than that. One of us could take

you home and leave the others to enjoy the holiday, if you can't join in nicely.'

'You wouldn't do that,' she smirked, which was not far from the truth, as to-ing and fro-ing to the campsite would have been almost impossible in the space of the weekend, as we were several hours away from home.

'Try me,' I said, as convincingly as possible.

I thought I had finally got through to Keeley because, for the next hour or so at least, she cut out the cheek and the aggravating behaviour and joined in perfectly well with a game of swing ball with Jonathan and the boys.

Later in the afternoon we went to play crazy golf on the campsite and I hoped that Keeley's good behaviour would continue. However, after struggling with the first hole a few times she started to lose her patience.

'I can't do it! I'm useless!' she shouted, after whacking the ball far too hard and hitting it out of play in temper and frustration.

'No, you're not useless, you're just learning and you'll get better,' I soothed. 'You just need to take your time. You can do it, Keeley. Come on, have another try! Put the ball back on the starting spot and try again.'

Keeley took a deep breath.

'OK,' she said through gritted teeth.

I was glad to see she now looked more determined than angry as she replaced her golf ball on the dot at the start of the hole. Her face was etched with concentration and she focused intently on the castle gateway she was aiming for, as she took a very firm swing. I was willing this to be a good shot, but the ball missed the target by quite some distance, smashed into the castle's turret and ricocheted back down the green matting. As if to taunt her, it rolled this way and that before eventually coming to a stop back at her feet, almost precisely on the starting spot.

Carl and Phillip burst out laughing. I couldn't really blame them; it actually was quite a comical moment that you really couldn't make up.

'I wish we'd filmed that!' Phillip laughed. 'We could have sold it to *You've Been Framed*!'

Not surprisingly, Keeley didn't see the funny side of this at all.

'What are you fucking laughing at!' she screamed.

The boys' eyes widened and they both looked shocked and embarrassed. The crazy golf course was busy that day and there were groups of people all around us. Several looked over, some raising eyebrows and others nudging one another.

'Keeley!' Jonathan said firmly. 'There is absolutely no need to use language like that.'

'Fuck off!' she shouted at him at the top of her voice.

Keeley then started to raise her golf club in the air, and so I dashed swiftly to her side and put my hand on her arm, as I was worried she might try to hit someone or take a swing at something with it.

'Keeley!' I said. 'This is completely unacceptable. You need to calm down and have a think about your behaviour.'

'OWWWW!' she bellowed. 'Get off my arm. You've hurt me! OWWWW!'

I flushed with embarrassment. I could feel the other holidaymakers looking over at the commotion, and I was afraid they might think I had actually hurt Keeley. The reality was that I'd barely even touched her, let alone hurt her.

I am acutely aware that any physical contact with a child must be very carefully monitored. We can't even hug a child without asking their permission and, right from the day she moved in, I'd checked with Keeley that she was happy for me to give her a hug at bedtime. She had agreed to this, and that is why we had a routine in place where I gave her a hug at her bedroom door before she tucked herself into bed. I wouldn't have laid a finger on her if she had told me she didn't want a hug, because the child's wishes must be respected at all times. In some cases, where a child has been physically or sexually abused, we might be advised to only give them a group hug with other adults and children in a circle, so there can be no danger they feel threatened, and there is no risk that they might be drawn into making an inappropriate complaint against you.

I had most certainly not taken hold of Keeley with any force, and had only placed my hand lightly on her arm because I was worried about what she might do with the golf club. Her reaction was completely irrational, and extremely irritating.

'Keeley, I am not having this,' I said. 'You are behaving very badly indeed. I want you to stop shouting and creating a scene, and I want you to come and sit on that bench over there with me, right now.'

'All right then,' she snarled, looking at the bench I'd nodded towards, which was positioned just outside the golf course.

What I really wanted to do was march her straight back to the caravan, but that would not have been sensible at all in the circumstances. Social Services always advise us that it is safe practice to avoid being alone with a child as much as possible when they are in this type of mood, as that way you are less likely to be accused of something you haven't done. Even though Keeley had embarrassed me in front of lots of people here, it was the right thing for me to stay in full view, so that if it came to it I would have witnesses to prove I did nothing to harm Keeley.

'Are *they* carrying on?' Keeley said, pulling a face at Jonathan and the boys, and muttering 'losers' under her breath.

'Yes,' I said, ignoring the insult. 'There is no reason why the boys shouldn't play on.'

'Good.'

Keeley tossed her hair back over her shoulders, threw the golf club to the ground and marched angrily beside me as I led her to the bench.

'Why did you make it seem like I hurt you?' I asked, when we were seated next to each other.

'Dunno.'

'Well, can you have a think, please, Keeley? I know I

couldn't have hurt you, because I only placed my hand very lightly on your arm. I would never want to hurt you.'

'It did hurt. I've got bruises on that arm.'

I sighed. Keeley was very good at coming up with an answer to everything, and I realised I had to be very careful here. For once, I was very sure I knew the real story, but now she'd mentioned the bruises I was reminded that I had to always give the child the benefit of the doubt, however slight that may be.

'Right, I didn't know you had bruises on that arm at the moment, and I am sorry about that. It's very important that you understand that I didn't know about the bruises, and that I would never have touched your arm had I known it was going to hurt you. I didn't mean to hurt you.'

'OK,' Keeley muttered.

I was glad Keeley had accepted my apology. If she hadn't then I would have offered her the chance of calling her social worker, or talking to the duty social worker. They would probably have asked to speak to whoever was present when the incident took place, which was another good reason for me staying put. As it was, I could now simply write in my report exactly what had happened, and the fact it took place in a busy public place.

Keeley then surprised me by taking the conversation in another direction.

'My granddad used to hurt me,' she suddenly blurted out. 'I used to tell my mum, but she didn't tell anybody.'

'Your granddad Eric? He used to hurt you?'

'Yes. When he was looking after me. He didn't look after

me, though, because he hurt me, in the box room, where my mum locked me up. I told you he was weird, didn't I?'

'Yes, I remember you told me he was weird, but you didn't tell me he hurt you, in the box room.'

Keeley nodded vacantly and began playing with her hair, wrapping her finger around one of the thick curls. Then she turned to look at me, her big brown eyes set intently on mine. I wondered what she was going to say next, and I think I even held my breath.

'Angela, can we get a candyfloss when we go to the fairground?'

'Yes, Keeley, we can, if they sell it,' I said, exhaling and trying to smile. Keeley grinned with delight, showing all her lovely white teeth and looking like the innocent eight-year-old girl she should have been.

Very sadly, it was clearer than ever that Eric had taken some of her childhood from her. How much, and in what way, I didn't know. All I could do was hope Keeley would feel able to share some more of her story, but would she?

12

'Go on, stab him!'

After enjoying a fish-and-chip supper the five of us set off to the fairground, which wasn't far from our campsite. I hoped a fun evening out might be just the tonic Keeley needed. She had been a little bit quieter than usual after talking about her grandfather. I'd made a note of exactly what she had told me and would phone Social Services once we were back home, but for now I just wanted Keeley to enjoy the rest of our weekend break, and hopefully make some memories that she wouldn't be afraid of revisiting in years to come.

We decided to go to the dodgems first, which delighted Phillip. Carl wasn't really bothered about going on, but he reluctantly agreed to share Phillip's car, which meant Jonathan would ride on his own and I would take Keeley in with me. The music was blaring and the lights flashing, and Keeley had a steely glint in her eyes when the cars powered into life.

'Come on, Angela, let's get the boys!' she said, and I

obliged by steering towards the rubber bumper of Phillip and Carl's bright blue car.

I clipped it just enough to give them a gentle jolt and Phillip roared with laughter while Carl turned round and said a slightly strained but playful, 'Oi! Leave us alone!'

'Scaredy-cat, scaredy-cat,' Keeley taunted, pointing her finger at Carl. I didn't see his reaction because the boys whizzed off, chasing after Jonathan around the next corner. I did gently ask Keeley not to tease Carl, though, as I desperately didn't want anything else to go wrong today.

After another couple of laps I got us hemmed into a bit of a traffic jam and Phillip shouted, 'We'll get you out!' before crashing square into the back of our silver car. I jolted my neck a bit and Keeley was flung as far forward as her seat belt would allow.

'Wanker!' she shouted angrily, putting her middle finger up at Phillip and holding it aloft for what felt like an age. Once again I could sense other people looking over disapprovingly, and to my deep embarrassment the tattooed young man who was running the ride shouted, 'Oi! Less of that, young lady!' and shot me a dirty look, as if to say: 'Can't you control your kid?'

'Oh my God!' I snapped, pulling Keeley's hand back into the car. 'Stop it, Keeley! Stop it this minute.'

'Wankers, wankers, wankers,' she went on, getting louder and louder.

'Stop it, Keeley!' Jonathan called as he cruised past, looking at us instead of where he was going. He was so distracted he then promptly crashed into a broken-down dodgem car, which made him spin around wildly on the spot.

'For heaven's sake . . .' he shouted, as he tried to regain control, not to mention some semblance of decorum. 'What on earth . . .'

I looked up and saw the boys passing us once more. Phillip was now creased up laughing and even Carl was trying to keep his face straight. I was furious though, and when we finally got off the ride Jonathan looked mortified.

'I could hear you all over the circuit,' he said to Keeley. 'You can't use language like that. It's completely unaccept-able, do you understand? And as for the finger signal . . . I never want to see that again. Never!'

She wrinkled her nose and jutted her chin towards Carl and Phillip.

'It was *their* fault! They started it!'

The boys just shrugged and sniggered, clearly thinking this was too ridiculous a scenario to bother arguing about, especially with a little girl.

'Honestly, Keeley, the boys didn't intend to jolt us so hard,' I said, 'and in any case that's what happens some-times on the dodgems. You need to apologise to all of us for creating another scene like this, and you need to do it properly.'

Keeley thought about this for a moment, and then she stepped forward and stamped as hard as she could on Phil-lip's foot before running off into the crowds. Phillip yelped and called her a 'little cow', and Jonathan shouted at me to stay put while he gave chase.

I comforted Phillip and reassured him we would deal with this.

'You'd better,' he said. 'She's driving me mad.'

'Me too,' Carl muttered. 'I'm sick of her.'

As we waited for Jonathan to bring Keeley back, the two boys shared several complaints they'd clearly been stewing about for a while. It turned out Keeley had pinched Phillip hard on the hand when they were in the back of the car together the previous week, and she had continued to walk into both of their bedrooms unannounced, often when they were getting changed. On one occasion she had unlocked the bathroom door from the outside, using a coin, and barged in when Phillip was in the shower. He was particularly livid about this invasion of privacy, and who could blame him? Keeley had apparently pointed and sneered and made rude remarks about his body. He wasn't the most physically confident boy, and in any case, no thirteen-year-old lad wants to be mocked while naked in the shower.

'Why didn't you tell me?' I asked.

There was a silence and both boys looked sideways at each other.

'With me it hasn't really been a big deal,' Carl said eventually, 'and I thought she'd get bored, but she hasn't. She's much worse with Phillip, though.'

Phillip was looking at the ground, and I could see that he was flushed in the face and feeling embarrassed.

'Why didn't you say anything, Phillip?'

'I suppose, like Carl, I thought I could deal with it myself. She's only eight, isn't she? I thought I could handle it, but she's just so annoying. She's a nightmare. I've never met anyone so irritating before, Angela, and she knows exactly which buttons to press and how to lie her way out of trouble.'

Carl nodded. 'That just about sums it up,' he concurred. 'We're no match for her, which is a bit embarrassing. She's an expert in bad behaviour, and how to get away with it.'

Moments later Jonathan reappeared, looking extremely harassed.

'Where's Keeley?' I said.

'She ran into the ladies' loos,' he panted. 'You'll have to go in, Angela.'

The boys rolled their eyes. They were clearly not impressed, or surprised, at being in the middle of another one of Keeley's dramas.

I dashed through the crowds to the far side of the funfair, where the ladies' toilet block was, and found Keeley sitting inside, on the corner of a counter next to a washbasin. She was angrily kicking the hand dryer on the wall. Several women and young girls were looking at her nervously, and she was staring back at them defiantly.

'Keeley, there you are! Please stop kicking, you might break the dryer.'

All the women turned to look at me and one tut-tutted loudly, showing her disapproval.

I wanted to shout, *Don't treat me like that! I'm a foster carer and, believe me, I'm doing my level best with this child. It's not her fault she's like this, and it's not mine either!*

I didn't, of course. Instead, I focused completely on Keeley. She had now begun kicking even harder. All my instincts told me to get hold of her, lift her off the counter and remove her from the toilets, but I didn't want to touch her in case she accused me of hurting her again.

'Keeley!' I implored. 'Please! You will be in serious trouble if that gets broken.'

'So will you!' she replied.

'Me? It's not me doing the damage, Keeley. It is you who is behaving badly. Now stop it at once.'

She gave the dryer one last kick and then stopped and looked me straight in the eye.

'Are you angry with me, Angela?'

'Yes!'

'Good!' she said gleefully, and then she jumped off the counter and walked out the door.

We struggled through the rest of the weekend with Keeley's unpredictable behaviour dictating the mood of the group. She was narky, sulky and ungrateful, whatever we said or did to try to gee her along and rescue the trip. I took her to visit the castle we'd talked about and, as it was just the two of us while the boys went fishing, I thought this might have been a success. Sadly it wasn't. She was just as difficult to be with and I had to face the fact that it was nigh on impossible to predict anything at all to do with Keeley's behaviour.

At one point the two of us watched a re-enactment of a battle and Keeley completely threw herself into the drama of it all. For a few minutes I was delighted, thinking I'd found something that had captured her imagination and would let her lose herself in fantasy for a while.

'Kill him!' she suddenly screamed when one soldier got the better of his opponent and charged forward with his sword.

There was a menacing tone in her voice that alarmed me, and when I looked at her face she was practically snarling.

'Go on, stab him!' she shrieked, jumping up and down and waving her fists in the air. 'KILL, KILL, KILL!' she chanted.

At one point an elderly gentleman turned around and looked at Keeley in mock horror.

'It's not real, my dear!' he guffawed, but she seemed oblivious to everyone around her and continued to bay for blood.

'Keeley, calm down,' I had to say in the end.

'Shut up, Angela,' she retorted. 'You're so boring, did you know that?'

I had a long chat with Sandy over the phone as soon as I could on the Monday morning following our trip. I felt we needed some support, and there was a lot to discuss. Luckily we were due one of our regular placement meetings shortly too, which were held every six weeks and also attended by Keeley's social worker, Joan, plus Sheila Briggs. The aim of these meetings is to monitor the progress of the placement, make sure everybody is happy with the arrangements – Keeley included – and to ensure that everyone concerned is up to date with any relevant news or change in circumstances.

After we spoke on the phone Sandy and Joan then came to the house and had a word with us all. Joan spoke to Keeley in private, which is standard practice prior to a placement meeting. Sandy asked me how it was going with the star charts, and using time out, which were the two strategies that had been suggested at the core meeting to help improve Keeley's behaviour.

'To be honest, Sandy, I decided pretty quickly that neither were going to work very well with Keeley. She craves attention, so time out aggravates her even more. I have persevered with the star chart, but I don't think it's helping. Once she's had the reward she goes straight back to behaving badly. It's not teaching her anything, I don't think.'

Keeley had actually achieved ten stars and had been thrilled to pick out a new outfit for one of her dolls. Now she was working towards the next ten, and she had already decided which felt-tip pen set she wanted. I couldn't take the stars away when she behaved badly, though, as that would not have been fair at all, and I'd actually been working quite hard to spot good behaviour and reward Keeley. I think if the truth were told her behaviour hadn't changed at all as a result of the star chart, and the weekend in Wales proved the point.

'The only thing that really works with Keeley is giving her attention,' I said. 'Ideally one to one, and preferably from me rather than Jonathan. She's never happier than when the two of us are making something together.'

Sandy listened carefully as I detailed the events of the strained weekend, and especially when we discussed Keeley's allegations that I had hurt her. As our support social worker, nipping this situation in the bud was clearly Sandy's most pressing concern. It would cause difficulties for everybody, including Keeley herself, if Jonathan and I had to be formally investigated. Just like with Keeley's previous foster carer, we could be suspended from caring for children while the investigation was carried out. This would mean Carl and Phillip might have to move to other placements, which would be extremely disruptive, and clearly this situation had to be avoided at all costs.

'I'll ask Joan to also arrange a visit,' Sandy said decisively. 'As Keeley's social worker, I think she should be the one to spell out the potential consequences of her accusations and general bad behaviour. How does that sound?'

I agreed to this plan. It was clear Sandy trusted me, and as usual she had recognised the priority and honed in on it. I felt better after speaking to her, and I looked forward to Joan's visit. The weekend in Wales had left me feeling quite unsettled. Normally with kids, once I feel I've identified their issues and worked out some strategies to help them move forward I feel I'm making progress. It isn't always fast, but I nearly always have a sense that the child is at least heading in the right general direction. With Keeley it was different. It was as if we were constantly taking one step forward and two steps back, and so any support Joan could provide would be very welcome indeed.

13

'You all hate me!'

Joan had arranged to visit one afternoon after school, and I'd explained to Keeley in advance what was happening.

'Joan is due to arrive soon, and she would like to ask you how you're getting on,' I reminded Keeley on the day in question. 'I've told her about the trouble we had in Wales and she is going to discuss it with you.'

'Why?'

'Because we all want to help you improve your behaviour.'

'But I'm fine now. Why is everyone still going on about it?'

'Are you really fine?' I asked, raising my eyebrows. 'I hope so, Keeley, but I want to make sure.'

She seemed to accept this and went up to her room to do her homework before Joan arrived, but it wasn't long before I heard Phillip shouting at her to 'Get lost!' and I went charging up the stairs.

'I don't believe it!' Phillip shouted. 'She's coming in my

119

room again, Angela. She won't stop! Will she ever stop? I wish she'd just get lost.'

'He hurt me!' Keeley retaliated, placing her hands on her hips.

'What?' Phillip said, looking shocked.

'You heard. Look at my face!'

It turned out that Keeley had been running in and out of Phillip's room, poking him in the ribs, flicking things over on his desk and generally making a terrible nuisance of herself. In an effort to stop her he had piled up some bags and books behind his door, and the next time Keeley tried to barge in, the door clattered, and she hit her face on it.

'Phillip, why didn't you come and get me when this started?' I asked, though as I'd already started to realise, as a teenage boy, he was finding it very hard to admit a little girl was tormenting him. He saw it as an affront to his machismo, and he didn't want to admit defeat.

'I was just trying to get my work done, Angela. I couldn't be bothered coming all the way downstairs, it's so annoying and a waste of my time. She kept promising she wouldn't come in again and then she did. Oh my God. I'm so sick of this. Can I have a lock on my bedroom door, please?'

This was something I had actually been thinking seriously about, and had discussed with Jonathan. We'd never done it before, but with Keeley persistently breaking the rules we were feeling extremely uncomfortable. We have always been very carefully about sticking to the fostering guidelines we'd been taught, but now Keeley was making it impossible for us to do so. We were regularly reminded in training about the possible risks involved in allowing access to bedrooms, and some of the stories made the hair on the back of our necks stand up. Allegations of theft were scenarios we could easily guess at, but there were other, more shocking examples too. One little girl had taken matches from a teenager's room without him knowing, and then started a fire in the garage. A male carer had been accused of deliberately walking in on a young teenager while she was undressing. He was ultimately cleared of any wrongdoing, but needless to say we did not want to find ourselves in a stressful and dangerous situation like that. Fostering was not just a job to us, it was our lives, and we had to be one hundred per cent safe and transparent in everything we did, every single day.

When Joan arrived I discussed putting locks on the doors. After hearing why, she didn't hesitate in saying she thought this was a sensible idea, and that she would arrange for us to receive the formal permission required from Social Services to sanction our request. The locks on the outside of the doors would only be used when the rooms were empty, to stop someone going in when we weren't there, and we would also be allowed to put a simple bolt on the inside at the bottom of the boys' doors, so that when they were in their room Carl and Phillip could secure their door shut without being actually locked in, which would have been a fire risk. There would be no lock on the inside of Keeley's door, as she was too young to be locking herself inside a room.

I was relieved to have Joan's support and I told her this. Then I asked Keeley to come downstairs, which she did willingly. In fact, when Keeley came into the lounge she looked like butter wouldn't melt in her mouth. She had Jinty in her arms, and she started talking very sweetly to the social worker about dolls and teddy bears.

'Did you have a favourite doll, when you were little?' she asked Joan, who had kindly remarked what a pretty dress Jinty was wearing.

'Yes, I did, Keeley. She was called Tilly-Jo and she had red plaits. I've still got her somewhere. I think she's in my loft.'

Keeley giggled and hugged her doll. 'I'd never put you in the loft, Jinty!' she whispered in her cloth ear. It was extremely hard to believe that this was the same little girl who was capable of displaying such bad behaviour as we'd seen in Wales, and at other times.

'It's lovely to see you enjoying playing with your doll,' Joan said, 'but I've been hearing that you haven't been behaving so nicely all the time, have you, Keeley?'

Keeley shook her head sadly from side to side.

'Do you know why you have been causing trouble and swearing?'

Again Keeley shook her head, and now big tears formed in her eyes and began dripping down her cheeks.

'Here, have a tissue,' Joan said kindly, fishing one out of her handbag. 'I'm not here to make you cry, or to make you feel bad. I'm here because I want to help you, and Angela wants to help you. Everybody will be happier if you behave better, so is there anything you can tell us that might help us to help you?'

Keeley shrugged and looked at the floor. 'I don't mean it,' she said eventually. 'I don't like being naughty.'

'OK,' Joan said gently. 'I'm sure you don't. How about we draw up a contract? I would like you to agree to three things, Keeley. How does that sound?'

'What?' she said, looking worried.

'They are not difficult things. First, no bad language. Second, if you feel like you are going to lose your temper, count to ten and go and sit quietly on your own before you react, and thirdly, think about how other people around you are feeling, and if you are making them feel bad, then again you must stop, count to ten and walk away.'

Joan had clearly thought this through before she arrived, which impressed me, and she handed Keeley a piece of paper with the three points clearly set out.

'If you can do these things before my next visit, I think you will deserve a big treat, what do you think, Angela? I think it will also make it much easier for Angela to continue being your carer, which is what you want, isn't it, Keeley?'

Keeley nodded, and I readily agreed to provide a treat if and when appropriate.

'Thanks for your help, Joan,' I said, feeling a surge of gratitude for having her professional support, and a structure of sorts in place.

However, when Joan had gone I was left feeling a bit uneasy, and I wasn't immediately sure why.

'What's the matter?' Jonathan said as he leafed through the telephone directory, looking for a place to buy locks for the bedroom doors.

'I'm not sure Joan's contract is going to help,' I found myself fretting. 'In fact, I've got a horrible feeling it's not going to solve Keeley's problems at all.'

'Why not? We've had contracts with kids before and they are usually very useful.'

'Yes, but this one is really just a more official version of the star chart and time out. The only difference is that she's effectively being asked to put herself in time out. I know Joan is very experienced and she's seen good results with these types of contracts, but I can't help thinking that Keeley is just not going to get it. What's more, I can see she's very fond of me, and I know she likes it here. I'm not sure how it's going to affect her, thinking that if the contract doesn't work the placement may not be able to continue.'

'You may be right, but we don't know, do we?' Jonathan said reasonably. 'I do think you've got a point comparing it to the star chart and time out, but the idea that Keeley's bad behaviour might cause the breakdown of the placement could be just the thing that makes her turn a corner. We'll have to cross our fingers and hope for the best.'

We had the placement meeting the following week, at which everything we'd discussed with Sandy, Joan and Keeley was reiterated, agreed by Sheila Briggs and recorded on file. All three members of the Social Services staff praised our efforts, acknowledged the work we were doing and wished us luck in implementing the strategies discussed, and finally making better progress with Keeley.

It gave us a lift to know we had this professional backing, and that we were appreciated, but unfortunately our spirits didn't stay raised for long. We had an extremely difficult week after the locks were fitted to the bedroom doors, because Keeley decided to find new ways to irritate the boys, and particularly Phillip.

The first trick she pulled was to steal some raw vegetables from the fridge, break off little bits and stick them in his shoes or his school bag.

'Keeley! I know this is you! Leave me alone!' he said, tipping curled-up bits of peppers, onions and carrots onto the hall floor in exasperation.

'What?' she said, giving her best 'butter wouldn't melt' gaze.

'I'm watching you!' he snapped. 'I really mean it, Keeley. I'm gonna catch you in the act and you'll be sorry!'

When I tackled Keeley I got the usual denial and indignant 'what would I do that for?' response, but one day I found the remains of the vegetables she'd broken up in her bedroom, behind her door. I had told her I was cleaning her room that day and so I had to assume she had either forgotten about the vegetables or wanted to be found out. When I spoke to her after school, I came to the conclusion it was probably the latter.

'Keeley,' I said. 'I found the same vegetables you have been putting in Phillip's shoes, in your bedroom.'

'So?'

'Well, nobody could have put them there except you. The boys can't have gone into your bedroom as you have the locks outside of the door which I lock every day. I am the only person who goes into your room, when I tell you I am going to clean and tidy it for you, and I certainly didn't put them there.'

'Angela, I've got no idea how they got there,' she scowled defiantly. 'I think you're just trying to get rid of me!'

'Get rid of you? No, I am certainly not trying to get rid of you, Keeley. The last thing I want is for you to have to move out, but please remember what Joan said. If your behaviour doesn't improve it might be impossible for you to stay, as we can't have the boys being aggravated and upset like this. It's not fair.'

I felt a pang in my chest as I said this. As I'd feared, the contract strategy had backfired. Instead of encouraging good behaviour it had made Keeley feel tested and insecure. In fact, the only message the contract seemed to have given her was that if she didn't behave she might have to leave. It was a stick, not a carrot, and I felt terribly guilty for even agreeing to use it. Keeley was a vulnerable little girl, and it just seemed awful to have put her in this position. I thought of all the lovely things about her. Keeley was brave and resilient. She had a sense of fun, a love of learning and a sweet and loving nature, given the right circumstances. It was my job to provide the environment in which her good qualities would grow and she would flourish, but could I honestly do that? I had three children to care for, not just one, and I had to think about the boys as well as Keeley. They deserved to feel safe and comfortable and happy, just like Keeley did, but was it possible for all three to live in harmony under one roof?

'Can't they move out, if they don't like it?' Keeley said, using her sweet voice now.

'No, they can't. They like it here and they want to stay. The best thing would be if you could all get along nicely.'

'I'd rather just live with you, Angela,' she said.

'That's a nice compliment to me, Keeley, but you know that can't happen. We all have to get along, that's the way it is. The boys aren't going anywhere, and nor is Jonathan.'

'Pity,' she mumbled.

'Pardon?'

'Nothing. I didn't say anything.'

The next day an almighty row erupted when Carl went to have a shower and discovered that 'someone' had put his hair wax all over his sponge.

'It wasn't me, you dickhead!' Keeley shouted when he confronted her. 'You're a lying bastard, you did it yourself to get me into trouble! You're trying to get rid of me too. You all hate me!'

When I intervened Keeley accused me of taking sides and favouring the boys, even though I chose my words carefully and didn't accuse her of anything I couldn't prove.

'Why don't you count to ten and go and sit in your room quietly and think about this,' I suggested, which was met with another angry rant.

'I told you! You're just trying to get rid of me, Angela! You hate me like everybody else. You just want me out of your sight!'

Later that evening I asked Keeley to take a shower.

'No, I won't,' she shouted. 'You'll probably accuse me of doing something else I didn't do if I go in the bathroom.'

'Why would I do that, Keeley? I don't like having unnecessary arguments, actually. I am asking you to have a shower tonight because your hair needs washing and you have had PE in school today, so you need to wash. That is the reason.'

'I don't believe you. It's a trick.'

'It's not a trick. It's for your benefit, not mine, and I certainly am not asking you because I want to aggravate you. Why on earth would I do that?'

'You just would, to get rid of me.'

I realised I was on a hiding to nothing here. Keeley had never been brilliant at showering properly. She often emerged from the bathroom with damp but unwashed hair, or grubby feet and fingernails that she clearly hadn't washed thoroughly. I'd talked to her about this many times and offered her endless encouragement, complimenting her when she did smell fresh and talking to her about how much better a person feels when they are clean. Nothing worked, and this time I decided to completely change tack.

'You know what, Keeley,' I said with a sigh. 'It's probably not worth you having a shower anyway, because you don't do it properly.'

'I do!' she argued.

'No you don't.' I replied calmly.

'I do!' she insisted, getting more animated and annoyed with me. 'I'll prove it, and you can't stop me!'

With that she flounced off to the shower and had what was probably the most thorough wash she'd had in all her time with us. It was a small victory, though I still wasn't at all sure I was winning the war; in fact, I was feeling as if I was only just keeping my defences up.

I discussed this with Jonathan later that evening, and he recounted a small success story he'd also had with Keeley, that he hadn't got round to sharing until now. She had been playing in the back garden while he was in the shed, looking for some tools to do the bedroom locks. Keeley clearly decided she would try to disrupt whatever Jonathan was doing, and she started knocking on the shed windows and doors and running away.

Jonathan thought she probably expected a similar reaction to the one the boys typically gave her whenever she knocked on their bedroom door or the bathroom and ran away. This stunt, which she pulled frequently, inevitably got their backs up, which was just what she wanted to achieve. (Another of her habits, incidentally, was to turn the bathroom light off and on repeatedly when one of the boys was in the bath or the shower as, very inconveniently, the switch was on the landing.)

Anyhow, on this particular occasion Keeley's plan to cause irritation completely backfired, because instead of telling her to stop annoying him by knocking on the shed,

Jonathan didn't react at all for about five minutes. Then, when Keeley was distracted – for some reason she was stuffing lumps of gluey paper into the cracks in the patio – he nipped out of the shed and hid behind a tree. The next time Keeley went and tapped on the shed window he leaped out from behind the tree shouting: 'Who goes there!' in his best pantomime baddie voice. Keeley squealed in surprise and Jonathan laughed.

'What were you hiding there for?' she asked, giggling and jumping up and down excitedly. 'You made me jump out of my skin!'

'I don't know, Keeley. I just felt like it. What were you tapping on the window for?'

'I don't know. I just felt like it. It's not a crime, is it?'

'No, what can be wrong with knocking on an empty shed?'

Clearly, we'd hit on something here. If we could call Keeley's bluff or use distraction techniques and humour to dissipate her plans when she was trying to aggravate and annoy, we might just be able to turn a corner in terms of her behaviour.

14

'Everything was fine until he came in!'

It was the carnival at the weekend, which I was really looking forward to, as so far the bonnet making had proved to be the best antidote of all to Keeley's bad behaviour, and I hoped this would be a satisfying and fun day.

'There's a fancy dress competition open to all the children,' I told her. 'If you like I can make you a costume.'

'Can I go as anyone?' she asked.

'Not quite. The theme is fairy tales. You can go as any character you like from a fairy tale.'

She thought carefully about this, fetched her felt-tip pens and some paper, and started writing down some ideas. Cinderella and Snow White were top of the list, but then she suddenly started shouting, 'I know, I know! I want to be the cat out of *Dick Whittington*.' It turned out that Keeley had seen this pantomime performed at a local theatre the previous Christmas and so she knew the story well, and had loved the character of the cat. I was quietly pleased, as although I'm always willing to have a try at making things, I'm not a natural dressmaker or artist, and at least a black cat was an easy costume to make.

Keeley was absolutely thrilled to bits with my efforts and she joined in enthusiastically when we made a cardboard mask complete with pipe cleaner whiskers. I added some ears to a hairband and sewed a tail onto a black leotard I picked up in the charity shop. With her long, black curls to compliment the outfit Keeley looked really good, and I asked her if she would let me take some photographs so she could remember the day. I explained that she could put the photos up in her bedroom if she wanted to, and that they could ultimately go in the memory book that I would put together for her, to help her remember her time with us. She was delighted with this idea, and I will never forget how she posed and pouted for the camera.

'Do another one like this, Angela!' she called, making every possible cat shape she could think of and curling her wrists up to make her hands dangle like paws. She was a natural performer, I realised, and I asked Keeley if she fancied finding out about a popular theatre group that was run locally for kids. I knew the lady who ran it, and offered to have a word with her.

'Oh, I'd really like that,' Keeley said, eyes widening. 'I'd love to be on stage. Would you come and watch me?'

'Of course I would. I'll find out when the group meets, and let's see if we can sort something out.'

Keeley was equally delightful when we put the finishing touches to the bonnets, just before we set off to the carnival. Jonathan fetched us a basket full of beautiful spring flowers, which we tied to the brightly painted hats using floristry tape and ribbon. They looked a picture, and the girls we'd made them for were thrilled to bits when we handed them over. I'd made an extra one for Keeley, as promised, and we carried it with us in a cardboard box, ready for her to put on when the fancy dress competition had finished.

'Do you think I'll win?' she asked excitedly, as she lined up alongside lots of fairy-tale princesses, a Goldilocks, Pinocchio and Jack from Jack and the Beanstalk.

'Who knows?' I said, smiling. 'You've got as good a chance and anyone. You look great!'

In the event Keeley took third prize and was given a book voucher for W H Smiths, which she was very pleased with. One of the Cinderellas and Pinocchio took first and second prizes, which Keeley accepted graciously. 'I think they did look the best,' she said, adding wistfully, 'my mum would like that Cinderella dress. She loves pretty dresses.'

This comment made me feel slightly uncomfortable. We'd been to a few supervised visits with Keeley's mum by now, each of them very similar to the first. Keeley always put on her most sparkly dresses and her mum picked her up and spun her around, sometimes with her hands under her dress, on Keeley's bare legs. The supervising social worker had had several words about this, I'd learned from Sandy, but it didn't seem to stop Tina behaving inappropriately. It was a difficult situation, because it did appear that Tina's low mental age was responsible for her behaviour, rather than something more sinister. She picked Keeley up like you might a young baby girl in a frock, when nappies and tights made it acceptable to touch the legs. Clearly, though, at eight years old Keeley was no baby, and her mum really should have known better.

Anyhow, the carnival was great fun, and I didn't allow those uncomfortable thoughts to cloud the enjoyment of the rest of the day. After the fancy dress competition, Keeley and I admired the floats and we both cheered and waved when we spotted the one on which the girls' choir was assembled, resplendent in their bonnets. Keeley was transfixed when they began their repertoire with a very joyful and upbeat song that got the crowd clapping and tapping their feet.

'I'd love to be in a choir like that,' Keeley said.

'Would you? Well, these girls are a little bit older than you, but perhaps you could see if you could join the choir at school?'

She thought about this for a moment, and I was hoping she might be as taken with this idea as she was about joining the theatre group. I think by this point in time, with so many fights and arguments already behind us, I was prepared to encourage anything of this nature that might distract Keeley from misbehaving.

'No, I can't do that. The teachers don't like me and they won't let me join the choir, and the girls are all the stuck up ones. They don't like me either.'

Keeley delivered this verdict very calmly, as if she accepted this was her fate and wasn't even going to bother trying to challenge this situation.

'I don't think it's true to say the teachers don't like you,' I said. 'The teachers don't like some of your behaviour some-times, but that does not mean they don't like you.'

Keeley didn't look convinced but she didn't argue, and so I carried on talking while I had her attention, and she seemed to be in a fairly responsive mood.

'As for the other girls, how do you know they don't like you? Perhaps you just need to get to know them.'

'No, they are stuck up. They look down their snooty noses at me, Angela. They think they are better than me.'

'Why do you think that?'

'It's true. They think they are better than me because they live with their mums and dads and I don't.'

I felt my heart tighten when she said this, because I knew there was probably some truth in what she was saying. Before I started fostering, I had no idea of the pre-judice that exists against children in care. Many people don't even know they are doing it and it isn't necessarily intentional, but unfortunately the mere mention of 'foster care' can provoke misguided judgements in some that can lead to discrimination against a child. Sadly, some people with no experience or understanding of fostering often jump to conclusions about a child's intelligence, their per-sonality and even their future prospects, purely because they have the label that they are in care. Most damagingly, some people imagine that a foster child is responsible for their circumstances, or that there must be something wrong with them because they have 'ended up' in a foster home. I've seen this in peoples' eyes and in their reactions many times, and I always want to say to them: 'This child was not born bad. This child was born into a bad family situation. She did not ask to be a foster child. Please understand the difference! It could have happened to you, or me, but it happened to this child. It is not her fault. She has as much right as you and I to be treated fairly and without prejudice.'

I didn't press the point about the choir, instead changing the subject and telling her a bit more about the theatre group I thought she might be interested in. It was actually a musical theatre group, I told her, and I explained that the previous year I'd watched a terrific performance they put on of *Mary Poppins*.

'Who is Mary Poppins?' she asked, which gave me another pang in my chest.

I must have been about Keeley's age the first time I watched the film, in black and white, with my family. Since then I'd watched it dozens of times, often with foster kids snuggled up on my settee. In my mind it was a part of childhood that you simply couldn't escape. Even if Keeley hadn't yet watched the film, it seemed very sad that she hadn't even heard of it.

'Mary Poppins is a magical nanny,' I said. 'It's a lovely film; we'll have to watch it together next time it's on. Seeing it on stage is lovely too. I'll keep my eyes open and see if there's a performance coming up locally. Would you like to go and see it?'

Keeley nodded.

'Do you have to play a musical instrument to be in the

theatre group?' she then asked. 'Because if you do then I'll have to forget it.'

'No, not at all. Some of the children do play instruments, I think, but mostly they sing and dance or act, or do a bit of everything. We'll find out more, shall we?'

'Yes,' she said emphatically. 'As long as none of those girls from the school choir go.'

I couldn't guarantee that, of course, but I didn't say this. Instead I promised Keeley I'd phone up Mrs Crowther, a very enthusiastic, middle-aged lady who'd run the group for years, and make enquiries.

Keeley enjoyed the carnival so much she didn't want to go home. She asked me to take her photograph several times; first when she was wearing her bonnet, again on the spinning teacups ride and also when she tried her hand at hook-a-duck and won a light-up necklace, which she loved and wore for the rest of the day.

'Can I hold your hand?' she asked when we finally set off home.

'Of course,' I said. 'Have you had a nice day?'

'The best ever. Thank you, Angela.'

That evening Keeley followed me around like a little shadow.

'Can I sit next to you?' she asked when we put the TV on in the early evening. 'Can you plait my hair? Can you help me change Jinty's clothes?'

It was lovely to see her in such a good mood and of

course I obliged, but when Jonathan came in and I told him about our day, she started behaving quite strangely.

'I'm absolutely shattered!' he declared after we'd caught up on each other's news. 'It's been such a busy day in the shop.'

'You do look tired,' I said. 'Shall I make you a cup of tea?'

'Oh yes please, I'd love one, thanks, Angela.'

Keeley narrowed her eyes and spoke to Jinty, who was sitting between us on the settee. 'Can't he make it himself?' she asked. 'Why does Angela have to do it?'

'Would you like a cup of tea, Keeley?' I asked, trying to brush over her remark. 'I'm happy to put the kettle on, and I could make a big pot for all of us to share. The boys will be back any time too.'

She let out an exaggerated sigh.

'Boys!' she huffed, again talking to Jinty. 'I wish they would go away. Far, far away and never come back.'

I couldn't ignore this.

'Keeley,' I explained. 'I know we've had a lovely day together, just you and me, but Carl and Phillip, and Jonathan, are all in this evening and this is their home too. There's no reason we can't enjoy the evening together, all five of us.'

She totally ignored me and stayed sulking in the living room while I stood up, ready to go downstairs to make the tea.

'How was the carnival then, Keeley?' Jonathan asked, as I was leaving the room. 'I heard you won a prize. Well done!'

She pretended she hadn't heard, but Jonathan told me

later that he wasn't easily put off, and he'd persisted with his questions.

'Did you take some photographs? What did you win?'

'None of your business, nosy parker!' she'd shouted, staring intently at Jinty.

'I beg your pardon!' Jonathan had exclaimed. 'I hope you weren't speaking to me like that, Keeley?'

Again she spoke to the doll. 'What was that noise? Did you hear something?'

She lifted Jinty up to her ear. 'What was that you said? Oh, yes, just a silly old man!'

'Keeley!' Jonathan said. 'Will you please stop being rude and ignoring me. I've been trying to ask you about the carnival. I heard you had a great day. How was it?'

Jonathan was shocked to see that now Keeley put her hands on her ears and began humming loudly, shaking her head from side to side.

'What on earth is going on with all this humming?' I asked, when I came back into the room with the tea tray. 'Why are you making that noise, Keeley?'

She carried on, and Jonathan relayed what had just happened.

'Keeley, if you don't start behaving properly I'm afraid I might have to send you to bed early.'

She took her hands away from her ears and lowered the volume of her humming.

'Did you hear me, Keeley? I said, please behave yourself or I will have to send you to bed early tonight.'

Keeley finally stopped humming, and then she got to her feet, hurling Jinty at Jonathan as she did so.

'It's all his fault!' she screamed. 'It's all his fucking stupid fault! Everything was fine until he came in!'

Keeley was eventually sent to bed half an hour early that night, after being given three warnings to apologise and curb her behaviour, which she repeatedly failed to do. In fact, she got worse instead of better as the evening wore on, and she completely ignored Carl and Phillip when we had dinner together. Her language was shocking too, and she called me a 'fucking bitch' as I put her to bed.

'I hate you all,' were her final words as I switched off the light, feeling absolutely wrung out.

15

'Is this what is wrong with Keeley?'

The next morning Keeley came down for breakfast and seemed to have completely forgotten what had taken place the evening before.

'Can I play out?' she asked, looking out of the kitchen window and across to the rec.

It was quite early and I told her that she could, once she had done her homework and tidied her bedroom.

'OK, thanks!' she smiled.

She ate some toast and marmalade and had a glass of milk, and then she told me she was going to have a shower first, then tidy her room and do her homework.

'I've got spellings,' she said. 'Will you test me later?'

'Of course. I'd be happy to.'

Though I found them unsettling, I'd become accustomed to Keeley's unpredictable moods by now and Jonathan and I had agreed that we should try to always enjoy the calm before the next storm, because otherwise we would be permanently at loggerheads.

I explained this to Sandy when she phoned, as she did once a week to check how we were getting on. This call was in addition to the support we received at the regular six-weekly placement meetings, and Sandy wanted to know if there were any concerns we wanted to raise.

'Well, we are still seeing a lot of bad behaviour, and her moods are unpredictable,' I said, 'but at other times she is a delight to be with. There is no rhyme and reason to it. We try to make the most of the good times, of course.'

'Do you feel you are coping with Keeley, despite the behaviour issues?'

'Yes, I do, but I have to admit she is not an easy child to look after. Normally I'd be seeing a general improvement in the child's behaviour by now, but Keeley's progress is erratic, to say the least.'

'I see,' Sandy said, encouraging me to go on.

I was careful not to sound as if I was losing patience with Keeley, as overall I didn't consider that I was.

'You know what it's like with most children, Sandy,' I continued. 'Nearly every child is on their best behaviour when they begin a foster placement, aren't they? Then, after this so-called "honeymoon period", they might have a bit of a relapse, and then they usually get back on track, settle down and show a steady improvement, don't they?'

'That's generally the way it goes,' Sandy conceded. 'And you and I should know,' she added, a nod to the many years' experience we had between us.

'Well, with Keeley it's not like that,' I went on. 'She's not like any other child I have come across before. It is very difficult to gauge how she is going to behave, and Jonathan and I have said several times that it feels like for every one step we take forward, we often take two steps back.'

Sandy paused.

'I was at a conference the other week,' she said. 'And a case study was discussed that reminded me of Keeley.'

I was all ears as Sandy went on to discuss the child in question. This young girl was seven years old and, like Keeley, she had also been brought up by a mother with a low mental age, who had failed to bond with her daughter.

'The young girl was accused of being an attention seeker,' Sandy explained. 'But in fact she had "attachment disorder", because she hadn't bonded with her mother the way she should have done from birth and in her early years. She was reaching out to one particular carer as she wanted to form an attachment with that person, but this was often misconstrued as attention-seeking behaviour. Often it was very bad behaviour the girl exhibited, but the point was she was doing this to try to bond with her carer, because she wanted to be noticed and not ignored, as she had been as a baby and toddler. She didn't know how else to behave, as she hadn't learned how to form a normal relationship. Ultimately, love was what she needed and wanted, but she asked for love in an unpleasant manner.'

'I see,' I said, my mind going into overdrive. 'Is this what is wrong with Keeley? Do you think Keeley has this "attachment disorder"?'

'I honestly don't know,' Sandy said. 'There is certainly nothing in her file about it, and of course I don't know exactly what she's discussing in therapy. All we know for sure is that she suffered emotional and physical abuse at home, and possibly sexual abuse. Clearly, I don't want to start putting a label on Keeley and guessing at a medical diagnosis; that would be very wrong of me. The case study did ring bells, though. I thought it might be useful for you to hear about it, just in case it might help you deal with Keeley in some way. There's a leaflet I picked up that gives some tips for carers and parents that might be useful for you to see. I'll pass it on.'

'Thank you,' I said. 'The girl's story certainly does have similarities to Keeley's. Thinking about it, I'm sure I've got some notes on attachment disorder, actually. I remember it was mentioned at a training session not that long ago. I'll go and dig the notes out.'

'Good idea,' Sandy said. 'I don't think it can do any harm to do a bit of research, as long as we're not jumping to any conclusions.'

'Precisely,' I agreed. 'Forewarned is forearmed, I always say. At least it might give me some clues to help me understand Keeley a bit better.'

Sandy said she trusted me to use the information sensitively. Social workers and foster carers generally knew little about attachment disorder in those days, and far fewer children were diagnosed with it compared to today. Now there is a wealth of help and information available to all foster carers. Research into attachment disorder has not only increased but become much more widely recognised and distributed, and of course there is now a huge amount of material online, including support groups and discussion boards accessible everywhere from Mumsnet to Facebook.

After the call I went straight upstairs to find my old notes, which I kept in rows of lever arch files on a large bookcase in my bedroom, precisely for times like this, when I wanted to refer back so some information we'd been given at training. It didn't take me long to locate them, as I'm meticulous about dating everything and I had a fairly good idea when the session took place.

I sat at my dressing table and began to read, my eyes hungrily scanning the page.

> The first three years of a child's life are crucial to switching on their capacity to bond with other human beings. If somehow that bond is not developed it can make it extremely difficult for the child to function in society. Healthy brain development depends on the child's interaction with their mother, or parent figure, in these critical early years. If a child is not given eye contact or a loving touch, or soothed, nurtured and fed consistently, and when necessary, nerve connections crucial to forging human bonds and relationships are not formed. The results can be very damaging and far-reaching. A child who develops attachment disorder is prone to behavioural and interpersonal problems.

Alarmingly the notes, which had originated from a research centre in America, went on to state that some experts believe such damage to brain development in early childhood might be 'irreparable and irreversible'. Being in a stable and loving home and receiving effective therapy 'could go some way towards helping the child progress', I read, but that was where the information ran out.

My mind flashed back over some of the incidents we'd had with Keeley, and particularly those involving other children she had fallen out with. There was no doubt she had behavioural and interpersonal problems, and now I'd read this, things seemed to make a little more sense. After all, how could a child like Keeley, starved of basic care and bonding from birth, be expected to form relationships as naturally as a child who'd been nurtured and soothed and shown boundless love and affection? I wanted to hug her and tell her everything was all right. Nothing was her fault. Having a diagnosis that labelled her as an 'attachment dis-order' sufferer seemed irrelevant. We knew she had been emotionally abused and was having therapy, and from now on I felt that Jonathan and I had to work on the basis that what happened in her early years had potentially left her with the problems she had behaving herself and getting along with others.

When I told Jonathan all this he was quite upset and started thinking back over the times he'd told Keeley off.

'How could we not have worked this out?' he said. 'It was obvious, really, wasn't it?'

'Everything becomes clear in hindsight,' I said. 'Besides, I don't think we have done anything wrong. It's one thing understanding the root of the bad behaviour, but we can't ignore it or not discipline her, can we?'

'You're right,' he said. 'And besides, we're making some assumptions here, as we have no medical proof backing up this theory. I guess all we can do is carry on doing our best for Keeley, bearing all this in mind.'

The leaflet Sandy gave me was useful and gave us further food for thought. It described a method of caring for children called PACE. This was totally new to me then, more than ten years ago, but is a well-respected model for caring for troubled and difficult youngsters that I'm now very familiar with.

PACE was developed by an American parenting expert called Daniel Hughes, and is a way of interacting with the child to make them feel safe. The acronym stands for Playfulness, Acceptance, Curiosity and Empathy, and it focuses on the whole child, not simply the behaviour, with the aim of helping the child to start to look at herself and let other people into her life, so that she can begin to trust others.

In a nutshell, PACE encourages the carer to connect with the troubled child in the way loving parents bond with babies and toddlers. For example, when you play, you should use a soft, light tone of voice, focus on fun and try to delight in just being together, as you would with a very young child. Jonathan was particularly good at being playful and did it naturally, like when he hid behind the tree in the garden and surprised Keeley. I was better at enjoying an activity together, like making the bonnets, but from now on, armed with this insight, Jonathan and I resolved to both up our game as much as possible.

The acceptance element of PACE is focused on making sure the child knows you accept them for who they are deep down, no matter what outwardly bad behaviour they display. Thankfully, I think we'd done quite well with this, always telling Keeley it was her behaviour we were upset by, not her as a person. We'd have to carry on reinforcing this idea whenever we had the opportunity.

Next, curiosity is concerned with encouraging the child to reflect on their own actions, and to learn how to talk about why they have behaved in a certain way. Crucial here is that carers must not be judgemental.

Finally, being empathetic is about the adult actively showing the child that they care about their feelings, which lets the child know they are not alone, and that they have support and comfort on hand when they need it. Hopefully we had been doing OK on this score; empathy is a basic tool of fostering, but again Jonathan and I would make sure we used it more often from now on.

To our relief, we read that if combined and followed well, the four elements of the PACE model can help troubled children, including those with attachment disorder, to bond and interact with others. This was welcome news. With or without a diagnosis of attachment disorder, Keeley could be helped, and help her we would.

Looking back, we were perhaps more optimistic than we should have been. Despite being armed with this helpful leaflet, and Sandy's support, the information we had was scant and we had an awful lot to learn. In the weeks to come I scoured the library and the Internet for any more information I could find on caring for children who had gone through early life traumas or suffered emotional abuse as babies and toddlers. There was a fair amount of material available if you looked hard enough, but it wasn't an easy task. Thankfully things have improved dramatically, and research continues into how an abused or troubled child's brain is formed and functions.

Jonathan and I are still learning, all the time. Back then we had to try to muddle through as best we could with the resources available to us and, unfortunately, we didn't always manage very well.

16

'We are out of our depth with Keeley, aren't we?'

Calls from the school telling us Keeley had been in trouble for a variety of reasons started to steadily increase as time went on. Giving cheek to the teachers, bullying a younger child, throwing food at another little girl across the lunch hall, pinching and kicking in the playground – the list of Keeley's misdemeanours went on and on.

Each time I'd try my best to connect with Keeley, often using the PACE method to encourage improved behaviour, but my efforts weren't always rewarded.

'You must not have been feeling very happy when you threw the food in the lunch hall,' I'd say, attempting to be as empathetic as I possibly could, to show Keeley that I was open to hearing her side of the story. 'Do you know why you were feeling unhappy? Do you think you can tell me why you felt so unhappy you wanted to throw food at another little girl?'

'She's a cow, that's why!'

'Please don't say that, Keeley, it's not kind. I would

prefer it if you could tell me how you were feeling when you threw the food.'

'I was pissed off, Angela. Isn't that obvious? Are you thick?'

'Please don't be rude to me, I don't like it. I want to help you. I'm sorry if you weren't feeling happy in the lunch hall. I don't like to think of you feeling unhappy. What were you thinking about?'

'She's a cow! I told you! Durgh! That's why I did it!'

It was very frustrating to have Keeley answering back like this but I took comfort from the fact that the PACE method, and our years of experience as foster carers, meant we had the best chance possible of making positive progress with Keeley.

I felt confident that I was doing the very best I could in such difficult circumstances, and I reminded myself often that this was not Keeley's fault, and that I had to try to understand her, not judge her.

I'd found online, using my extremely slow and temperamental dial-up Internet that is laughable by today's standards, a complex description of how the brains of children with attachment disorder function differently to those of children who have grown up in a loving and nurturing environment. This was pioneering research back then and I don't think I fully understood what the weighty scientific document I stumbled across was describing. All I knew was that it confirmed what I'd already gleaned from Sandy and my other reading: Keeley's brain had potentially not developed in the way it should, because of the emotional abuse she had suffered at such an early age.

Today, I understand that instead of processing information rationally in the front or 'thinking' part of her brain, in an emotionally abused child like Keeley the information goes straight to the middle of the brain, tapping into old memories and stored reactions. This means, for instance, that if another child shouted rudely or aggressively at a child with attachment disorder, instead of thinking, 'why are they doing that?' or 'should I tell an adult?', the troubled child is likely to automatically revert to how she reacted to being shouted at when she was very small. Back then her default position was probably to defend herself by shouting, fighting back or getting very angry, frightened or upset, and so that is how she reacts as an older child too. Put simply, an emotionally neglected child's brain might not be wired to handle situations rationally, which is why bad behaviour often ensues.

I didn't give up, even when Keeley was very rude and dismissive.

'The teacher's feelings were hurt when you called her a rude name. Why do you think you did that? Can you tell me how you were feeling when you used that rude word?'

'I don't care!'

'Look, Keeley, I'd like to help you stop swearing, because it gets you into trouble, and I don't like to see you getting into trouble.'

'It's not my fault! She hates me! She's a bitch! She's a cunt! He's a wanker.'

If Jonathan tried to talk to her it was even worse. She blanked him completely, trying to pretend he wasn't even there. On one occasion I attempted to at least get Keeley to acknowledge Jonathan was sitting at the table with us, and wanted to talk to her.

'Where is he?' she said defiantly, pretending to look straight through him. 'I can't see him? Jonathan who?'

He took it in good spirit, considering, and the next time Keeley ignored him like this at the dinner table, Jonathan took a serviette out of the dresser and wrapped it around his face, putting a pair of sunglasses over the top.

'What are you doing, Jonathan?' Carl said.

'I'm not Jonathan!' he laughed. 'I'm the Invisible Man.'

Carl and Phillip burst out laughing. They all knew the character from the television show and Jonathan's impression was very funny, but Keeley studiously refused to crack her face.

All of these incidents and responses were recorded and passed on to Social Services via my daily notes, and Sandy assured me that, where appropriate, this kind of information was then handed over to Keeley's therapist. I wished I could talk directly to the therapist as I felt we could have helped each other to help Keeley, but I also understood and fully accepted that any therapy like this is confidential. A child needs to know he or she can talk openly and without fear, in order to achieve the best possible outcome.

Sandy had written in Keeley's file that we had discussed attachment disorder, and that she had provided me with information about PACE, but I was still never given any feedback or specific detail about Keeley's mental health. I have no idea if the therapist even read the Social Services notes, and certainly nothing seemed to improve in terms of Keeley's behaviour; in fact, it got worse still.

One day Jonathan and I went to collect Keeley for her therapy session and found, once again, that she had been sent out of the classroom. This time it was because she had sworn at another little girl, torn a page out of the child's workbook and stamped on it. Keeley was red in the face and looked fit to explode when she was asked to wait in the school office while we trod the now familiar path into the deputy head's office for another 'quiet word'. Once more I found myself reassuring Mrs Tiller that Jonathan and I would talk to Keeley and do our best to help her control her behaviour.

'I'm trying all the time to show Keeley that I understand life has been hard for her in the past, and I'm doing everything I can to help her improve her behaviour, but it's a slow process,' I said, feeling really quite inadequate.

'I do understand, Mrs Hart,' Mrs Tiller replied, 'and of course I am not criticising you.'

'I know,' I nodded, although looking back, I can see that I did feel some personal responsibility, and Jonathan did too. We were Keeley's foster carers after all, and we weren't making progress in helping Keeley behave better, so it was very difficult not to be self-critical.

On the journey to the therapist's that day Keeley studiously ignored Jonathan, which was something she was doing more and more often. It was extremely irritating, and I felt sorry for Jonathan as he always made an effort to entertain her, however badly she treated him.

'Shall we play a game?' he'd say, smiling. 'Shall we put some music on?'

Nothing worked, but he wasn't easily put off. Often he told a joke, or he told a daft story against himself, but Keeley didn't respond at all. On this day, as I often did, I pointed out that it was upsetting to Jonathan to be ignored like this, and I told her that if there was a reason she didn't want to engage with him then she must tell me.

'I'm here to help,' I said. 'It would be much nicer if we could all get along. What can I do to make the situation better? I don't like to have an atmosphere like this in the car. It would be better for everybody if you stopped ignoring Jonathan.'

'Can you sit in the back with me?' she asked.

'Why, Keeley?' I replied. 'You know I always sit in the front.'

'Because I feel sick.'

'Do you mean you feel travel sick?'

'No, just sick.'

'Do you want us to pull over so you can get some fresh air?'

'No, I just want you to sit with me, in case I'm sick.'

I sighed and told Keeley I didn't like sitting in the back of the car, as I do have a tendency to suffer from quite severe travel sickness myself if I can't see the road directly in front of me.

'You can still look out the window when you are in the back,' she retorted in a very rude and surly tone of voice. It really annoyed me.

'I really don't want to sit in the back,' I snapped, rather too harshly. Looking back, I was feeling at a low ebb after talking to the deputy head, but nevertheless I should have been more patient. Now I felt even worse for talking to Keeley that way. Jonathan put his hand on my knee reassuringly, and he took over.

'Look, if you think you are going to be sick, tell us and we will pull over,' he said sympathetically, but Keeley didn't reply to him and simply let out a loud, disappointed and very exaggerated sigh.

Twenty minutes later Keeley vomited all over the back of the car. Of course I felt horribly guilty and partly responsible for having taken such a dim view of her worries about being sick. I had honestly thought that she had been trying to manipulate the situation, using her supposed sickness as a way of getting me in the back of the car and cutting Jonathan off even more than she already had done. I'd been wrong, and now the situation had escalated, which I mentally cursed myself for. Keeley was as white as a sheet, clutching her stomach and groaning.

'Oh my God, Keeley, we'll pull over and sort this out,' I said. 'Are you OK?'

She was covered in sick and staring at me blankly.

'Can you hear me, Keeley? Goodness me, whatever have you eaten?'

Jonathan took the next available turn off the bypass we

were travelling on and thankfully we pulled into a super-market car park moments later. I used some tissues from my handbag to clean up Keeley's face, while Jonathan sprinted into the store to buy a bottle of water and a packet of wipes. I kept talking to Keeley, telling her not to worry, reassuring her that she would be feeling much better soon, but she was still silent and staring.

'Jonathan will be here soon,' I soothed. 'We'll get this mess cleaned up. Do you want to get out of the car?'

Keeley slowly shook her head.

'OK, well just shuffle along the seat then, Keeley. I'll open the window and . . . oh, my goodness!'

I looked down at the pool of vomit on the back seat and the floor of the car and squinted in shock.

'What have you eaten, sweetheart?'

'Nothing,' she muttered.

'But what is that blue stuff. Keeley, it's Blu Tack! Have you been eating bits of Blu Tack?'

She nodded.

'I stole it. From Miss Fraser's cupboard,' she said, suddenly brightening up and looking and sounding victorious.

'But why? No wonder you've been sick! Oh my God, why did you do that?'

'Dunno,' she said. 'Because I wanted to? Dunno. Sorry.'

Jonathan arrived back with the water and the wipes and I left him to clean the car while I took Keeley into the toilets inside the supermarket, where I managed to change her into her PE top and wash away the bits of sick that had got into her hair. While I was doing this I noticed several sections of hair that were shorter than the rest. It looked very much like she'd been at her hair with a pair of scissors again, but this was something I'd have to tackle later.

'Honestly, Keeley, I can't believe you've eaten Blu Tack. You must have had lots of it. Didn't you realise you shouldn't have been eating it?'

'Yes, but . . . I didn't care!'

'You didn't care? Why on earth not? Why would you make yourself sick like that?'

As I spoke I was aware I wasn't handling this situation very well. I shouldn't have been critical or judgemental and I should have focused on Keeley's feelings and gently encouraged her to open up about why she had done such a thing, but I really wasn't in the mood. It had been a hell of a day and I felt at the end of my tether.

'Dunno,' she repeated. 'Sorry.'

'OK,' I said, forcing myself to stay calm and not mishandle the situation any more than I already had done. 'What's done is done. Now come on, let's get you to your appointment. Do you feel well enough to drive on?'

'Yes,' she said. 'Will you sit in the back with me though?'

'Yes,' I said through gritted teeth.

This was not a good situation and I was feeling uncomfortable, out of sorts and irritated. We completed the rest of the journey mostly in silence, and when Keeley went in to see her therapist I felt like crying.

'This is a nightmare!' I said to Jonathan.

'I know,' he said, shaking his head.

We sat statue-like for a while in the waiting room,

neither of us knowing what to say or do next. Normally, Jonathan would have reassured me that things were going to turn out all right, that this was just a bad day and we'd look back and maybe even laugh about it before too long, but he didn't. He looked worn out and his brow was furrowed with worry.

'We are out of our depth with Keeley, aren't we?' I said eventually, my voice several octaves deeper than normal, as my throat was so tight with worry and upset.

'I hope not,' he said unconvincingly, 'I mean, things can't get any worse, can they?'

'They can, and I think they will,' I said.

Unfortunately my prediction was right, though I could never have foreseen the chain of events that unfolded next.

17

'Eric made me do things if I lost at cards'

One Saturday night, in July, Jonathan and I were invited out to a friend's birthday party and my mum came over to babysit for Carl, Phillip and Keeley. We didn't go out until 8 p.m., everybody had eaten and the last thing I said to my mum as we left the house was, 'Just relax and enjoy yourselves!'

The boys were planning to watch a James Bond film and Keeley and my mum were going to play a few board games, and perhaps watch the video of *Mary Poppins* that I'd rented. I'd promised I would rent the film if it wasn't on television any time soon as Keeley still hadn't seen it, and my mum said she'd love to watch the old favourite again.

Everybody seemed to be in a good mood when we left, although I did have a strange feeling in the pit of my stomach as Jonathan and I drove off.

'Do you think they'll be all right?' I asked nervously.

'Of course! Your mum is an old hand at this now. She'll keep them all occupied, no problem at all.'

'But what if Keeley is difficult?'

'Look, your mum can cope. She'll keep Keeley entertained brilliantly, you know she will. Besides, the boys are doing their own thing, so there's less opportunity for an argument to break out, isn't there? Relax, it'll do us good to have a night out.'

I gave a half-hearted nod, trying to convince myself Jonathan was talking sense, as he undoubtedly was. The two of us hadn't had a night out together for a long time. Jonathan was quite right; it would do us the power of good to let our hair down a bit, away from the children and the stresses of home, and we really did have nothing to worry about, did we? My mum was holding the fort as she had done very successfully on many other occasions, the kids enjoyed her company and if anything did go badly wrong, we were not far away.

The party was in a function room in a hotel just across town and it was already in full swing when we arrived. Loads of our old friends were there, the buffet table was groaning under the weight of a fabulous array of salads and finger foods, and the DJ was playing a really good mix of classic dance tracks and some popular favourites that got everybody on the dance floor.

I chatted to a few people and Jonathan and I had a dance, but to be honest my mind kept wandering back to home. What if Keeley was giving my mum a hard time? What if something happened and we were out at a party? What would Social Services think of us? Looking back, these thoughts were unnecessarily bleak, but that was how

I was feeling, and I just couldn't switch off and fully engage with the party or our friends.

The last straw was when the words I'd spoken after Keeley was sick in the car came into my head, the words I'd said after Jonathan questioned: 'things can't get any worse, can they?' 'They can, and I think they will,' I'd responded.

Now I just couldn't get the words out of my head and I told Jonathan I felt tired and out of sorts, which was true, and that I didn't want to stay late. In the end we left before most of the other guests, although hopefully not too early so as to be rude. I counted every minute, just wanting to get home and make sure nothing had gone wrong.

'What's the matter, Angela?' Jonathan asked when we got back into the car.

'I can't put my finger on it, really,' I replied. 'I just wasn't in the mood, and even though common sense tells me they'll be fine, I couldn't help thinking about the kids, and worrying.'

Jonathan nodded sagely. 'I know what you mean. After trying to put your mind at rest I must admit, I found it a bit of an effort tonight too.'

We got home to find my mum sitting tensely in the kitchen, which was half-lit.

'Mum!' I exclaimed, my stomach dropping like a stone. 'Is everything all right?'

Normally she would be watching television in the lounge, or at least relaxing on the settee, reading or doing a crossword, and it alarmed me to see her in the kitchen like that, stiff and in the shadows.

'Yes, dear,' she said calmly. 'All the children are in bed. Keeley went up hours ago and the boys both turned in at around half past ten. I haven't heard a peep out of them.'

'I'm glad to hear it!' Jonathan smiled. 'For a moment there, you had me worried, Thelma. Why are you sitting in the kitchen in the dark?'

He switched on the main light and went to put the kettle on.

'Oh! I didn't realise how dark it was! Silly me. Now, if you don't mind I won't stay for a cup of tea. Would you take me home, Angela?'

Neither of us had had a drink and Jonathan volunteered to run Mum back to her house, which was only a few minutes' drive away.

'No, don't worry, Jonathan. Angela can take me, can't you, dear? Come on, I'll get my coat.'

It was one of those moments when you know not to argue, and I dutifully escorted my mum to the car. As soon as we'd turned the corner she asked me to pull over for a moment.

'What is it?' I asked, feeling very worried about what she was about to say. I wanted to blurt out, 'It's Keeley, isn't it? What has she done?' but I bit my tongue.

Mum looked uneasy, like she wasn't quite sure how to tackle this situation. Normally she's very self-assured and forthright, so of course this added to my fears. I held my breath, wondering what was coming.

'The thing is, Angela, I know that everything about the

children is confidential, and you never tell me, or anybody else, anything about their backgrounds, do you?'

'No, that's right,' I said slowly. 'It's always been like that, hasn't it?'

'Yes,' she said. 'But tonight, something happened that I think I need to tell you about. It's something Keeley said, something I think I should share with you, because it might be very important.'

My heart was thumping in my chest now.

'Go on,' I said, exhaling and then dragging in a deep breath. 'If you think it's important to tell me, please go ahead, and then I can decide if I need to pass it on to Social Services.'

Mum put her hand on mine.

'It's terribly sad, Angela. I don't know how you deal with these children, knowing what they've been through.'

'What happened, Mum? Please, just tell me now.'

'Well, the boys gave up on their film halfway through and asked if we could all play cards together. Keeley wasn't keen because, as you know, she does like to have one's full attention, doesn't she? The boys said they'd teach her how to play a few games though, so she reluctantly agreed.

'"I know how to play," Keeley told them. She seemed to be quite angry when she said this, and I thought she was cross that they'd assumed she couldn't play, perhaps because she was younger than them, and a girl . . .'

Mum's voice trailed off.

'Go on, Mum,' I encouraged.

'Well, everything was fine to begin with. Keeley actually

could play cards, very well indeed, as it happened. The boys were impressed, and so was I. I've never seen Keeley concentrate so hard. She was watching every move like a hawk and she won the first few games easily.'

'And . . . then what happened?'

'Well, Keeley lost a game, and then she went, well, I honestly don't know how to describe it, Angela.'

Mum looked forlorn and tongue-tied.

'Did she lose her temper? Is that it? How did she react, Mum?'

Mum was still clearly struggling to find the words but she took a sip of breath and gamely carried on.

'Keeley panicked, Angela. I think that is the best word to describe it. She started shaking and crying hysterically. I've never seen anything like it. It was such a sudden and shocking reaction, like she'd seen a ghost, and been scared out of her skin. Then she ran away and locked herself in the bathroom. It took quite a lot of coaxing to get her to come out, and I'm afraid I resorted to bribery.'

My mother tapped her handbag and gave a weak smile. 'I had a bag of pick and mix and I told her she could choose whatever she wanted. I hope you don't mind.'

'No, Mum, I don't mind at all. I'm glad you were there. I'm glad you got her out of the bathroom.'

'Yes, I was very relieved. She seemed to calm down quite quickly, once she'd had the sweets. I got her a glass of milk and asked her if she was all right, and did she want to talk about what happened. Eventually she said that she did want to talk about it, and then she told me something that

I'm hoping might mean a little more to you than it does to me.'

'What did she say?'

'Well, I'm sorry to say that she told me if she lost at cards "Eric" made her do things to him.'

'OK,' I said, feeling an icy grip around my heart. 'Thanks, Mum. Is that exactly what she said, and is there anything else at all?'

Mum didn't know that Eric was Keeley's grandfather, and I wondered if this was deliberate from Keeley. Had she chosen not to call him granddad as she so often did, because she didn't want my mum to know this detail?

Mum thought for a moment before she spoke again.

'Well, she said it was rude things that he made her do. "Eric made me do things if I lost at cards. Rude things." That's precisely what she said. I know you have to be careful about these things, and that's why I was sitting in the kitchen when you came in. I wanted to remember it all as accurately as possible, and to tell you as soon as I could. I was thinking it through, and if you hadn't come in as early as you had I was going to write it down.'

I thanked my mum and reassured her that I would handle things from here on in, and that she didn't need to worry about Keeley. 'It's very good that she has talked to you,' I said. 'I know it's upsetting, but I think it can only be a positive thing for Keeley. Thank you for being there, and listening to her.'

'Well, I hope you're right, Angela, but what a dreadful

thing for a young girl to have been through. I was very sorry I'd agreed to play cards.'

'No, you shouldn't be. You have done nothing wrong at all and, as I say, telling you might be a good thing; it might help her. Usually it helps when children talk, and unburden themselves of things that have upset them in the past.'

The boys had apparently just shrugged and left Keeley to it, thinking she was simply having a particularly bad strop as she lost at cards, which was no bad thing. I have always been extremely cautious about protecting each child's privacy within the house, and the last thing I wanted was for the boys to start speculating about Keeley's past.

I relayed the entire conversation to Jonathan, made the necessary notes and phoned Social Services as soon as possible. As a result, Joan arranged to come and see Keeley a few days later. I told Keeley why Joan was coming, gently explaining that the social worker needed to talk to her about what she had said to my mum about Eric.

'Your mum's an interfering old bag!' she snapped.

'Keeley, my mum cares about you a great deal. She had no choice but to pass on what you said to her. We all care about you, and that is why I have had to pass it on to Social Services. This needs to be looked into properly, and you know the rule. If there is something you say that I feel needs to be passed on, then I have to do so. It's for your own good. That is the only reason this rule is in place, Keeley, to help you.'

She stormed off and we didn't discuss it again, but when

Joan came round Keeley was polite and cooperative. I wasn't present for the conversation, but afterwards Joan explained that Keeley had quite readily agreed to go to the police interview room in the next town, to talk about what her grandfather had done.

I knew about this interview room from past experience with several other children. It's a specially adapted room in an ordinary-looking house, designed to help children feel at ease by reducing the fear they might have about going to a police station to give an interview, or make a statement. The room is fitted out with cameras and tape recorders and there are dolls of both sexes, which the children can use to demonstrate what happened to them, in case they can't find the words.

Joan phoned later to give me the date and time of the appointment, which was after school at the end of the following week, and told me that she had explained to Keeley that Jonathan and I would be taking her there and back and waiting in another room while she talked to the police. We immediately started making arrangements for the shop to be staffed and for the boys to be babysat by my mother that afternoon, and I told Keeley that if she had any questions at all or just wanted to talk about the appointment then she should feel free.

'No, thanks,' she said rudely. 'I don't need your help.'

18

'You and Jonathan are bullying me'

Ever since her arrival we'd continued having trouble trying to encourage Keeley to shower on a regular basis. I'd noticed that her knickers and school trousers were often damp when I came to wash them too, and she was still hiding wet knickers in her bedroom from time to time. I was constantly reminding Keeley to go to the toilet as soon as she needed to, and not to wait until she'd had a bit of an accident, but she clearly didn't listen and refused to acknowledge there was even a problem.

'But there is a problem, Keeley,' I'd said on more than one occasion. 'Your knickers are wet and your school trousers are damp.'

'How can they be?' she'd say. 'I always go to the toilet when I need to.'

'Well they are wet, Keeley, so you need to be more careful. It can't be nice for you, walking around with damp clothes on.'

Even when I found wet knickers hidden under her toys

or in the corner of her room, which I did on a fairly regular basis, she wouldn't admit a thing.

'I don't know how they got there,' she'd say defiantly. 'It wasn't me.'

'But who else was it, Keeley?'

One time I was actually holding the wet underwear in my hand but Keeley still claimed she had no knowledge of how her knickers could have possibly got wet, or how they came to be stuffed under her rows of dolls.

'Someone must have come in and spilt water in my room when I wasn't looking,' she said, and on another occasion she tried to completely ignore me and started talking very loudly to her dolls instead.

'Who is doing this?' she said to Jinty. 'Somebody's messing with me, and I'm going to get them for this!'

She said the same thing when I tackled her about her hair, and why it looked like it had been cut in several random places, which I'd noticed after she was sick in the car.

'No idea,' she said brazenly, and even when I eventually found clumps of hair stashed under her pillow and rug she still claimed total ignorance.

'I'll get them,' she said, waving her fist. 'Whoever's doing this to me, I'll get them. Nobody messes with me!'

The day after Keeley had agreed to go to the police interview house I told her she really needed to have a shower, as she'd made excuses the day before and I had reluctantly let her off because of the social worker's visit. Now, though, her hair was overdue a wash and she didn't smell very fresh at all. Despite the problems we'd had with the wet knickers and her resistance to take regular showers, up until now I'd tried to avoid getting into personal conversations about how Keeley smelled, because it's such a sensitive issue and I didn't want to upset or offend her. Most of the time she didn't smell too bad – just not especially fresh – but on this particular day I couldn't ignore it, as she smelled very strongly of urine.

'You need to go and have a shower, Keeley,' I said in the early evening. 'I'd like you to go up now, please, because the boys will be in soon and they will both need to shower too.'

'No,' she said flatly. 'I'm not having one. I don't need one. I had one two days ago.'

'Yes, you do need one, Keeley,' I said.

'Why?'

'Well, you don't want your friends in school to call you smelly, do you?'

I didn't say this lightly. I felt it was the only way to get through to Keeley when she was in such a defiant mood, and I really couldn't let her off the hook again or she would have been absolutely stinking.

'What friends? I don't like anyone at school. Why would they call me smelly? If they do then they're not my friends anyway, are they? I'll sort them out!'

I sighed. Thankfully, it wasn't true that Keeley had no friends. In recent weeks she had started talking about a little girl called Ellie who lived a few streets away from us, and the two of them had begun to come out of school together every day, playing and chatting happily. I'd been delighted to see this, as I knew from Keeley's records that she had never had a special friend before. There was even talk of Keeley being invited to Ellie's house for tea and on a cinema trip, which was great news.

'You do have friends,' I said. 'What about Ellie?'

'What about Ellie?'

'How would you feel if she thought you were smelly?'

'Why would she think that?'

'Because when you don't have a shower and your clothing gets a bit damp then you smell of urine, Keeley, and it's not a nice smell.'

'What's your ine?' she said, scowling.

'Urine – you spell it u-r-i-n-e – is wee. It's what you smell of if you don't wipe yourself properly when you have been to the toilet, or if you don't go to the toilet quickly enough and you have a bit of an accident.'

'I always wipe myself when I've had a poo,' she said.

'Yes, but you need to wipe yourself when you have a wee too.'

'That's daft. Why would I need to wipe myself then?'

'Because if you don't then your knickers get a bit wet, and then you get smelly. That's just the way it is; it's the same for everybody.'

'I can't believe you're calling me smelly! You're not supposed to be nasty to me; I'm going to tell the social workers about this. I can't smell anything at all. I think it's all in your head, Angela.'

Jonathan had been quietly reading the paper in the corner of the room, but he intervened at this point.

'Please don't be rude to Angela,' he said. 'She is not making things up for the sake of it, Keeley, she is trying her very best to look after you and you need to listen to her. Everybody needs to have a shower, every day if possible. If you didn't have one yesterday, there is no argument at all. You have to have a shower today. Why are you so against it? I'm sure you'll feel better afterwards.'

Keeley pointedly ignored Jonathan, refusing to even look in his direction.

'Keeley,' I said. 'Please don't be rude to Jonathan, he's talking to you.'

'Who is talking to me?'

'You know who is talking to you!' I said, exasperated. 'Jonathan asked you a question, so kindly answer him.'

'I don't know who you are talking about. If you mean *him* I'm not talking to *him* and I'm not doing what *he* says.'

'Right, Keeley, I've had enough of this. I'm going to have to take something away from you if you don't behave.'

'Like what?'

The first thing that came to my mind was the theatre group. I'd made contact with Mrs Crowther by now and she had told me Keeley was very welcome to go along the following week, which she was looking forward to. I knew she'd have been very upset if this was cancelled and it would really teach her a lesson, but I'd also learned over the years that you never take away a positive activity from a child. The theatre group would be an opportunity for Keeley to meet other children and to feel part of the community, and it might provide a very good outlet for her. She needed it, and pulling the plug before she even got started could backfire badly on us.

I bit my tongue and thought again.

'Our next cinema trip,' I said hastily, remembering we'd promised to take her to see a new film that was coming out. 'You won't be going to the cinema if you can't be civil to Jonathan or do basic things we ask, like taking a shower.'

Keeley thought about this for a moment and then suddenly decided she was going to have a shower after all.

'It's no big deal!' she shouted as stomped upstairs. 'I was going to have a shower anyway. There was no need to threaten me! That's bullying!'

'Cup of tea?' Jonathan grinned when she left the room.

'I think I could do with a double brandy, but tea would be lovely, thank you!'

Keeley had been in the shower for about ten minutes when the boys came home. Phillip was covered in mud from playing football and asked how much longer Keeley would be in the bathroom.

'I expect she'll be finished shortly,' I reassured. 'Just give her a few more minutes.'

Having been so reluctant to shower, I imagined Keeley would have the quickest wash she could get away with, but this didn't appear to be the case. Ten more minutes passed and Keeley was still in the shower. Phillip had gone upstairs and waited patiently in his bedroom at first, but then he started calling to Keeley to hurry up, with no response.

I went upstairs to investigate, as I could hear Phillip was starting to get aggravated, and so I shouted through the bathroom door to Keeley.

'Are you OK in there, Keeley? Are you nearly finished? Phillip's waiting to go in next and he's covered in mud!'

I could hear the water running but there was no reply at all, and so I tapped on the door. Still I got no answer. I was getting a little bit concerned by this point and so I knocked again, probably a little bit harder than I intended to, rapping my knuckles quite sharply on the door several times and calling, 'Keeley, are you all right in there, sweetheart?'

To my surprise the door fell open as I knocked, and a cloud of steam enveloped me. I blinked and then stared in surprise at the sight before me. Unbelievably, Keeley was sitting on the toilet seat; still in the same set of clothes she'd had on earlier, and playing with her dolls. She clearly hadn't been anywhere near the water, but the shower was switched on to full power, blasting hot water down the plughole.

'Keeley! What is happening here?'

Her face was an absolute picture. For once she had been caught completely red-handed, and yet Keeley still had the nerve to try to fib her way out of trouble.

'I've been having a shower. You aren't supposed to come in here like this! What are you doing?'

'I knocked on the door and it opened by accident. Didn't you hear me knocking?'

'No, because I am having a shower, *obviously*.'

'But you weren't, were you? It looks to me like you switched on the water but didn't get in, because you are sitting there on the toilet instead, fully clothed and playing with your dolls.'

'Well I'm doing that *now*, but I had a shower *before*.'

'Then why is your hair dry?'

'Because I dried it.'

'What did you dry it with?'

'God, you really are thick sometimes, Angela! I dried it with a towel. What else would I use?'

'There is no need to be rude, Keeley. And why is the shower still running?'

'I must have forgotten to switch it off, *obviously*.'

'And did you remember that the boys were waiting to use the shower after you?'

'I forgot. I can't remember everything, you know. I'm only eight years old. You and Jonathan are *bullying* me. I'm going to tell Joan, when I tell her about everything else you do, like calling me smelly. You're nasty old people and you are bullying an eight-year-old girl!'

Keeley then marched out of the bathroom. Phillip had heard the commotion and he now came out of his bedroom, with his towel under his arm. He and Carl had started to keep their towels, toothbrushes and any personal toiletries in their bedroom for fear of what Keeley might do. There had been rows on several occasions about the fact she'd used the wrong towel, and the boys had accused her of putting hair gel on the toilet seat and taps, and spraying deodorant on the mirror and window. One time Carl said he caught her scrubbing pen off the legs of one of her dolls, using his new toothbrush, but she always denied everything.

'At last!' Phillip grumbled, shooting a dirty look towards Keeley as she headed to her bedroom. He was clearly in a very bad mood and looked thoroughly fed up.

'Well, some of us like to get washed *properly*,' she retorted, flicking him a defiant look over her shoulder, which made my jaw drop.

I could see I wasn't going to get her to shower tonight and so I decided to cut my losses and try again in the morning, before school. Unfortunately, the next day she was even more belligerent.

'You are always telling me not to be late and to hurry up and get ready, and now you want me to have a shower *and* wash my hair, and all before school when I'm in a rush anyhow. I don't understand you, Angela. Do you want me to be late or something? Do you want me to get told off by the poxy teacher again? I'll do my hair but I haven't got time for a shower.'

With that she slammed the bathroom door and then spent twenty minutes locked inside, forcing the boys to use my bathroom or they would have been late for school. When Keeley finally emerged she had wet hair but it wasn't soaked through, and I imagined she'd simply wet it and brushed it through.

'Why haven't you washed your hair properly?' I asked, trying to contain my exasperation.

Keeley just looked at me, with her hands on her hips, rolling her eyes.

'I asked you a question, Keeley. Why have you just wet and brushed your hair?'

'Because I hate my hair, all right? Is that good enough for you, Angela? I'm trying to get rid of the curls, if you must know. I don't want curly hair. I want nice straight hair.'

'But you were supposed to be washing it, weren't you? Couldn't you wash it and then brush it, or better still, ask me to dry it straight?'

'I told you, I didn't have time. Did you want me to be late? I think you did, so you could bully me and tell me off all over again. I know your tricks!'

When I got back from the school run I discovered the toilet was completely filled to the brim with reams and reams of toilet roll. I put on a pair of rubber gloves and fished it out, and then I saw two pairs of knickers floating in the water. I could have cried. I felt tired out and incredibly irritated as this behaviour was so unnecessary.

When I went to check Keeley's room and fetch her dirty washing, I then found that she'd gone to school in the same pair of trousers she'd had on the day before, even though I'd specifically told her to wear clean ones that smelled fresh.

'Do you know, I could write the script for what she says about the toilet roll when she gets home from school,' I said to Jonathan when we were in the shop together later that morning.

'So could I,' he said.

Then, at exactly the same time, we both said: 'It wasn't me! I don't know what you are talking about!'

We burst out laughing, which released a bit of tension, but of course it really wasn't funny. Keeley was testing us to the limit, and if we didn't laugh I think we would have cried.

19

'You don't know the half of it, Angela!'

At lunchtime the phone rang.

'Hello, Mrs Hart?'

I recognised the voice immediately. It was Mrs Stone, the school secretary, and I felt a lump form in my throat.

'Yes, it is. Hello, Mrs Stone, is everything all right?'

'Not really. Have you got a moment?'

She asked me if I could call into the office when I collected Keeley that afternoon, explaining that Keeley had kicked, punched and threatened a group of children because they had called her 'fishy pants'.

'I see. I'll come in later, of course.'

Unbelievably, about an hour after that conversation the phone rang again. This time it was the head of year from Phillip's school, informing me that he had been involved in quite a serious fight, in which he had punched another boy in the face and given him a bloody nose. To make matters worse, Phillip had been extremely abusive towards the teacher who intervened. He had been given a warning and told that if there were any repeat of such behaviour he would be excluded from school for a period of time, most probably a week.

I felt mentally and physically exhausted, and Jonathan and I had a hard job keeping our spirits up in the shop for the rest of that afternoon. Customers came in chatting happily about the sunny weather we were having, or a special occasion they had to buy for and, of course, we were as polite and upbeat as possible. It wasn't easy though. As Jonathan commented dryly after one particularly chatty customer left the shop clutching a pretty bouquet: 'Being a foster carer is no bed of roses, is it?'

'No,' I said. 'You can say that again.'

'Being a foster carer is no bed of roses, is it?'

I smiled. It was a very lame joke, if you could even call it a joke. We were standing behind the counter, surrounded not only by roses, but also by all sorts of beautiful flowers and colours and glorious smells, and I found myself giggling. Even raising a smile on my lips in the circumstances was no mean feat, but once again Jonathan had managed it. Being able to share a bit of humour and have a laugh is undoubtedly one of the reasons I've been able to carry on fostering, even when things have got this tough. Without a smile and the occasional unexpected giggle I might have buckled under the strain on many occasions, but Jonathan has kept me going.

When I arrived at Keeley's school I had a couple of minutes to chat to her before the teacher came to see me, and

Keeley predictably blamed everybody but herself for her behaviour.

'Those kids were rude and nasty! They were bullying me!'

'I'm sure the teacher will talk to the children responsible for calling you rude names, but you have to take responsibility for what you have done, Keeley.'

'I didn't do anything.'

'Yes, you did. You kicked, punched and threatened a group of children. You cannot do that, Keeley, no matter what they say to you.'

'So I just let them get away with it?'

'No, that's not what I'm saying.'

'It is! It so is! You don't care about me! You just want me to take all this shit and shut up.'

'No, Keeley, I most certainly do not want that to happen. What you should have done was to tell a teacher that you were being called a rude name, and not got involved in fighting with the children who were taunting you.'

'They deserved it. They all deserve to go to hell! I'll kill them if they do it again.'

The teacher appeared and, after reiterating that Keeley had to focus on what she had done wrong, not what the other children had said or done, she told Keeley she would miss some of her play time the next day. The teacher explained that she would be talking to all the children involved individually too, and disciplining them accordingly. Then we were allowed to leave, by which time Keeley appeared to have calmed down considerably, and she even smiled very sweetly at the teacher as we left. She looked her in the eye and said that she was sorry, which appeared genuine.

'I'm glad we've got all that straightened out,' the teacher said, giving me a relieved and satisfied look as she picked up a pile of books and prepared to move on to her next task.

'So am I,' I replied, though I was thinking to myself that the teacher didn't know Keeley the way I did, and she hadn't heard her say she would kill the other children if they did it again. I didn't for one minute think Keeley was serious about committing a violent act, but I knew she was capable of switching very quickly from being all sweetness and light to being manipulative and mean. The teacher may have dealt with this one little battle, but she certainly hadn't won the war.

'How would you like to go shopping?' I asked Keeley when we got in the car.

I'd thought about this on the drive to school. Keeley's hygiene was the crux of the problem, and telling her off for blocking up the toilet with tissue and knickers, or harking on about what she had done at school was not going to help her shower more regularly, or wear clean clothes. If she didn't clean up her act, quite literally, she was going to risk being called 'fishy pants' all over again, so I needed a positive plan.

'Shopping? What for?' she asked suspiciously.

'Some smellies and nice things for the bathroom.'

I wanted to buy Keeley some bubble bath of her choice and some battery-operated candles, in the hope that creating a pampering experience in the bathroom might encourage her to have a soak in the bath, as we were clearly on a hiding to nothing with the shower. This was something I'd heard another foster carer had done successfully, and I'd actually been planning on suggesting this before the phone call from the school. Now things had reached a head I decided we had no time to lose.

'Why do you want to do that for me?' Keeley said. 'I'm bad. I've been naughty.'

'You're not bad, you've got yourself into trouble, as all children do, but you've apologised now. You're going to miss some playtime and then hopefully it will all be forgotten.'

'So you want to buy me nice things? Why aren't you cross? Why aren't you telling me off or taking away treats?'

'The teacher has already taken away some of your playtime. You're a clever girl, Keeley, and I think you have learned a lesson. I think you understand that next time something like this happens you need to tell a teacher instead of fighting back, so that you don't end up in trouble again. Am I right?'

She nodded.

'Good. So, let's go shopping, shall we?'

'Fine, if we have to!' she said rather cheekily, but I let that pass. For some reason she seemed to be looking for some more conflict, but I wasn't going to give it to her.

Before I started fostering I wouldn't have thought it was very sensible to treat a badly behaved child to a shopping trip and a few luxuries immediately after being called up to the school, but experience had taught me that working with Keeley instead of battling against her had a much greater chance of creating a positive outcome.

Having been born in the fifties, I'd been raised with traditional post-war values and strict but fair discipline. If I stepped out of line I had my sweets or my pocket money docked, or I was sent to bed early without any cocoa. There was no arguing about this; my parents' word was final and defying them was simply not an option. Good manners and absolute respect for adults was the order of the day, and treats had to be earned with hard work and excellent behaviour.

Times had inevitably changed, and parenting techniques in general had become less stringent. As a foster carer I'd had to take giant strides in my way of thinking and, whenever possible, with all the children I fostered I much preferred to encourage good behaviour than to punish bad behaviour. Over the years I've become programmed to constantly remind myself that when you are dealing with a child who has suffered trauma as Keeley had, it is not the child's fault that they are behaving badly, and they need praise more than they need criticising.

Keeley's disclosure about her grandfather making her do 'rude things' had given me a very sharp reminder of this fact. She was not a typical eight-year-old girl, and she needed to be cut an awful lot of slack.

I took Keeley shopping, feeling optimistic about my bath plan and, thankfully, my efforts paid off. She was in a really good mood by the time we got home, and was looking forward to having a lovely, relaxing soak in the bath later that night.

'Thank you, Angela,' she said thoughtfully, looking out of the window. 'I don't deserve this.'

'You do,' I said. 'Everybody deserves to feel good about themselves. I think you'll feel really good after a bath. I always do.'

Dealing with Phillip's problem that day was trickier, even though it was handled in a phone call and I didn't have to go up to the school and speak to his teachers. He too had some issues from his past that impacted on the way he behaved at times, and I was always careful to factor this in whenever he stepped out of line.

'I'm sorry to hear you got into a fight and swore at a teacher,' I said when he arrived home from school by bus that evening.

I'd spoken to the head of year and knew the details, but I asked Phillip to tell me what had happened. He had been involved in similar fights in the past and Phillip's standard apology and explanation was, 'I lost my temper, I'm sorry,' which I always fully accepted and understood. This time, however, he came out with something I wasn't expecting.

'It's Keeley,' he said. 'It was her fault.'

'Keeley? What's she got to do with it? She goes to a different school. What are you talking about, Phillip?'

'You don't know the half of it, Angela!' he yelled, banging his fist on the kitchen table. 'I can't take it anymore!'

20

'You can't solve everything, you know'

After his outburst, blaming Keeley for his fight at school, Phillip started to cry. Over the course of the next half hour or so he reluctantly told me about a string of tricks that Keeley had played on him, which he'd been too embarrassed to tell me about before. Her spiteful behaviour included elbowing him in the ribs whenever she walked past him and nobody else was looking, singing very loudly next to his wall when he was trying to do his homework, smearing toothpaste and hair gel on his bedroom door handle, refusing to let him into the bathroom when he needed the toilet, and teasing him relentlessly with the phrase, 'I know why you're in care!'

Not surprisingly, that last taunt seemed to have tipped the balance and really made his blood boil.

'Is that right, Angela?' he asked nervously. 'Does she know why I'm in care?'

Phillip had been rejected by his mother after she remarried several years earlier, which is what led to him being placed in care. His slightly older sister still lived with their mother, which was very difficult for him to accept. His sister had physically abused Phillip, burning him with cigarettes and matches, and she had played psychological games with him throughout his formative years.

I reassured him that Keeley had no idea why he was in care, reiterating that this was something I would never discuss with anybody other than Jonathan, under any circumstances. Keeley was making this up to aggravate him, I told him.

'Well she's succeeded!' he said. 'She's making my life a misery!'

The bad blood between Phillip and Keeley was not a passing phase; unfortunately it persisted, spreading like a rotten smell throughout the house. Despite enjoying the shopping trip and her pampering experience in the bath, which she thanked me for several times, Keeley soon snapped back into to being extremely difficult. In fact, she behaved appallingly every day leading up to the police interview. Her back chatting, spitefulness towards the boys and rudeness towards me, and particularly Jonathan, seemed to be non-stop, and she was full of anger. We understood this under the circumstances, but it was still very tough to live with.

One afternoon I spoke to Sandy on the phone about the arrangements for Keeley's interview, and I told her how bad things were.

'Have you thought about giving her an old telephone

directory and letting her rip it to pieces when she is in a rage?' she asked. 'I've heard it's a good way for children like her to vent their anger, in a safe way.'

I was so desperate I tried this the following night, after Keeley had scratched Phillip and drawn blood on his arm during a scuffle in the kitchen. Apparently he'd found Keeley standing on the worktop, trying to hide his favourite mug on top of the highest wall unit.

'I'll report you to my social worker,' he'd threatened.

'Fine! They won't do anything! I bet you've complained to them before and they haven't done anything, have they? You're stuck with me, you daft fucker.'

Phillip tried to grab her and she scratched his arm with her fingernail. I came in on the tail end of the scrap. My gut instinct was to take hold of Phillip's arm immediately and inspect the cut, but of course I had to put on a pair of gloves first. Fumbling with the box of disposable gloves I kept in the kitchen, I felt like bursting into tears but I bit my lip and stopped myself. I had similar feelings to these for days and days, as I tried to draw on an ever-decreasing pool of patience, goodwill and energy. I kept telling myself that things would get better, because how could they get any worse?

Keeley looked at me triumphantly when I decided to take Sandy's advice later that day and give her an old tele-phone directory to destroy. Keeley made a huge mess all over the dining room with it, which she crossly refused to clear up, and I was left feeling even more frustrated and defeated. That method of anger management was later deemed to be unhelpful and we were taught that trying to keep a child calm worked better. This advice has changed since, and now the thinking once again is that children need to release their anger in a physical but safe way, though not necessarily with a telephone directory.

Anyhow, in Keeley's case keeping calm appeared to work best, and after I'd bought her the smellies, soaking in the bath seemed to do her good. She loved the bubbles and electric candles, and after her bath that night she finally emerged in a much better frame of mind.

'Can I watch telly before bed?' she asked.

Keeley was dressed in pink pyjamas, wrapped in a fluffy white bathrobe and cuddling Jinty. Her face was glowing after her warm bath, and she looked very pretty, and positively virtuous.

'Yes,' I said, 'as long as you are polite to everybody, we have no more arguments, especially with the boys, and you go to bed on time. Do we have a deal?'

'Yes,' she grinned, fluttering her eyelashes. 'It's a deal, Angela.'

That was the only real chink of light over several days. I left her contentedly watching the television and retreated to the kitchen, where I made myself a large mug of sweet tea and indulged in a chocolate biscuit.

The next night when she took her bath, I noticed that Keeley was only in the bathroom for a very short time. She could have only had a very quick dip, and she certainly hadn't been in there long enough to have a soak or a proper wash.

What's more, she told me the electric candles had broken already, which was very disappointing, as we hadn't had them for very long.

'I'll take them back to the shop,' I said. 'I think we should be able to exchange them. They should last for a lot longer than this.'

Unfortunately, when I did just that, returning them to the shop and complaining about the quality, I was left red-faced, because the shopkeeper opened the battery compartments and found they were full of water.

'I'm terribly sorry,' I explained. 'The person who used them must have splashed water on them without realising.'

'Actually, I think it was more than a splash,' the shopkeeper replied, mopping up the mess on her counter with a handful of tissues. 'Both candles would appear to have been totally submerged.'

'Oh,' I replied sheepishly. 'Well, I'll buy another set then and tell the person who used them to be more careful next time.'

This proved to be a complete waste of money, because Keeley clearly couldn't resist dipping the new set of candles in the water either, and a day later they were broken too.

'Keeley, what did I say to you about keeping the candles dry?'

'I did!'

'You didn't, because look at the water inside the battery compartment. Look, I've opened them up. It's exactly the same as last time. You must have put them under the water.'

'I didn't.'

As frequently happened with Keeley, I couldn't confidently continue the argument. I hadn't actually seen her put the candles in the water, although of course there was no other logical explanation. After that she started to refuse to have baths and we went back to having regular discussions about how she needed to have daily showers instead, and wash herself properly using shower gel and a sponge. She rarely did, and we were back to square one with Keeley coming home from school smelling of urine and wearing damp knickers and trousers.

I'd discovered that, despite me telling her to place her dirty trousers in the laundry bin every night, Keeley was wearing the same pair every day and putting the clean ones I laid out for her in the wash. I only noticed this because the pair she favoured had some red stitching on the front pockets, while the other pairs were all completely black. When I tackled her about this she said she didn't know what I was talking about.

'But Keeley, I know you are wearing the same trousers every day because you only have one pair with red stitching.'

'Exactly! Why can't they all have red stitching?'

'Then would you wear clean ones every day?'

'No, because the other kids would think I was trying to be posh if I wore clean trousers every day!'

I could see I was allowing myself to be drawn into yet another confusing and nonsensical argument that I wasn't going to win, and I bit my tongue once more. One evening I gathered up all the trousers, took out my sewing kit and added red stitching onto all the other trousers. Then I made a point of emptying Keeley's laundry bin every night so she had no choice but to wear a clean pair from her wardrobe, which thankfully she didn't seem to mind doing now as they all had the same red stitching.

'You're amazing!' Jonathan said when he found me hunched over the trousers, needle and thread in hand.

'I don't think so,' I said, trying to smile but finding it difficult. 'I'm not sure I'm doing an amazing job at all.'

'You are,' he assured, though I could tell that Jonathan was struggling to be positive too.

He hadn't been sleeping very well, which wasn't like him, and he'd been grumpy with the boys about things that didn't normally bother him. For example, Phillip had a habit of scattering dry mud from his football boots in the hallway. Typically, Jonathan would issue a firm but light-hearted reminder that he should take his boots off outside, or he'd say something like: 'Phillip, are you leaving that mud there for the magic cleaning fairy to come and clear away, or shall I fetch you the dustpan and brush?'

The next time it happened, however, Jonathan snapped.

'What did I tell you about taking your boots off outside?' he said, sighing in exasperation and flapping his arms about. 'Look at this mess! I won't tell you again, Phillip. Have a bit of common sense, please! You're thirteen years old, not five!'

We were both feeling the strain, but neither of us really knew where to go from here. Keeley's placement was only in its third month, and we didn't want to give up on her.

*

When the day of the police interview finally came round I was feeling stressed and nervous.

'God, I hope this makes a difference,' I said to Jonathan.

'So do I, but we have to be prepared for the fact she might be even more difficult to deal with afterwards. It's going to be very tough for her, going in there and talking to strangers about her past. It could affect her in a very negative way. She's going to need our support.'

Jonathan was right, but even though I dreaded Keeley being even more out of control I actually felt better instead of worse when I really thought about what he said. Jonathan had put things in perspective for me. This was a very difficult time for Keeley, and whatever she was experiencing was much tougher than whatever I was going through. This is a thought that's recurred many times with different children throughout my fostering career, and is one that keeps me focused and still coming back for more. At the end of the day, the kids need care, and it's my job to provide that, no matter how hard it gets for me. That's the nature of the job, it's what counts at the end of the day, and it's worth it, always.

Keeley was monosyllabic on the journey to the police house and when we arrived she didn't say a word as a smiley female police officer, dressed in civilian clothing, escorted her into the interview room. It was decorated to look as much like an ordinary living room as possible, albeit one with cameras on the walls and tape machines on the coffee table. Jonathan and I glimpsed Keeley being shown to a comfortable settee scattered with cushions, and then we were swiftly directed to an adjacent room to wait for her.

The rule in these interviews is that police officers can't prompt a child to talk, for the same reasons that foster carers have to use the mirroring technique in conversations when a child is making a disclosure. Anything the child says to us or to the police might be used in court, and so it is imperative that nobody can claim words have been put in the child's mouth.

Jonathan and I sat uncomfortably on a pair of plastic chairs, making small talk but both struggling to focus on anything but Keeley and what she was going through next door. Twenty minutes later she emerged with the female officer, who was looking sympathetic and telling her not to worry.

'Mr and Mrs Hart, you are free to take Keeley home now.'

The officer looked downbeat and gave a slight shake of the head as she spoke to us, but I wasn't sure if this meant the interview had been unsuccessful, or if the officer was upset about what she had just heard.

I desperately wanted to know how the interview had gone, but it wasn't my place to ask. Social Services would be informed and Jonathan and I would be filled in on a need to know basis only, so maybe we would never find out.

Keeley barely said a word all the way home. She had Jinty with her, and she spent the whole journey plaiting and un-plaiting her hair.

'Are you struggling there, Keeley?' I asked. 'Can I help you?'

She kept her eyes on the doll.

'No. You can't help, Angela. You can't solve everything, you know.'

21

'I don't want to give up on her ...'

Jonathan and I had a lot to discuss at Keeley's next placement meeting, which was coming up soon. We wanted to talk about Keeley's effect on the boys and particularly Phillip, plus Jonathan and I had prepared a long list of the behaviour issues we'd encountered that we felt we needed to pass on and ask for advice about.

'I'm really very worried they'll think we're not coping,' I said after we talked before the meeting about the many problems we'd had with Keeley's rudeness, spitefulness and general lack of discipline.

'We have to face the facts,' Jonathan replied flatly. 'Maybe we're not coping. Maybe the right thing to do would be to admit this? I mean, if Keeley has got deep-rooted attachment issues that are causing her to behave badly, maybe we're not qualified enough to help her? We're trained foster carers, not psychologists or qualified mental health professionals. Plus we haven't even been given a diagnosis, so we're working in the dark really, aren't we? I don't think anyone could accuse us of not doing our best, but perhaps our best is not good enough?'

My heart sank when he said this. The same thing had crossed my mind several times recently but I'd been hoping, perhaps naively, that the roller-coaster ride would start to slow down, if not stop. Optimism is one of the characteristics you need in spades as a foster carer. You have to stay strong and see each day as a new challenge, come what may. I'd been doing this with Keeley for months and I'd also been telling myself not to take anything personally.

However badly Keeley behaved with Jonathan and me, I constantly reminded myself that we were not the ones who caused her pain and trauma in her early childhood. It was not our fault that she behaved the way she did, and we had to keep offering her unconditional care and support to help her cope with her past and move forward. The trouble was, of course, it wasn't just mine and Jonathan's life that Keeley was affecting and disrupting, and we couldn't expect the boys to deal with her the way we did.

'I think we're doing OK in the circumstances,' I said, trying hard to give Jonathan an encouraging smile. 'It's just very tough because we have the boys too. That's what's making it difficult, but we'll get there, I'm sure.'

Jonathan looked disheartened, and I didn't like to see him like that.

'Will we really? I'm not at all sure, Angela. I think perhaps Keeley needs to be the only child in a placement. Look how she is when she is with you on her own. Generally speaking, she's like a different girl. I'm loathed to say it, but she'd be better off with carers who aren't looking after any other children, wouldn't she?'

The words hung in the air for a moment. I knew Jonathan was right and I couldn't argue. I'd thought this myself but never voiced it, and it upset me to acknowledge this now. Thankfully, the boys themselves had never asked if we could move Keeley out, or if they could move, so I took some small comfort from that. There were times when all three children had played games like Cluedo and draughts around the kitchen table together, and managed to get on well and even have fun. They were rare times though, I had to admit. Things clearly weren't great for the boys and their lives had certainly not improved with Keeley's arrival, but at least they weren't desperate. That's what I had been telling myself as I tried my best to make things work.

'You're right, in theory, Jonathan, but,' I stuttered, 'I don't want to give up on Keeley . . . She's been through enough in her life already. Perhaps she should never have been placed with us when we already had the boys, but we can't change that now, can we? We have to make the best of things. Surely we can do it?'

Now it was Jonathan's turn to dig deep and offer me some encouragement.

'If we acknowledge that we think Keeley would do better as the only child in a placement, it doesn't mean we're incompetent or that we're no good as foster carers. Keeley is just a particularly difficult child to look after, and having the boys makes it much harder. It's nigh on impossible to juggle the three of them successfully.'

Jonathan was talking a lot of sense, but it was still upsetting and I couldn't help putting up counterarguments.

'What if we suggest it's best for Keeley if she is moved to a single placement, and then she is placed somewhere even more unsuitable? And what if she knew this came from us and felt we'd let her down? What might that do to her? It could be catastrophic!'

Jonathan shared my worries but reasoned that Social Services would not move Keeley anywhere unsuitable; they would only move her if the right single placement became available. That was the hope, although deep down we both knew we had no control over this, and there were no guarantees.

'It wouldn't be in anybody's interests to move her into another placement with other kids,' Jonathan went on, trying to put both his own mind and mine at rest. 'I think we should just be honest at the placement meeting. We need to explain that, from our experiences, we think Keeley would be better off in a single placement where she can receive one-to-one care, but that for the time being we are managing as well as can be expected, and we are very happy to keep Keeley with us until the right placement is available.'

I reluctantly agreed with this. I cared deeply for Keeley and I had more to give, but we had three children who all deserved excellent care, and if Keeley had a better chance of receiving this in a different foster home, we would of course fully support this.

*

Following the heart to heart I'd had with Phillip I later spoke to Carl, who unfortunately provided me with a further catalogue of Keeley's misdemeanours. The bathroom seemed to be creating the most problems, as for some reason Keeley appeared to be hell bent on preventing the boys from using it as much as she possibly could, even though she still wasn't showering properly herself.

'One time I walked in on her by accident,' Carl reluctantly admitted. 'I thought the bathroom was empty, but when I went in she was sitting on the floor chewing gum and playing with her dolls. Not only that, it was Phillip's chewing gum that he'd "lost" from his school bag.'

'I see,' I said, making a mental note to remind Keeley to properly lock the door when she was in the bathroom, 'and what did Keeley say when you saw her like that?'

'She shouted at me to get lost because she was having a shower. I argued and said she wasn't showering, instead she was sitting there chewing gum, but she wouldn't move. In the end I had to wait about half an hour for her to come out.'

'Why didn't you tell me? I could have helped, and you could have used my bathroom instead of being forced to wait.'

Carl shrugged. Like Phillip, I think he was embarrassed to be locked in a losing battle with a little girl. He was not a confrontational person by nature, and so he had been trying to get on with things as best he could. However, I could tell from the way he spoke that this had led to a great deal of resentment.

'She's one of those people you can never win with,' he lamented. 'Do you know what I mean?'

I knew exactly what he meant, though I didn't say it.

'I'm pleased you've told me this,' I said. 'It's important that Jonathan and I know what is going on, so we can help everybody live together with the minimum of trouble and arguments.'

The mention of Jonathan's name prompted Carl to speak again.

'She said something about Jonathan,' he said, looking worried. 'I know it's not true. I told her she needs to be careful about making up lies.'

'What did she say? Don't worry, Carl, I won't tell her you told me.'

He swallowed hard and shifted in his seat.

'OK, thanks, Angela. She said, er, she told me that Jonathan hurt her.'

'Did she now, in what way?'

I felt like cold water had been pumped into my veins, and I braced myself for what Carl might say next. When you have a child who has been physically abused or sexually abused, their experiences can give them ideas that other children wouldn't even dream of, or they can bring past experiences into their current situation and conflate the two. For example, one child we had staying with us used to deliberately cross and uncross her legs in front of Jonathan, flashing her underwear to try to provoke a reaction, as this is something she had been encouraged to do at home, when her mother had men in the house. Jonathan had to tell the girl to stop each time she did it, and he always removed himself from the scene as quickly as possible. Then he had to report the situation to Social Services, as much to protect himself as to keep the girl's file up to date.

'Keeley showed me some bruises on her arm, and she said Jonathan had done them,' Carl told me.

'Did she say how?'

'She said she was crossing the road at the retail park and he grabbed her arm really hard for no reason and pushed her onto the pavement.'

'I see.'

'I know Jonathan wouldn't hurt her,' Carl said apologetically, 'and anyway she's always got bruises, hasn't she?'

I didn't want to discuss her bruises with Carl, but unfortunately this was still true. Even though Keeley had far less marks than in the beginning, she was never bruise free, and this was something I had to constantly keep an eye on and report on. Jonathan was convinced that the number of bruises she had seemed to correlate to her levels of anger and discontentment and her outbursts of bad behaviour, and I think this was true, although it was quite hard to tell. She had been lucky enough to have joined a form at school which was taken for weekly swimming sessions, so I never did book her in for lessons at our local pool, having decided I would wait until her school course was over before I took her swimming again. This meant I never saw all her limbs at once, so it was difficult to know from one day to the other how many bruises she had.

Keeley would still never admit that she made the bruises

herself. On her legs, I noticed they were sometimes in neat, circular patterns that looked very deliberately placed, but Keeley continued to claim she either had no idea how she got them, or that she must have bashed herself by accident.

Occasionally, when I thought Keeley was doing well and hurting herself less, I asked her if I could count the bruises so I could reward her if she had less than the last time I counted. When I suspected she might have more than last time I avoided counting because it would have been counterproductive, as I didn't want to create a scene and I certainly didn't want to punish her in any way for the self-harm.

'Thanks, Carl,' I said, being very careful not to say anything negative about Keeley, or to accuse her of anything I couldn't prove. 'I'm glad you told me that. I'll deal with it, and I won't mention your name. You don't need to keep any secrets from me. You can trust me to handle Keeley. Please don't hold anything back that you think you should share in future.'

After the conversation with Carl I thought back to a week or so earlier, when Keeley had started to misbehave near to the supermarket in the retail car park, as I think this must have been where her concocted and exaggerated story had come from. Keeley had offered to take the trolley back after we put the shopping in the boot of the car and so Jonathan went with her, which she wasn't happy about as she clearly wanted to mess about. She then wheeled the trolley in circles and tried to jump on the back of it, and Jonathan had inevitably told her off, because it was dangerous to do that around so many cars.

'You're always a spoilsport!' she complained, and then she rooted herself to the spot and refused to budge.

'Keeley, we're in a car park!' Jonathan implored. 'Please stop this! It's not the time to mess about.'

Just then a car started to back out of a space rather too quickly, heading in Keeley's direction. Jonathan was worried the driver hadn't seen her, and so he instinctively took hold of Keeley's arm and pulled her to the safety of the kerb. Jonathan had the trolley in one hand by now and he did pull her a little bit awkwardly if the truth were told, but he certainly wasn't gripping Keeley's arm tight enough to cause a bruise.

'Stop! You're hurting me!' she cried, in an echo of the way she'd accused me of hurting her arm at the crazy golf course, when she misbehaved on our weekend break to Wales and I feared she might lash out with her golf club.

Thankfully, on this occasion, there were no passers-by listening or giving sceptical looks, so at least Jonathan didn't have to suffer that humiliation. Nevertheless, this incident was logged in my notes for Social Services, complete with a verbatim account of what was said.

'I'm not hurting you, Keeley!' Jonathan had hissed. 'I'm trying to stop you from getting hurt!'

'You are hurting me! STOP!'

'I'm not! And I can assure you that I would not have touched your arm at all if you hadn't been in danger!'

Keeley sulked all the way home and was in a foul mood

for the rest of the day, which put Jonathan and I in a bad frame of mind too. The fact she had complained to Carl about this on top of everything else, and made Jonathan out to be the villain of the piece, was incredibly frustrating.

22

'Can I have another cuddle?'

Keeley was getting ready for bed when I had that conversation with Carl. I thought about what I would say to her, and I decided that I would leave it until I found the right moment, perhaps the following day, when she was going to her first theatre group class and may be in a more responsive mood. I always find that sleeping on a situation helps, as you can see things clearer the next day. Also, if you feel angry, you may say something you regret.

I was very pleased that Ellie, her best friend from school, had also decided to join the group. I arranged with Ellie's mum, Hazel, that I would pick the two girls up from school and take them to the club. In turn, Hazel said that if they enjoyed it she would take them the following week.

Keeley and Ellie came out of school that afternoon skipping, giggling and babbling ten to the dozen, as they often did. I gave them a drink of juice and a snack each in the car, and they talked excitedly about what the club would be like, and what songs and dances they already knew. It was a joy to listen to them. Anybody witnessing this scene would not have believed that Keeley was the same girl who could be so rude and troublesome, and who had suffered the emotional abuse she had.

The principal of the theatre school, Mrs Crowther, invited me to stay for the first session and she was wonderful with the girls. The group had just started work on a new production that they were putting on later in the year. The parts hadn't been cast yet and Mrs Crowther was encouraging all the children to show off their singing and acting skills. Keeley and Ellie were given song sheets and very happily joined in with a chorus.

'Super, girls!' Mrs Crowther said, clapping. 'Let's hear it again from the top. And off we go!'

All the children were enthused by Mrs Crowther. She had been on the stage in the West End in her day and, even though she must have been well into her sixties by now, she hadn't lost any of her exuberance, which was energising just to witness.

'Can Ellie come for tea?' Keeley asked afterwards. 'Pleeeeaaasee, Angela!'

Both girls pleaded with me in the car, and so when we got to Ellie's house I asked Hazel if it was OK.

'Of course!' She smiled at the girls, who had run up to the front door together to plead in unison. 'It's lovely to see you two getting on so well. How was the theatre group?'

'Really good!' they chorused.

'You don't want to go again, do you?' Hazel teased.

'We do! We do! And next week can Keeley have tea at our house?' Ellie begged.

'I think that'll be absolutely fine, if it's all right with you, Angela?'

'I'm sure that can be arranged,' I smiled. 'As long as you can manage all three?'

Ellie had a little brother who was just over a year old, and he was wedged on Hazel's hip as she stood at the door.

'Oh yes, I'm sure I can.' Hazel smiled. 'Jake loves being fussed over and I'm sure he'll get plenty of attention with two girls in the house!'

Keeley was on a full care order with us, rather than a voluntary care order, which would have meant her mother retained parental responsibility and I might have needed to check with Social Services before allowing her to go to another person's house. As it was, with Keeley I was trusted to make day-to-day judgements like this, about whose house she was allowed to visit and which clubs she could join. This isn't always the case and the rules can alter depending on the different social workers and parents you are dealing with. Similarly, when it comes to sleepovers, some social workers will tell you that they are happy for you to make the decision, depending on how well you know the other family, and if you trust them. Other social workers are adamant that permission can only be granted for an overnight stay if all of the adults in the hosting family have been police checked. This, of course, is easier said than done. It can be awkward asking someone you don't know very well if they would mind going to the trouble of being police checked, and some people view it as an imposition and an inconvenience they would rather do without, especially when there is only a kids' sleepover at stake. It can sometimes work in the foster carer's favour, as if you don't want a child to go for a sleepover you can use the fact a police check is required as a very good excuse, which I have done on occasions in the past.

Anyhow, I was very confident I was doing the right thing in agreeing that Keeley and Ellie could spend time in each other's houses. It's a wonder I didn't have my heart in my mouth, knowing Keeley as I did, but I really didn't. I'd never seen her looking as happy and carefree as when she was in Ellie's company and she was in such a good mood that afternoon, I actually felt more relaxed than I ever had with her.

Once we were back at our house, Keeley took Ellie over to the rec with a pile of dolls, which they pushed enthusiastically on the swings and launched down the slide, and I watched from the living room window as they joined in with a skipping game with a few other girls from the neighbourhood, some of whom Ellie already knew. I gave the girls their tea before Carl and Phillip got in as they were both really hungry, and the two of them sat at the kitchen table tucking into bowls of pasta, still chattering away and full of fun.

Jonathan came in from the shop as I was serving up two bowls of strawberry ice cream.

'Ooooh, good timing!' he joked. 'Both for me, are they? Thanks, Angela.'

'No, they're ours!' Keeley giggled.

'Did somebody speak?' Jonathan said as he picked up both bowls and two spoons and sat at the table, pretending to be about to tuck in.

'Let's get him!' Keeley said. 'Come on, Ellie!'

Keeley ran around the table and pinned Jonathan's arms to his sides while calling, 'Go on, Ellie! Get our ice cream! Nobody can steal our ice cream!'

Ellie slid the two bowls to the other end of the table while Jonathan put up a pretend fight.

'OK, I give up! I surrender!' he said after a minute or two of wriggling in his seat, acting as if he were trying but failing to break free from Keeley's stronghold. 'But I'll get you next time! No bowl of ice cream is safe from me! I'll win next time!'

When it was time to take Ellie home, both girls groaned but then put their shoes on willingly, climbing into the car and buckling their seatbelts without a fuss. It was so refreshing to get through such mundane tasks without a battle, and I felt almost euphoric when I dropped Ellie off.

'They've had a lovely time!' I told Hazel. 'It's been a real pleasure to have Ellie over.'

'That's great to hear,' Hazel replied. 'They do seem to get along really well. I'll speak to you nearer the time about the arrangements, but take it that I'll do the lifts and Ellie can come here for tea next week.'

The girls cheered and burst into a little impromptu chorus they'd learned at the theatre group.

ANGELA HART

'I think we've got a pair of proper drama queens here,' Hazel commented and I thought that, for once, it was fantastic to hear that term being used in a positive way about Keeley.

'Maybe Keeley being a "drama queen" is the way forward,' I said to Jonathan that night.

'You could be right, Angela,' he replied, knowing exactly what I meant. 'I never thought I'd be agreeing with a statement like that, but I think we might be on to something. It certainly seems to suit her to be on a stage, singing and dancing.'

At bedtime I praised Keeley to the hilt for her good behaviour, and I gently talked about how lovely it was to see her enjoying herself rather than having fall-outs. I certainly didn't want to burst her bubble after such a good afternoon, but then again I couldn't ignore the issues I'd discussed with Carl. I'd promised him I would talk to Keeley when the time was right, and I felt this was the moment, as she was in such a responsive mood.

'I bet you feel much happier when you are having fun and being a good friend,' I said.

'Yes, I do.'

'Maybe you could try and be better friends with the boys? I know they are older and you don't have things in common like you do with Ellie, but you might be surprised how well you get on with them, if you try.'

'Maybe,' she said.

'And the same goes for Jonathan, too. He is on your side, Keeley, and he cares very much about you.'

'Does he?'

'Of course he does. You know, when he pulled you onto the kerb that day in the retail park?'

'Yes.'

'He did that because he was very worried that you may be hit by the car. Your safety was the most important thing in that moment, and Jonathan was looking out for you, because he cares and wants the best for you.'

'OK,' she said quietly.

I left it at that, and when I said goodnight to Keeley at her bedroom door she asked me for an 'extra big cuddle,' which of course I provided.

'Thanks for a good day, Angela' she said.

'You are welcome, Keeley. Night night.'

'Can I have another cuddle?'

'Of course!'

She hugged me tight and then got into bed and curled up under her quilt, looking angelic with her shiny curls splayed all over the pillow.

'Sleep tight, Keeley. See you in the morning.'

23

'I wish I could just live with Angela'

Keeley had been with us for three months now, and the day had arrived for our second six-weekly placement meeting, to be attended once again by Jonathan and me, the social workers Sandy and Joan, plus Sandy's boss Sheila Briggs.

For several days beforehand Jonathan and I had talked late into the evening, picking over the conversation we'd had about coping with Keeley, and what we should say at this meeting. It wasn't an easy decision, but we both agreed that despite the good behaviour we'd recently enjoyed, seeing Keeley getting along so well with Ellie, it was still wise for us to broach the subject of Keeley moving to a single placement, if and when the right one became available. We had to do what was right for her, we told ourselves. We might be judged by Social Services for suggesting such a move; perhaps even viewed to be struggling to cope or even failing, but if that was the case, then so be it. Our priority was Keeley's wellbeing, and all we wanted was the best for her, and for the boys.

*

I felt nervous when I took my seat around the table in the Social Services office. I was very familiar with these meetings, having attended hundreds by this point in my fostering career, but this was the first time I had gone into one with the intention of suggesting a child would ultimately be better off living with somebody else. Jonathan looked nervous too, his worried expression and the sheen of sweat on his brow reminding me of the day when, some seventeen years earlier, we waited to hear if a panel of officials had decided whether or not we were fit to be passed as foster carers.

As usual, the meeting started with a discussion about the formalities required in every placement, such as routine check-ups with the doctor, dentist and optician, and school attendance and progress. Jonathan and I answered all of the questions to everybody's satisfaction, and then Joan spoke. As Keeley's social worker, she had spoken to her a few days before the meeting to ask how she felt about the placement, so that this information could be passed on. Joan told the meeting that Keeley had commented: 'I wish I could just live with Angela,' and that this was not the first time she had intimated this. Sandy, Jonathan and I all conceded that we were not surprised to hear this, as the three of us had discussed the fact Keeley seemed to enjoy one-to-one attention from me more than anything else.

Sheila Briggs took up the reins, and to my surprise she began to catalogue how Social Services had hoped to put Keeley in a single placement from the start, following the breakdown of her other placements. This, according to her file, was on the advice of her therapist.

'Mmm, I see, bonding issues,' Sheila said, reading from notes. 'Hence the recommendation for a single placement, and hence Keeley's comments about wanting to live just with Angela.'

Jonathan and I gave each other a look. We both knew that sending Keeley to us had not been first choice for Social Services. She had come to us because of our specialist training, and as we understood it there were simply no other foster carers with our training available at the time. If we hadn't taken her in then she may have ended up in a special unit, which would probably have been much worse for her than living with me and Jonathan, Carl and Phillip. I had no regrets about agreeing to have Keeley move in with us, but I felt irritated. I just wished somebody had spelled out from the start that Keeley had 'bonding issues' that warranted her therapist to recommend a single placement. As it was, we'd been left to our own devices, trying to piece together Keeley's confusing jigsaw with little else but Sandy's anecdotes from a conference and a few photocopied hand-outs.

'Can I ask,' I interjected, as soon as I saw an opportunity. 'Is there anything on the notes that says Keeley has attachment disorder?'

'No, I don't think so,' Sheila replied, asking me to elaborate as she continued scanning pages in Keeley's file.

I explained briefly about the conversation with Sandy, who supported me by chipping in with some details about the conference she'd attended, and then Joan concurred that she too had wondered whether Keeley had attachment disorder, but that to her knowledge this had never been confirmed by any of the several medical experts Keeley had seen since her time in care. It was frustrating that nobody in the room seemed to know the full facts about Keeley's mental health, although in our experience professionals often don't like to label youngsters. In any case, I thought that at least this conversation had set the scene very well for me to give my views about Keeley moving into a single placement. I went on to hold the floor for quite some time, explaining how we felt Carl and Phillip were suffering as a result of having Keeley in their lives.

'If we just had Keeley on her own I am sure we would manage well,' I said, being ever-mindful of the fact I didn't want to be seen as incapable. 'But the fact is the boys were with us first and there are no plans in place at the moment for either of them to move out. I'm afraid that the situation with Keeley might escalate.'

'Can you elaborate, Mrs Hart?' Shelia Briggs said once more.

'Yes, I can. Keeley sets out to deliberately aggravate the boys and, as we've discussed and put in writing already, she is sometimes physically aggressive towards them. So far the boys have not retaliated by fighting back, but she is pushing them all the time, particularly Phillip. He can be volatile given the wrong set of circumstances and I'm worried he might hit back if, for example, Keeley carries on digging him in the ribs or scratching and bruising him.'

I felt guilty speaking about Keeley like this, and I went on to talk about the positive progress we'd made lately too, and in particular how she had made a good friend in Ellie and joined the theatre group.

'I can see you and Mr Hart are very competent carers and you are doing your level best,' Sheila remarked. 'But I understand that this is not necessarily enough, in this instance. I do agree that we need to make renewed efforts to find an alternative home for Keeley.'

Joan pointed out that we were all in a difficult situation: it had been hard enough finding specialist carers for Keeley. Now she needed a single placement with two specialist carers; one carer on their own would not work with a child like Keeley, as they would be under too much strain and it would not be safe for them.

'I'm afraid this is like looking for a needle in a haystack,' she said. 'Those places are incredibly rare, and it could take years for one to come up.'

I felt deflated, but I suppose this should not have come as a surprise. For many mainstream foster carers, it is just not feasible to commit to the extensive specialist training that Jonathan and I had over the years. We were in the very fortunate position of running our business in tandem with fostering, and because we were both self-employed and able to cover for each other, we managed to fit everything in.

Sheila then said something else that I really hadn't anticipated.

'Joan, can you bring the meeting up to date on the situation with Keeley's family, and is there any possibility of her living with another relative?'

As far as I was aware there was only Tina and Eric. I hadn't considered there might be a larger family tree after all.

'On her mother's side, there are no other relatives besides the grandfather, Eric, and we've drawn a blank so far in tracking down Keeley's father,' Joan said. 'However, the good news is that he has not been absent throughout Keeley's life, as we first thought. It appears he has been in contact with Tina several times over the years, and the last time he saw Keeley was about two years ago.'

This surprised me. I'd always believed that Keeley's father had disappeared off the scene when Keeley was a baby and too young to remember him, but clearly this was not the case. Keeley had never once mentioned her dad, but then again Keeley barely talked about her mum unless a contact session was taking place. I calculated she would have been about six years old the last time she saw him, though, so she was definitely old enough to remember him.

Sheila then asked Joan to step up whatever efforts had been made to contact Keeley's father, and then she moved on to another matter: the police interview.

Scanning the file in front of her on the desk once more, Sheila nodded and said: 'I see that the police interviewing hasn't led to any further action.'

Jonathan and I exchanged yet more glances. We had heard nothing at all since we took Keeley to the interview house, and we had no idea what had gone on since, if anything.

Joan nodded. 'Yes, that's right. As you'll see in the notes, unfortunately Keeley wouldn't talk to the officers. She wouldn't say a word. When they asked her why this was, after agreeing to be interviewed, she said she had seen a programme on the television that week in which a girl had gone to the police about her dad hurting her. The dad was sent to jail and Keeley said she didn't want her grandfather to go to jail.'

I cast my mind back to the week of the police interview, and to my dismay I recalled Keeley watching her favourite soap opera, which at the time was dramatising an ongoing police investigation. I normally watched the programme with her, but it was the night she scratched Phillip and I gave her the telephone directory to rip up, and I remembered that I'd left her to it and retreated to the kitchen for a cup of tea and a chocolate biscuit and five minutes' peace and quiet. I regretted this now, but then again, would I have stopped Keeley watching the episode had I sat down to watch with her? Probably not, and I had to accept that what was done was done. This unfortunate coincidence was out of my control and, in any case, who knows whether she would have seen it through with the police? Jonathan and I were nervous enough waiting outside the interview room, so goodness only knows what it was like for Keeley to be inside, surrounded by strangers and with such a difficult story to tell. It would be very hard for any child not to clam up and decide the easier option was to say nothing.

The placement meeting was concluded with a discussion about Keeley's mother. Tina wanted to come to our house for the next contact session, so that she could see Keeley's bedroom and would be able to picture where her daughter was living. Jonathan and I were quite happy to agree to this. We'd seen Tina on many occasions by now at the weekly contact sessions but we had never had a proper conversation with her, as Jonathan and I always sat outside while the contact officer supervised the visit. I was sure Keeley would enjoy having her mum come to us for a change, and I thought it would also be an opportunity for Jonathan and I to get to know her better, which could be no bad thing. The social workers agreed that Jonathan and I could supervise this contact session by ourselves and didn't need a contact social worker to be in the house with us, and a time was set for the coming Friday, when Tina would be driven to our house by a member of staff from Social Services, who would also take her home afterwards.

That evening I told Keeley her mum was visiting after school on Friday.

She thought about this for a moment and then told me she wasn't sure if she wanted her to. Keeley had never objected to seeing her mum before and always seemed to quite enjoy it, so I asked her why it was she felt this way.

'Dunno. It'll just be weird, that's all.'

'You like seeing your mum though, don't you, Keeley?'

'Yes, but it's a bit weird, her coming here, that's all.'

She didn't say any more, apart from to tell me not to

worry because she could see that I was frowning, which I thought was very sweet of her.

I understood what she meant by it being 'weird' having Tina in our house. This was Keeley's territory, a place where she was safe from any bad memories and the abuse she had suffered in the past. We still had no evidence about whether or not there had been any sexual abuse from mother to daughter, or indeed from her grandfather. After the failed police interview I doubted we ever would, but the physical and emotional trauma Keeley had been through when she was in her mother's care was not disputed.

Seeing her mum on neutral ground, away from the family home, had clearly been something Keeley could handle. Before I became a foster carer I would not have believed that even this would have been possible. I imagined that if a child had been abused in any way by a parent or relative, be it emotional, physical or sexual abuse, then they would not want to see them at all, but of course I've learned that this is rarely the case. Almost every one of the fifty children I've looked after has shown themselves to be incredibly resilient and forgiving, no matter what parents or other abusers within the family have subjected them to.

One boy we looked after for a short while had been put in foster care at the age of three. He was eleven by the time he came to us, and his mother had been promising she would have him back 'soon' every few months for the past eight years. He picked himself up after every disappointment, his enthusiasm to return home and his loyalty to his mother unabated. I heard that she finally took him back in when he was seventeen and earning money, which unfortunately is not unusual. Then he stayed for just a few months, until his mother got fed up with him and kicked him out. Apparently, even then he remained her most loyal supporter.

I thought long and hard that evening about Keeley's reaction to her mother's visit. I could completely see how meeting in a council building differed entirely to meeting in our house, or indeed any family home. The Social Services' supervised contact room was fairly nondescript and it smelled like all council buildings – a little bit dusty and stale, with a faint whiff of disinfectant. This environment was a bonus to many children as it reduced the danger of bad memories being triggered by the smells and objects of home, plus the institutionalised setting made it seem safer and more controlled than a visit in a private house.

I remembered how I assisted on a training course in the late nineties, during which Jonathan and I learned how reminders from home are very powerful, and can work in both a positive and negative way. For example, a child may arrive at their new foster home with a smelly old blanket, a broken toy or clothing that is too small for them. Whatever condition their belongings are in, and even if it looks like rubbish that is only fit for the bin, you must not, under any circumstances, throw any of their personal items away. I had to do a role play at that particular training session, in which I played an insensitive foster carer who was greeting a child for the first time.

'What's in your bin bag?' I had to say.

'My stuff,' the person playing the foster child replied.

'Give it here, then. I'll help you unpack. Oh God! That stinks! That has to go in the bin right away!'

The child then helplessly and unhappily watched this so-called rubbish being thrown out. The simple but powerful message was that one person's trash is another person's treasure, and for some children taking away what might be their only physical reminder of a person or a place is potentially very damaging, and can make it much harder for them to settle into their new environment. The child is already going through a period of great change, and it is your job as a foster carer to help make them feel as comfortable as possible, and not to add to their anxiety.

I've also learned through training that sometimes objects and smells have the opposite to a comforting effect, and can instead trigger traumatic memories. One child we looked after became extremely upset when a teenager in the house used a particular aftershave, because it reminded her very powerfully and instantaneously of her abuser. It was like a switch. One minute she was happily playing a game and the next she was ashen-faced and shaking. It took her several hours to calm down after she smelled the aftershave, and several days to tell me why she had this reaction. Needless to say, I had to ask the boy not to use the aftershave again, and fortunately he readily agreed with no questions asked.

I discussed all of these thoughts with Jonathan, because I could feel myself getting stressed about the visit. I'd fretted that Tina's own perfume might linger in our house, and whether this might trigger Keeley in a bad way, after her mum had left. I wanted, and needed, Jonathan's opinion.

'How do you think we should handle Tina's visit?' I asked him. 'Is there anything we can do to make it go as smoothly as possible, avoid any potential problems?'

'First of all, we have agreed to the visit and it's not our decision to change the arrangement,' he said, trying to work through the problem systematically and reasonably, searching for any answers that could quell my concerns. 'Social Services have set this up and we trust they know what they are doing, don't we?'

'That's right. I'll pass on what Keeley has said about her mother coming to our house, though. They don't know she's said it's a bit "weird".'

'OK, yes, of course. We also know that Keeley is fine having contact with Tina at the offices, don't we? So the problem is not actually in seeing her mother, it's in her mother coming here.'

'Exactly. So the real question is, Jonathan, what is causing that reaction? It's not because her mother's scent or clothes or anything like that brings back memories from the past, because that would happen in the offices too.'

'Right, Angela. And so, therefore, the problem has to be that here she is simply worried her private space is being invaded, which as you've already said is quite understandable. We simply need to reinforce the fact to Keeley that nothing will change once Tina has been in the house.

Keeley is just as safe, we will look after her just the same, and Tina's visit is not going to alter what goes on here.'

Conversations like these have been taking place between Jonathan and me for decades now. We laugh sometimes at how we have become amateur psychologists and detectives on our fostering journey. The training courses we've been on have been second to none, and we're both very comfortable with analysing situations, trying to put ourselves in the shoes of the child and, above all, being open-minded and willing to watch and learn.

24

'I'm not sure I can take much more'

'Babe!' Tina trilled when she arrived at our house. Keeley was in the hallway, dressed in her favourite denim-blue leggings and a fluffy sweatshirt with a rabbit on the front.

'Hello, Mum,' Keeley replied.

She looked very nervous, though she pulled a wide smile.

'What's up, babe?' Tina asked.

'Nothing,' Keeley said unconvincingly.

'You sure? Come here, give us a cuddle!'

Keeley obediently went up to her mum, and Tina lifted her daughter aloft.

'Why haven't you got a pretty dress on today, babe?'

Keeley looked very worried now. She had worn a dress to every one of the supervised contact sessions we'd had so far, as her mum always made a point of telling her how much she wanted to see her in all the sparkly, glittery frocks she had given her. The collection in Keeley's wardrobe had expanded since she'd move in: not only had she arrived with a suitcase full of dresses, but every few weeks Tina gave Keeley a carrier bag stuffed with more dresses to choose from, often more flamboyant than the last lot. They were never new and I assumed they came from charity shops. Some were so shimmery and clingy that I had to encourage Keeley to wear a cardigan over the top, or some tights, to try to tone down the glamorous look. The style didn't seem at all appropriate for an eight-year-old girl, especially on an ordinary Friday afternoon. On several occasions I'd tried to gently suggest that perhaps Keeley might be more comfortable in her jeans or leggings, but she always brushed this aside, often quite forcefully.

I was therefore as surprised as Tina was to see Keeley in her leggings and sweatshirt on this particular day, and I was interested to hear what she would say when her mum asked her why she wasn't wearing a dress.

'All my dresses are in the wash,' Keeley said brazenly, which made Jonathan and I share a look. He raised an eyebrow and I widened my eyes ever so slightly. We both knew it was a complete lie. She would have had to have worn at least half a dozen dresses a day to get through her collection between washes, but of course we didn't point this out.

'Really? But you've got loads, babe,' Tina said.

Before Keeley could answer I stepped in.

'Would you like to come through to the kitchen?' I said, steering Tina out of the hallway, where the four of us were still standing.

'OK, thanks,' she smiled. 'Nice house you've got here. Is Keeley behaving herself for you?'

'We are enjoying having Keeley with us,' I said. 'Would you like a cup of tea, Tina?'

'No, thanks, have you got any lemonade or cola?'

We never have fizzy drinks in the house as over the years we've had children staying with us who have suffered from ADHD, autism and a whole range of hyperactivity problems that might potentially be aggravated by fizzy drinks. We stopped buying them many years ago, as it simply wasn't worth the risk of having them in the house.

'Sorry, no,' I said, 'but I do have fruit juice or squash.'

'Nah! No, thanks! We don't like that, do we, Keeley?' Tina said, wrinkling her nose. She was looking at her daughter rather than me as she spoke, which struck me as really quite rude. I told myself not to get annoyed, though. I knew Tina's mental age was below her actual age, and I had to accept that it was not her fault that she behaved this way.

I heard Keeley agree that she didn't like fruit juice or squash, although I knew this wasn't true, and she was obviously just trying to please her mum. The visit carried on in a similar vein. Jonathan and I sat down quietly at one end of the kitchen table while Tina and Keeley occupied the other, with Tina focusing her attention entirely on her daughter.

A report on this would have to be completed, with notes of all the conversation that took place. We would rather not have had to intrude like this, but of course it was the rule that the visit was supervised, and Jonathan and I felt that at least if we stayed in the kitchen we could potter around a bit, which we took turns doing.

Tina talked to Keeley about television programmes she had seen and about how much money she had saved up for Christmas, so that she could buy Keeley loads of presents. Then she went on to describe a new jacket she had bought that she was highly delighted with, and exactly which outfit she was going to wear for bingo that night.

'D'you like this colour, babe?'

Tina waved her fingernails under Keeley's nose. Her nail varnish was fluorescent orange, to match her tight top and the sequin-studded belt she wore around the waist of her cropped white jeans.

'Yes,' Keeley said politely.

'Do you want me to paint yours next time I see you?'

'Yes,' Keeley said. 'Me and Angela have done some painting, you know.'

'Did you, babe?'

'Yes. We made bonnets for the carnival. Do you want to see mine?'

'No, you're all right, babe. I need to go to the toilet.'

With that Tina turned to me to ask if she could visit the bathroom.

I was disappointed that she hadn't shown interest in Keeley's painting, but again I had to concede that Tina wasn't being unkind or uncaring; she had her problems, and I had to keep that uppermost in my mind.

I directed Tina to the downstairs toilet along the hallway, and while her mum was out of the room Keeley closed her eyes and lay her head on the table.

'Are you OK, sweetheart?' I asked.

230

'Yes, just tired.'

'Do you want a drink?'

'Yes, please.'

'What would you like, water or orange?' I asked, as Keeley tended to choose one of the two.

'Oran—' she started, and then changed her mind. I realised she had remembered agreeing with her mum that she didn't like fruit juice or squash. 'Just water.'

When Tina returned she asked if she could see Keeley's bedroom, which we all knew she would want to do, as this had been put forward as one of the main purposes of the visit.

'No problem.' I smiled. 'Come on, Keeley, do you want to lead the way?'

Keeley nodded and scampered up the stairs with Tina, Jonathan and I in her wake. I'd asked Keeley in advance to make sure her room was tidy, and I was pleased to see it was looking very spick and span, with all her dolls lined up in neat rows, the bed made and no clutter or clothes on the floor. Keeley positioned herself in front of the wardrobe as soon as she went in the room, no doubt to stop her mum from looking inside and spotting all her dresses hanging up, washed and ironed.

'Do they make you tidy up?' Tina whispered.

'Yes,' Keeley said quietly.

'But do they treat you good, babe?'

'Yes,' Keeley said. 'They do.'

'That's good, but listen, babe, come here, I've got a secret to tell you.'

Jonathan and I were standing in the doorway of the bedroom, as we had to supervise Tina at all times when she was with Keeley. It was an awkward scenario, as even though the bedroom was fairly big and Tina and Keeley were now sitting on the bed several metres away and talking very quietly, we could hear every word being spoken.

'What?' Keeley asked.

She looked nervous at the prospect of hearing a secret from her mum, and I think Jonathan and I held our breath at the same time as Keeley did.

'It's about your dad.'

'Dad?' Keeley said. 'What do you mean?'

'You do remember him, don't you, babe?'

'Yes.'

'That's good. He has been in touch, you see. And he'd like to see you.'

'Really?'

Keeley put her hand over her mouth, as if stifling a shriek.

'Yes, babe. And then, if you wanted to, you could go and live with him!'

'Great!' Keeley squeaked, her eyes widening, although I could tell she was not exactly brimming over with enthusiasm. Her face was etched with concern, and who could blame her? She hadn't seen her father since she was six years old, and two years is a very long time in the life of a little girl.

Tina's revelation was certainly a surprise to Jonathan and me too: it had only been a matter of days since we'd heard mention of him being tracked down at all. Keeley hadn't even been aware of this much. None of the social workers had enlightened her, because of course nobody wanted to raise any false hopes, in case the search came to nothing or her father didn't want to know.

I felt very strongly that I wanted to intervene, as I felt it was now Tina who was potentially raising false hopes. Whatever happened next, there was clearly a long way to go before Keeley might be going to live with her dad, and I didn't think it was appropriate to be talking about this possibility so lightly at such an early stage. I held back, though. This was something I'd have to discuss with the social workers and then with Keeley, once I was armed with all the facts. Interfering now might aggravate Tina and upset Keeley and would have been wrong of me, so I kept quiet.

Tina left shortly afterwards, when a contact officer collected her by car. As usual she picked Keeley up and swung her around, and she planted a big kiss on her lips when she said goodbye.

'Love you, babe!' she said.

Keeley wiped her lips.

'Bye, Mum. I hope you have fun at bingo.'

'Thanks, babe! If I win I'll buy you a big present. What d'you want?'

Keeley thought about this for a moment.

'I don't know,' she said. 'Nothing, really.'

She looked quite forlorn as she said this, but Tina didn't seem to notice.

'Don't be daft! There must be something you want!'

'Not really. You might not win, anyway.'

When Tina had gone Keeley was in a very bad mood and the parting smile she'd given her mum slipped straight off her face.

'Why didn't you tell me about my dad, Angela?' she ranted once Tina had been driven away.

'Keeley, I didn't know he had been in touch,' I said truthfully. 'I will talk to Social Services on Monday and find out exactly what is going on.'

'You hate me, don't you?'

'Why do you say that?'

'Because you are keeping me here!'

'What do you mean?'

'You are a sad old woman and you just want to keep me here instead of letting me live with my family! You are a selfish old bag, just like your mum!'

I was completely taken aback. This attack was totally uncalled for, and I was doubly insulted that Keeley had dragged my mother into this. Of course, I should not have risen to an argument, but I was so incensed I couldn't help answering her back.

'How dare you insult my mother and me! I have done nothing but my best for you, Keeley. I am not keeping you here because I'm selfish! I'm a foster carer, and I've taken you into my home because I care about you and want to help you.'

'Liar! You get paid to look after me, don't you? That's the

real reason you do it, isn't it? You just want me here so you can get more money. Doesn't your shitty little shop earn enough money?'

'That is complete and utter nonsense and extremely rude. And I'll have you know that the business does very well, thank you. I do not foster for the money. I foster because I want to. But if you don't want to be here, then that's the end of it. I am not holding you here against your will, am I? I'll tell Social Services you want to leave, if that's what you want.'

'Fine!'

'And why are you insulting my mother? What has she ever done wrong?'

'She's selfish! She just wants her own way all the time. You make a big fuss of her when she comes round and you ignore me.'

'I do not,' I said, and then I bit my tongue. I hadn't spotted this before, but Keeley must have felt jealous of my mother, in the same way that she wanted Jonathan and the boys off the scene much of the time, so she could have my undivided attention.

I felt slightly calmer once I'd made this realisation, but with the calm came a great, crashing wave of guilt. I thought about the PACE model Sandy had introduced me to and I felt ashamed of myself. Where were the playfulness, acceptance, curiosity and empathy in my reaction? I'd handled Keeley's outburst really badly, but in the heat of the moment, and with my mum being criticised so callously, I hadn't been able to help myself.

'What's happening?' I said to Jonathan that night.

'Well, we both know what's happening. Keeley needs to be in a single placement. We're not going to win with her here like this, are we? We know that, deep down. This isn't the best place for her.'

'You're right. I don't want to let her down, but . . .'

'But what?'

'I'm not sure I can take much more.'

'I feel exactly the same, Angela. It's a very difficult situation.'

'I know,' I sniffed, 'but for the time being, and for however long, she is living with us and we have to do better.'

At that moment Keeley walked into the kitchen.

'Can I have a glass of milk?' she asked quite aggressively.

'No, you can't!' I retorted. 'Now go back upstairs, right now. I asked you to go to bed half an hour ago, so what are you doing still up?'

'I told you, you hate me! You don't want me here.'

'That's rubbish. Go to bed!'

Keeley turned on her heel and stomped up the stairs, while I dissolved into tears.

25

'You BITCH! I'm gonna get you!'

I spoke to Sandy on the Monday and passed on everything that had happened since the meeting, and I was told that it was true Keeley's father had been found, and that he wanted to see her. Everything had happened very quickly, it seemed, and Sandy had been on annual leave on the Friday, and was only just processing all the information herself.

'Would you be able to bring Keeley to a supervised contact session to meet him one afternoon next week, after school?'

'Next week? So soon? Gosh, yes, of course. Are you happy for me to tell Keeley all of this?'

'Yes, Angela. I've spoken to Joan this morning. She'll talk to Keeley in due course, but we're both happy for you to discuss the meeting with her. I guess the fact Tina has already mentioned it should help. It won't be a huge shock, and by the sounds of it Keeley will be quite happy to go along.'

237

It turned out that Keeley's father, Frankie, had recently returned to the area after working away for more than a year, and had been tracked down after rejoining a club he had previously been a member of. He lived on his own and had no other children, and he was apparently very keen to be reunited with Keeley. The following Tuesday was suggested as the best day for the meeting to take place, which suited me and Jonathan, and I agreed to make the usual plans to cover our commitments at home and in the shop.

I told Keeley all of this once she was home from school later that day, and she punched the air with delight.

'Yippee! I'm going to live with my dad!' she began chanting, running around the kitchen excitedly. 'I'm going to live with my dad!'

'Keeley, you're going to meet him, but that's all we know so far. It might not be possible for you to move back in with him. There's a lot to think about first and I don't want you to be disappointed. We'll have to see what happens.'

'You're just saying that because you're jealous! You don't want me here anymore but you don't want him to have me either!'

I took a deep breath, and at that moment the boys walked in together.

'I'm going to live with my dad, losers!' she taunted. 'You'll be stuck here, but I'm going to live with my dad!'

The boys looked at me and asked if this was true.

'We don't know yet,' I said. 'Do we, Keeley?'

'Well, I'm going to meet him, aren't I? Why would he

want to meet me if he didn't want to know me? I'm going to live with him, I'll show you! You're all just jealous!'

'As I say, we'll have to see what happens,' I said, and out of the corner of my eye I saw Carl and Phillip grinning as they gave each other a victory fist-pump before taking off their shoes and heading upstairs.

'Did you remember it's swimming lessons at school tomorrow?' I said to Keeley, deliberately changing the subject. 'And that you need to use the waterproof bag?'

'Yes. I don't need *you* to remind me!'

'That's good. Make sure you pack your bag in good time tonight, so you have everything you need.'

Keeley rolled her eyes.

'Nag, nag, nag, that's all Angela does,' she said to the wall.

'Angela isn't nagging,' I said, crossing the kitchen and talking in a singsong voice to the same patch of wall. 'Angela is just trying to make sure Keeley has everything she needs and has remembered to pack a waterproof bag, because Angela likes to look after Keeley, and do the best for her.'

Keeley gave me a sideways look, unsure how to react to my talking to the wall too. She opened her mouth to speak but then said nothing; I'd matched her at her own game, and I hoped I'd made a point.

Ever since the school swimming sessions started up we'd had a weekly spat about the fact Keeley refused to pack her costume and towel in the waterproof swimming bag I'd bought for her. After each session she came home with her books and pencil case wet through.

'I'm glad you've remembered,' I went on, turning to look at her now. I tried to make eye contact but she scowled and looked straight past me.

'Of course I have. I'm not stupid, you know. I don't know where the waterproof bag is though.'

'Are you sure?'

'Positive.'

'Right then, shall I give you a carrier bag to put your wet things in?'

'What for?'

'So your books and pencil case don't get wet like they did last week.'

'They didn't get wet.'

'They did, Keeley.'

She reluctantly took the swimming kit in the carrier bag the next day, but when I collected Keeley from school I found she had no swimsuit in the bag.

'Did you leave your costume at the pool by accident?' I asked.

'No.'

'Then where is it?'

'You're stupid, Angela! I'm wearing it, of course!'

When I looked at Keeley again I could see the bright yellow colour of her costume underneath her school polo shirt.

'Why did you do that?' I gasped. 'You'll get poorly wearing a damp costume for hours on end.'

'Felt like it.'

'Didn't the teachers tell you to change?'

'No. I don't think they noticed. It's no big deal. Keep your hair on, Angela!'

When we got home I found Keeley's knickers wrapped inside her swimming towel. She'd clearly wet herself; the underwear was soaked through and smelled strongly of urine. I realised this was probably the real reason Keeley decided to keep her swimming costume on, and I was in two minds about whether to talk to her about this. I didn't want another fight or for her to tell me any more fibs, but equally I couldn't just leave it.

'Keeley,' I ventured. 'When I went to put your washing in the machine just now I found your knickers. Did you keep your swimming costume on because your knickers were wet?'

'No, why would I do that?'

'So that you didn't have to wear wet knickers.'

'But I wore a wet costume. What's the difference? What does it matter?'

'OK, perhaps you'd like to keep a spare pair of knickers in your bag, in case one pair gets wet?'

'Why would I do that? I DON'T WET MY KNICKERS!'

As she bellowed this, Phillip walked into the kitchen, and he stifled a laugh.

'What are you laughing at, you little fucker?' she shouted at the top of her voice.

'Keeley, with language like that you'll be missing the next treat!'

'See if I care!'

'Cow,' Phillip muttered under his breath.

'Phillip! You mind your language too! I think you two should apologise to each other, right now.'

Phillip and Keeley both had their arms crossed and stood glaring at each other across the kitchen table.

'I'm not saying sorry to him,' she bellowed. 'He's a loser! Ha ha, I'm going to live with my dad and you're just a LOSER! You've got to stay here 'cos nobody else wants you!'

Phillip exploded.

'You BITCH! I'm gonna get you!'

Philip then launched himself towards Keeley. I stepped forward and just about managed to block his path, raising my arms as I did so and saying, 'Stop! That's enough!' Thankfully, Keeley had been standing close to the kitchen door, and at the same time she darted out of the room like a scalded cat and ran up both flights of stairs at breakneck speed. I heard the bathroom door slam very loudly, and then Keeley shouted at the top of her voice: 'Go to hell, everyone! I'm not coming out of here until it's time to see my dad!'

Moments later Carl arrived home from school, complained that he'd been sweating his head off in a stuffy classroom for hours, and said he was going straight upstairs to have a shower.

'Keeley's in the bathroom,' I said, still catching my breath.

'Bitch!' Phillip spat again.

'What's happened?' Carl asked, rolling his eyes as if to say, 'What now?'

Phillip said it didn't matter and that he didn't want to talk about it.

'I'm going to my room,' he huffed. 'I've got work to do.'

'Me too,' Carl said, backing away. 'I'll just wait for Keeley to come out of the bathroom, Angela. I can wait for my shower, don't worry. I don't want another argument.'

The boys both skulked upstairs, leaving me to prepare the evening meal with a very heavy heart.

There was a hand-painted wooden sign on my kitchen wall that said 'Meals and Memories Made Here.' It was a gift from a former foster child, Mel, who was now grown up, and when she presented it to me I'd been very proud to display it.

'Thank you for the memories,' she had written on the back. Mel's placement with us had been very successful. She stayed for just a few months before moving back in with her mother, and she had kept in touch ever since. When I thought of Mel I always felt grateful for being able to do the job I did. When things go well in fostering, it is the best job in the world. Helping a child turn a corner and move forward with hope and optimism or better prospects is incredibly satisfying, and I can't imagine any greater reward in any job. When things go wrong, however, it can hit you very hard and make you feel responsible for failing to improve a child's life, which is the worst feeling in the world.

Now I felt the sign was mocking me. What memories were we making for Phillip and Carl now that Keeley was disrupting their life in this way? And what about Keeley herself? I wanted her to thrive in our care, and to be able to look back one day and see how Jonathan and I had helped her, and given her some good memories. With things the way they were, I felt that the longer she stayed, the more unlikely this was.

As I cooked dinner I found myself willing Keeley's meeting with her father to go well. How she would react if it went wrong was not worth thinking about; she was difficult enough to deal with as it was. I even allowed myself to daydream about the prospect it might go extremely well indeed, and that Keeley really could go and live with her dad. Good things do happen in life, and this wasn't completely beyond the realms of possibility. After all, Frankie wanted to see his daughter and he had no other family responsibilities standing in the way. We'd been searching for a single placement, and perhaps he was the one who was finally going to provide it? The daydream seemed too good to be true, but I lived in hope; it could be her salvation, and ours.

To my surprise, Keeley appeared in the kitchen while I was still busy cooking.

'I'm sorry, Angela,' she said quietly. Her voice sounded slightly hoarse, no doubt from all the shouting she'd done. 'Can I hug you?'

'Of course you can, sweetheart,' I said, because however badly a child had behaved I would never deny them a hug.

She flung her arms around me and squeezed me tight, and then she asked if she could make a pattern in the mashed potato I'd just put on top of the fish pie I was making for dinner. This had become one of Keeley's favourite jobs in the kitchen whenever we had fish pie or cottage pie, and she did a different design every time.

'Of course you can,' I said again, thinking how I wished she was in this frame of mind more often, and how I was going to have to talk to her about what had happened earlier, even though I wanted this mood to last for as long as possible.

'There!' she said triumphantly, standing back and admiring her work.

I looked at the top of the pie and smiled. Keeley had used a fork and drawn a great big heart with the letter 'A' in the middle.

'That's for you,' she said. 'I'm sorry I'm not always good.'

26

'Who is Jonathan?'

On Thursday morning I reminded Keeley that Hazel was collecting her and Ellie from school and taking them to the theatre group, and that she would be having her tea at Ellie's house.

'So what?' she said to me.

Keeley was in a difficult mood and was stalling for time as she got ready for school. I'd wanted to suggest she took some spare knickers, as I didn't want to risk her being smelly going to the theatre group or to Ellie's, but she was in such an unresponsive frame of mind that I kept quiet, knowing she would only give me short shrift.

She dawdled over eating her breakfast and then had a row through the bathroom door with both boys.

'I'm doing my hair!' she shouted when they nagged her to hurry up.

Unfortunately, over the last few weeks, this had become a very tedious daily ritual. Keeley would spend anything up to half an hour in the bathroom, damping down her hair and brushing it, trying to get the curls out.

'Go and use my bathroom!' I called up to the boys. 'Don't be late! Don't argue!'

Jonathan and I had started getting up a bit earlier than usual so we could use our bathroom first, before the boys might need it. This was a nuisance, but it was better than having Carl and Phillip getting wound up before school, or being late.

Once she was dressed, Keeley went through her now all too familiar routine of spending ages putting on her shoes. By this stage I was well aware that her behaviour became worse when she felt she was irritating Jonathan or me or stressing us out. Therefore, we would busy ourselves doing jobs in the kitchen while the shoe drama played out.

On this particular day I could hear Keeley repeatedly throwing her shoes at the front door. This went on for a full ten minutes before I reluctantly conceded that I'd have to intervene.

'Keeley, we'd better get a move on. I'd hate you to be late today.'

'Why? Are you worried what the school will think of you?'

'No, I'm worried you might get into trouble. What if you get kept behind after school? You're being picked up by Ellie's mum, remember?'

'They won't keep me back. They're not allowed. You're just saying that to make me hurry up!'

'I'm not, actually. I've known children be kept back after

school many times because they can't arrive on time in the morning. Never mind, though, it's up to you.'

Keeley's eyes were blazing.

'These shoes are too small. I'm going to go to school with no shoes today, I can't be bothered with them!'

'OK. That's fine. Get in the car then. Perhaps you'd better take off your socks, as you'll get holes in them if you walk on the pavement like that.'

She narrowed her eyes.

'Are you messing with me?'

'No, why?'

She pulled off her socks, threw them on the floor and then decided to put her shoes on her bare feet.

'Ready then?' I said.

'Yes!' she spat.

Jonathan appeared and picked up the socks.

'Don't you want these, Keeley?'

'What does it look like?'

'I was only asking because I was looking for something to warm my ears up with.'

With that he wrapped each little white sock around his ears and gave a daft grin.

'You're not funny,' she said. 'You're stupid.'

I laughed. 'Well I thought that was quite funny!'

'You would, wouldn't you. You think the sun shines out of Jonathan's arse.'

'Well, I wouldn't put it quite like that, Keeley, but he is my husband and actually, yes, I do think he is a fantastic man.'

'Who is?'

'Jonathan, of course.'

'Jonathan who? Who is Jonathan?'

Keeley grabbed her bag, walked past Jonathan as if he were invisible, and then climbed in the car while I stuffed the socks in my handbag. When we got to school Keeley darted out of the car and ran across the car park without saying goodbye or even speaking to me. The bell rang the second she stepped foot in the playground, and so I went to the school office and handed in the socks.

'Can you make sure Keeley gets these?' I asked the receptionist.

'Of course,' she smiled kindly. 'In a forgetful mood this morning, was she?'

'You could say that,' I said through gritted teeth.

On the drive home I began to worry about how Keeley would behave with Ellie after school. I assumed Hazel knew that Keeley was fostered, as she'd heard her call me by my first name, and most people in the neighbourhood knew that Jonathan and I were foster carers. I wasn't sure though. I had Hazel's phone number and I wished I could pick up the phone and tell her so many things she didn't know about Keeley, to forewarn her, in case something went wrong.

I wanted to say: 'Please understand, Keeley has led a traumatic life, and next week she is meeting her dad. She hasn't seen him for two years. If she behaves appallingly, this is probably why.' Of course I couldn't, and I wouldn't.

The child's privacy is paramount, and I just had to cross my fingers and hope that if there were an incident tonight it would be something Hazel could take in her stride.

I couldn't relax for the rest of the afternoon. I gave a customer the wrong change in the shop and I had to call a gentleman back who had phoned to order a bouquet for his girlfriend, as I'd failed to ask him some basic questions, such as how much he wanted to spend, and was there any particular colour or flower his girlfriend wasn't keen on. Normally these questions tripped off my tongue automatically, but I was preoccupied thinking about Keeley.

When I finally went to pick her up from Ellie's house I was a nervous wreck.

'Hi Angela!' Hazel said breezily when she came to the front door. 'Do you want to come in for a minute, the girls are just washing their hands, they've been doing some cutting and sticking.'

'OK, thanks! Have they been all right?'

'More than all right. They are absolutely full of beans. They seem to be really enjoying the theatre group. They've both got a little part now. We'll have to go and watch the show when it's on.'

Little Jake was crawling around in his playpen in the kitchen, grizzling and bashing a rattle against the rails.

'Of course! That'll be lovely. I'm so pleased they're enjoying it.'

'Oh, they are. And they've played beautifully together. It's Jake who's been the most trouble this afternoon.'

'Oh dear, what's he been up to?'

'He's just been out of sorts really. He was fine earlier on, but he got a bit grumpy at teatime and started crying for no reason. I think he's just getting a bit frustrated maybe, seeing the girls charging round. He's not walking yet but I think he'd like to be haring round with them! He's teething too, so that doesn't help, does it?'

I had a horrible thought that Keeley might have done something to Jake, but of course I had no evidence of this and it would have been very wrong of me to voice this fear. The girls appeared, showing off a very impressive collage they'd put together with all sorts of coloured paper, silver foil, pipe cleaners and bits of glitter.

'Look what we made!' Ellie said.

'Look, Angela, look!' Keeley beamed.

'It's wonderful, girls!' I replied. 'Haven't you done well?'

They were both in a delightful mood and I felt a pang of guilt for even thinking Keeley might have harmed Jake. I mustn't let her history of pinching cloud my view of her. Of all people, she needed me to think the best of her and be a loyal and positive supporter. All I could do was stay vigilant.

'You've got some very interesting shapes and bits and pieces on there, I must say,' I went on, admiring the girls' art work.

'Keeley got the pipe cleaners off miss,' Ellie said, which unfortunately rang another alarm bell, as I was sure the teacher wouldn't go dishing them out. 'And the coloured paper!'

I thought back to the stolen Blu Tack and my heart sank

a little, but I couldn't be sure Keeley had helped herself in the stationery cupboard again without permission, and of course I kept these concerns to myself too. Instead I focused on the fact Keeley seemed to have behaved herself very well all afternoon, and that her friendship with Ellie appeared to be going from strength to strength.

'Can you go and put your shoes on, Keeley?' I asked.

'Yes!' She grinned, and she went straight to the hallway and put her shoes on without a fuss. She was wearing the socks I'd delivered to the school office that morning, but again I didn't comment. I didn't want anything to spoil her mood.

One the way back to our house Keeley told me all about the part she was playing in the production, and she asked: 'Do you think my dad will come to see the show?'

'I don't know, sweetheart. You'll have to ask him that yourself.'

'Yes,' she said. 'I might do.'

'How are you feeling about seeing him again?'

'OK, I think. Ellie's dad works away a lot as well. She said he always brings her a present when he comes home. Do you think my dad will bring me a present?'

'I don't know, sweetheart. I don't know him, do I? I've never met him, I don't know what he's like at all, or if he's the sort of person who likes to buy presents.'

She thought about this for a moment.

'I think he is, because once he bought my mum a present. It was a microwave oven, for her birthday. She didn't like it though. She said it wasn't a good birthday present. I thought that was mean.'

'Well, we'll have to wait and see.'

Just before bedtime Keeley headed downstairs, barefoot, to say goodnight, and Jonathan arrived home at the same time. He'd had a very long day, having visited a new wholesaler about fifty miles away, and he'd also been to see one of his relatives who happened to live nearby. He was taking his shoes off as Keeley crossed the hallway, and by accident he stepped backwards and trod on her bare foot.

'Oh, I'm so sorry!' he said as she yelped in pain. 'That was really clumsy of me, I'm really sorry, Keeley.'

I'd seen what happened and it really was an unfortunate accident, but Keeley was having none of it and started ranting and raving at Jonathan, and calling him every name under the sun.

'You hate me! You're mean! You're a nasty old man!'

'Keeley, I'm really sorry. I didn't mean to do that. It was just unfortunate you were right behind me . . .'

'Yeah, right! You did it on purpose! You don't care about me! You want me to get hurt!'

'Keeley, that's enough!' I shouted. 'You can turn around and go straight back up those stairs, right now. I don't ever want to hear you treating Jonathan like that again, do you hear me?'

I was very cross and I probably shouted at her louder than I ever had before. She looked alarmed and shot up the stairs, and I waited for fifteen minutes before going up to check on her. In the meantime I made a note about the incident in my diary for Social Services.

'Get lost!' Keeley shouted when I tapped on her bedroom door. 'I don't ever want to see you again, Angela.'

I left her for another fifteen minutes, and this time she yelled, 'What do you want?'

'I've come to say goodnight, and make sure you are OK.'

'Open the door then!'

I started to open the door, but Keeley had obviously had second thoughts about talking to me. She flew at the door, knocking it shut, and I nearly bashed my face on it.

'Keeley!' I shouted. 'What are you playing at?'

'What are YOU playing at, Angela? You're not allowed to shout at me, are you? I'm going to report you.'

'Right,' I said, exhaling deeply. 'If that's what you want to do, I will go and fetch the phone and the out-of-hours number.'

I started walking down the stairs and Keeley flung open her bedroom door.

'No! I don't want to phone up!'

'Oh, are you sure? I don't mind. I'm happy to get the number for you . . .'

'No!'

'Then what do you want, Keeley?'

She glared at me then said in a soft voice, 'A cuddle, that's all.'

I gave her a big cuddle, which she loved, and then she told me she really didn't like me shouting at her.

'I don't like shouting either,' I said. 'And I don't like you treating Jonathan like that. So, why don't we make a deal?'

'What deal?'

'Let's agree that I won't shout at you, and that you start to treat Jonathan nicely.'

'Deal,' she said before getting into bed and wishing me goodnight very sweetly, blowing me a kiss as I closed the door.

27

'Keep your nose out, you nosy old cow!'

'School was boring today,' Keeley said when Jonathan and I picked her up, ready to take her to meet her dad at the supervised contact session.

'Why was that?'

'We had to do lots of writing, and I don't like writing.'

'What did you write about?'

Keeley curled her lip. 'You had to choose a topic. The topics were all stupid things like "my day in space" or "my magic wand".'

'What did you choose?'

'Can't remember. I'll show you later.'

She sat staring out of the window all the way to the contact centre. I tried to get her to talk about Ellie, her dolls and anything else I could think of to keep her occupied. Her mind was clearly on her dad though. I wanted her to be the one to mention him if she wanted to, but she didn't. When we finally pulled into the council office car park Keeley looked pale and withdrawn.

'Are you all right, sweetheart?'

'Yes, fine,' she said. 'It's just my foot.'

'What about your foot?'

'You know, the one Jonathan trod on. I think it might be broken.'

With that she started to make a meal out of limping from the car, although when we'd picked her up from school earlier she'd been perfectly fine.

'Come on, lean on me if you want,' I said. 'I'll help you.'

She linked arms with me but ignored Jonathan when he asked if there was anything he could do to help. A contact supervisor met us at reception and Jonathan and I were asked to sit outside the room where Keeley's dad was waiting. We'd expected to be introduced to him, but we didn't argue.

'Can you look after my bag?' Keeley said, as she'd carried her school bag in with her.

'Of course.'

'You can read my story while you're waiting, if you like. My literacy book is in there.'

'OK, thanks. I'd love to.'

Keeley was taken into the contact room and Jonathan and I perched ourselves on two seats in the waiting area outside. I couldn't help thinking back to the days when fostering was just an aspiration. Then, I had no idea that when you become a foster carer you have to deal with parents as well as children. Laughingly, right at the very beginning, I mistakenly thought that kids in foster care must be orphans, because why would a child need a foster carer if they had a parent? It didn't occur to me that usually the kids still have one or even both parents, but that for some reason neither their mother nor their father could look after their child at that time in their lives. Meeting the parents of the kids in our care had been a huge eye-opener to me over the years and, as I've observed countless times, the vast majority of youngsters ultimately want nothing more than to be reunited with their mum or dad, no matter what the reason they are in care. I've also learned that kids typically don't imagine they will stay in foster care for very long; they see it as a temporary situation that is going to change any time soon, although this is often not the case at all.

Predicting how a child's foster journey will pan out is, of course, impossible. Whatever you are told is likely to happen, or whatever you expect may happen, usually never comes to fruition. Every placement is different, every child unique, and there are any number of external forces that can rock the status quo and completely alter how the future unfolds. Having said all of this, before this meeting was set up with her father, in Keeley's case I really did imagine she was going to be in some form of foster care for the rest of her childhood. After all, her mother was not capable of looking after her, hence Keeley being placed under a full care order, and her dad had appeared to be completely off the scene. *I should have known better*, I thought. You can't make assumptions like this in foster care, and while they are still living no parent is ever 'completely off the scene'. The majority do try to maintain some kind of contact, however intermittently, and you should always expect the unexpected.

I wondered how Keeley was getting on with her dad and my eyes wandered to the door of the contact room, and then to Jonathan, who was also looking deep in thought. He caught my eye, gave me a gentle smile and then picked up a local council newsletter that was on a shelf beside him. He started reading the front page, about a new housing scheme for the borough, and so I decided to read too.

I reached into Keeley's school bag for her literacy book, and as I did so I noticed there was a pair of damp knickers in there, wrapped in paper towels. My immediate reaction was to sigh, but then I realised that she must have taken my advice and packed a spare pair of pants that day, which I was pleased about.

I picked up the school book and turned the pages until I found the last piece of work she'd done, which was topped with today's date and entitled: 'The best day of my life'. I settled back in my seat and began to read.

The best day of my life was when I was five and a half. My mum and dad took me to the zoo and we fed the penguins some fish and had two ice creams! (Me and Mum and Dad, not the penguins!) My dad bought me a cuddly lion in the gift shop and I called him Lenny the Lion. He was my favourite toy, until I was six. We went on a little train and me and my dad had running races in the park. My dad is very fast and strong and he is more than six foot tall and very muscly, once he won a strong man competition at the fair! My mum is very pretty and when we had our photo taken the photo lady said: 'You look a picture' and we all laughed. We didn't buy the picture, I don't know why, I wish we had. My mum had on a nice dress and her hair looked lovely and shiny. I wish I was as pretty as her! She has nice hair, not curly like me. My dad let me win one of the races BUT!! I cut my foot on a rock and my dad carried me to the fountain and washed it, because it was bleeding lots of red blood. Then it was very hot and me and Mum and Dad all jumped in the water and had a BIG paddle. A man in the park told us off but we didn't listen, it was funny ha ha ha! We got our clothes wet so we lay on the grass in the sun and got dry. I was very tired and then we went home. My dad carried me for a bit. He said to look after Lenny, but when I was six Lenny got lost, and so did my dad – oh no! He went on a big adventure in the jungle and couldn't find his way back, but he is back now. I would like to go to the zoo again. The End.

I'd wanted to see Keeley's father and find out more about him before I read this piece of work, and now I was intrigued to meet him. This account surely had to be taken with a pinch of salt, as with any child's story, and I was very keen to know more. I showed the story to Jonathan to see what he made of it.

'Interesting,' he said, 'but Keeley is so unpredictable and has such an imagination at times, I wouldn't like to hazard a guess what is true and what isn't.'

'No, nor would I!' I said, allowing myself a laugh. 'Knowing Keeley, the bit about the jungle expedition could be fact and the rest fiction!'

Despite my scepticism I couldn't help being drawn into the story, though, and especially the timescale. We knew that the last time Keeley saw her father was when she was six years old, and so that part of it fitted; she could well have gone to the zoo with him and Tina when she was five and a half. Was it the case that Frankie had been out of Keeley's life for years and then reappeared when she was five, perhaps just for a short while? I wanted to know, and I was desperate to find out why he had disappeared completely for the past two years.

Eventually, the door to the contact room swung open and Jonathan and I instinctively got to our feet. Keeley came straight over to us and said politely, 'We can go home now.'

The contact officer was right behind her, making sure we were there to collect her.

'Thanks, Mr and Mrs Hart,' he said. 'See you next time, perhaps.'

Frankie didn't appear, and the contact officer returned to the room and shut the door behind him. Jonathan and I were both disappointed not to meet him, but even though we were curious for news we were careful not to press Keeley for information.

'How was it?' I asked. 'Are you all right?'

'Yes, it was fine, thanks. What's for tea?'

'Oh, I've done a cottage pie so we can heat it up when we get in.'

'Is there any pudding?'

'I've got ice cream or there are plenty of yogurts.'

'What flavour?'

'Strawberry.'

'I don't like strawberry.'

'But you chose it, and it was the one you enjoyed last time we had it!'

'No, I didn't!'

Jonathan intervened, and quite rightly so.

'How about some music?' he asked. 'Shall I put the radio on?'

'No, thanks,' Keeley said. 'I want to be quiet.'

'OK, sweetheart,' I said, reminding myself what a big step she had just taken. 'I read your story, by the way. I thought you wrote it very well.'

'Oh,' she said absent-mindedly. Then she turned to stare out of the car window, placing her hands over her ears as she did so.

No matter what the situation was with her dad, the one certainty was that Keeley had not seen him for two years, and the meeting must have had a huge emotional impact on her.

My mum was at our house when we got back, as she'd been keeping an eye on Carl and Phillip.

'Hello!' she said brightly, coming into the hallway to greet us. 'How is everybody?'

Keeley ignored her, kicked off her shoes and said she was going to watch television.

'I'm sorry, Mum. It's been a busy day.'

'Oh, I see. But good manners don't cost anything, do they, Angela? Should you be letting her get away with that?'

'Mum! Leave it, please. You have no idea what's been going on.'

I hadn't realised it, but Keeley heard this. She must have loitered on the stairs on the way to the living room.

'Yeah! Keep your nose out, you nosy old cow!' she shouted down.

'Well I never!' my mother exclaimed.

'Keeley, how dare you!' I shouted at the top of my voice. 'That is extremely rude and you are in a lot of trouble, young lady!'

'I thought we had a deal that you weren't going to shout at me, Angela?' she taunted.

'Well I thought we had a deal that you weren't going to be rude.'

'That was to Jonathan!'

'Well quite clearly I don't want you being rude to anyone! Kindly come down here and say sorry to my mum. You have no right saying that to her.'

'No, fuck off!'

My mother gasped in horror, and I steered her back into the kitchen, where Carl and Phillip were looking very uncomfortable.

'I'm sorry, boys. What a drama, and the minute we walked in the door. Come on, I'll sort the dinner out and hopefully things will calm down.'

They boys looked at each other, then at my mum, as if to say: 'What did we tell you?'

'I guess the boys have told you how difficult it can be sometimes?'

'Well, yes, they did mention a few things. Are you sure you're coping, Angela?'

'Of course I'm coping! This is my job! I know what I'm doing, Mum, and I can do without being questioned like this. Now, please, let's just get the dinner on the table.'

The meal was a trial. Keeley deliberately ate with her mouth open despite repeated requests from Jonathan and I for her to show good manners. This was something that she knew particularly annoyed Phillip, and he was getting really fed up.

'Can I eat in the kitchen, Angela?' he asked. 'I can't stand it.'

'No, why should you move? Keeley, behave yourself, for goodness' sake. You are spoiling the meal for everyone.'

'I'll leave the table then.'

'No, finish your dinner, but please eat nicely.'

She continued to shovel food into her mouth in vast quantities and then chew it slowly, with her lips open.

'I'm going!' Phillip said, and stormed out, leaving his unfinished meal on the table.

'Good!' Keeley said.

'I really think perhaps Keeley should have been the one to leave the room . . .' my mother began.

'Thelma!' Jonathan snapped irately, which was really quite unheard of in all the years we'd been together. My mother and I had had our spats, but Jonathan was typically the one who smoothed things over and tried to stop arguments escalating. 'Do you honestly think that is helpful? Do you?'

My mother's jaw dropped and Keeley started laughing.

'Yeah, shut up, Thelma!'

'Right!' I shouted. 'That's it! Keeley, finish your dinner and go straight up to your room.'

'I'm finished. Can I have pudding?'

'No, you said you didn't like the yogurt I've got.'

'I don't. I'll have ice cream though.'

She looked at me menacingly and I very nearly gave her the response I expected she wanted, which was for me to say she couldn't have any ice cream. I'd learned a lot about how Keeley's mind worked, though, and I knew this would give her the ammunition she wanted, so she could then accuse me of not only shouting at her, but refusing to give her food.

'You can have a small bowl of ice cream and then it's straight upstairs.'

My mother's jaw dropped even further, if that were possible.

'But, Angela,' she started.

'Thelma, please don't say any more,' Jonathan said

forcefully. 'With respect, Angela and I are in charge here. Please let us deal with this.'

The look on my mother's face was priceless. Written all over it was the question: 'Do you honestly think you are in charge? It doesn't look like it from where I'm sitting, giving a child ice cream after all this bad behaviour . . .' but thankfully she did as Jonathan asked, and said no more.

Jonathan and I went to bed exhausted that night.

'Thank God we've got the holiday coming up,' Jonathan said. 'We don't half need a break.'

'Are you serious?' I asked. 'Do you really think it will be a break, with the way things are?'

'Oh come on, don't be like that. A change is as good as a rest, as they say. Keeley's not bad all the time, is she? Perhaps if we get her excited about the holiday she'll behave better? It surely can't get any worse, and a bit of sea air never did anybody any harm . . .'

I looked at my husband with the utmost admiration. Somehow, he'd managed to find a glimmer of hope in what had felt like the darkest evening we'd had for a long time, and I lay in bed thinking positive thoughts about the fun we would have at the theme park, and the sun and the sand and the good times we'd have at the coast. School broke up for the summer later that week and the holiday was just two weeks off. Happiness was in touching distance; we had to keep going, because what choice did we have?

'What if she goes to live with her dad?' I murmured as I began to fall asleep.

'It won't happen that fast, if it happens at all. Let's enjoy the holiday. Maybe Keeley will leave us on a high. Wouldn't that be good?'

'Eternal optimist,' I mumbled, burying my head in the pillow.

28

'You mean you didn't read my report?'

Not long before our holiday I met Keeley's first full-time foster carer, the one she had lived with before moving in with the carer she had accused of giving her the bruise on her cheek. That investigation had been completed, incidentally, and the carer had been cleared. Sandy had passed this information on to me and that was all the detail I knew; Keeley had never mentioned it again and as far as I was aware she never knew the outcome of the investigation. I thought this was probably for the best, as who knew how Keeley would react if she felt she had been disbelieved?

Anyhow, Keeley's relationship with her original full-time carer, who was called Mandy, had been much better. Even though the placement ultimately broke down because of Keeley's bad behaviour, she had talked fondly about Mandy on several occasions.

Staying in touch with former carers is not something social workers actively encourage, but Jonathan and I have always made an effort to link the children up with their former carers where we think it's appropriate. We believe it helps foster children feel they belonged in the family, are remembered and maybe even missed, which is important to their sense of self, and in building memories and a child-hood history. The last time Keeley mentioned Mandy I casually asked if she'd like to see her again if it were possible, and she said she would love to see her, and her children.

Mandy was a mother of three, and when Keeley lived with her, which was just over a year earlier, her son Danny was about fourteen months old and her two little girls were aged five and six. It was a very lively household and Mandy stayed at home full time while her husband went out to work.

I spoke to Keeley's social worker and she readily agreed to put us in touch with Mandy, who was very happy to see Keeley again. I was pleased and relieved. In the past we'd experienced situations where children had wanted to see their former foster carers but the feeling wasn't mutual, and we had to gently explain to the kids that it wasn't possible.

Mandy and I arranged to meet in a local soft play centre, roughly halfway between our houses. Keeley was enjoying being on school holidays and was really excited, and when she spotted Mandy and the children she bounded over to them, chattering away happily and disappearing with the girls onto one of the big slides.

'That was easy!' I remarked.

'It was, wasn't it?' Mandy smiled. Her son was a toddler now and was planted on her lap, eating a Marmite sand-wich. Mandy stroked his hair and explained that she was taking a break from fostering for a while, which I assumed was because she had her hands full with her own children.

'I can't say I blame you,' I smiled. 'I think you've probably got enough to do, looking after your three!'

Mandy looked puzzled and for a second I wondered if my remark had been a bit clumsy, and that maybe she thought I was suggesting she couldn't cope, which of course wasn't what I meant at all.

'I did look after another girl after Keeley,' Mandy said apologetically, 'but it kind of put me off, to be honest, you know, what happened with her.'

She gave me what appeared to be a knowing look but I wasn't sure if she was referring to something that happened with Keeley or with the other girl she fostered. I obviously barely knew Mandy and so I didn't want to pry into something that wasn't my business.

'I'm not sure I do know . . .' I said cautiously.

At that moment Mandy's two daughters and Keeley arrived back, breathless and excited, asking if they could go on the bigger slide that you needed a rope mat for.

'Yes, if you're careful,' Mandy told her girls. 'Are you happy for Keeley to go on, Angela?'

'Yes, that's fine.'

'Yippee!' all three girls cheered. 'Can you sign the form, Mum?' Mandy's oldest daughter asked.

The rule was that an adult had to give permission for children under the age of eight to use the slide, and so Mandy had to go and provide a signature for her two girls.

She followed them to a desk near the slide, taking Danny with her, and I watched as she stood in a queue of parents.

My mind was whirring now. Had something bad happened with Keeley when she was living with Mandy, and if so why hadn't I been told about it? I knew the Social Services system well enough by now to realise that not every piece of information about a child filters through to the foster carer. Some children have files of records stretching to hundreds and hundreds of pages, and very often a social worker simply doesn't have the time to read through the full history when they take a child onto their caseload. Each social worker can be responsible for about twenty children at any one time, so reading every word written on each child is an almost impossible task. A summary or chronology would be extremely useful in each file, but this is rarely provided, again because of the time constraints on social workers.

Very occasionally I've suspected that Social Services have been deliberately selective with the information made available to foster carers, and particularly specialists like Jonathan and me. They ultimately have the best of intentions, of course, but I've wondered if they have held back on providing every scrap of information for fear of putting carers like us off, and being left with a child they cannot place. I don't blame them for this. The priority is placing the child in a foster home and the child's needs must always come first, and if a social worker can't place a child with a mainstream carer their options are already limited. There is also a school of thought that if you give the foster carer too much detail they might pre-judge what will happen when a youngster moves in, rather than discovering for themselves how to deal with a particular child. Again, I accept this is a valid reason for social workers to hold back a little when passing on a child's history because, after all, taking a child into your home is a journey of discovery and, as with any journey, it is best to embark on it with an open heart and mind.

However, we had an extremely good relationship with Sandy, and I didn't think for one minute that she would have withheld any important information from us deliberately. She'd told us all she knew about Keeley's background and the emotional abuse, and she'd gone the extra mile trying to help provide us with information about attachment disorder, hoping it might help.

Mandy reappeared, interrupting my thoughts.

'Sorry about that, Angela,' she said, taking her seat next to me while Danny trundled around pushing a plastic tractor. 'Now, where were we?'

'You were saying how you've given up fostering for the time being, because of what happened?'

'Ah, yes. I think you've been brave to take Keeley on, Angela. Have you got other foster children living with you, or children of your own?'

'Yes,' I said, knots tightening in my stomach. 'Two boys, foster children.'

'How old?'

'Teenagers.'

'OK, well I guess that's better than little ones, I suppose.

I would have thought they'd have found a single placement for a girl like Keeley though, wouldn't you?'

I realised that Mandy was talking as if she expected me to understand what she was referring to, but clearly I didn't.

'Mandy,' I said. 'I think there is something I don't know about. This thing that happened, I'm not aware of it. I wasn't even sure at first if you were talking about Keeley or the other girl you had in foster care after her.'

Mandy looked absolutely astonished.

'You mean you didn't read my report?'

'What report?'

'The very long and detailed report I provided to Social Services when I told them I could no longer look after Keeley!' she exclaimed.

Mandy ran her fingers through her short blonde hair and tears pricked her eyes.

'I put a lot of time and trouble into that report, because I felt very strongly indeed that Keeley needed to be in a single placement.'

'I'm sorry, Mandy, but this is the first I've heard about a report. Can you tell me what was in it?'

'Oh my God! I spent hours writing it up. I did such a detailed report on Keeley after she left my care! It must be buried somewhere in her file. Or maybe they didn't want you to see it. What on earth could have happened to it? I'm going to have words about this. What is it they say about foster carers being like mushrooms?'

'Pardon?' I spluttered.

I was feeling incredibly anxious now and just wanted to

know what had happened to make Mandy write a report, and ultimately step away from fostering.

'Haven't you heard that one, Angela? The saying is that foster carers are like mushrooms. Keep them in the dark and feed them shit!'

'Oh,' I said, 'yes, I think that does ring a bell. But listen, Mandy, right now I'm more concerned with what you wrote, and what went on, than what has happened to the report. Please can you tell me what the issue was when you fostered Keeley?'

'I can,' she said, biting her lip. 'But I hope you're ready for this, Angela, and I'm sorry to be the bearer of bad news.'

Before Mandy told me what the 'bad news' was I had to wait another five minutes, because Danny tripped and banged his lip on the tractor and needed a cuddle. Once he'd cheered up, Mandy then encouraged him to explore the small ball pool within sight of our table, as she clearly didn't want to have this conversation in front of him.

'Danny was just over a year old when Keeley came to live with us,' she said, watching her son intently as she spoke. 'And I think she must have been jealous of the attention he got.'

Mandy started to get upset and I handed her a napkin from the table.

'Take your time,' I said. 'I'm in no rush.'

Tears dripped from her eyes.

'Oh God, I'm sorry, Angela. I didn't expect to have to pick over all this again. I thought I'd got it all over with when I wrote the report. That's why I put so much effort into putting it all down on paper, so I didn't have to go over it ever again!'

'Shall I go and get us a cup of coffee and a biscuit?' I offered. 'Or do you just want a minute to yourself?'

'No, it's all right. I'll tell you now, before the girls come back again. Sorry.'

She dried her eyes and blew her nose.

'I don't know exactly when it started, but the thing is, Keeley began to pinch Danny, when I wasn't looking. I feel so guilty because I didn't spot it straight away. I have no idea how many times she did it, or when it actually started, but he'd had a lot of marks on him by the time I worked it out.'

'I see,' I sighed, giving Mandy a sympathetic look.

I desperately wished there was some mistake, that this could not possibly have happened, but unfortunately all I could think about was how Keeley had pinched herself and others during the time she'd been living with us. My mind flicked back to baby Jake too, Ellie's brother. Surely Keeley could not have harmed him too?

There was more than a ring of truth to what Mandy was saying, and I felt very sorry for her indeed. I can't imagine what it must have been like for her to discover her baby son had been hurt; it's every mother's nightmare to put their child in any kind of danger, particularly when they are so young and vulnerable.

'Did she hurt him?' I asked, dreading the answer. 'I mean, obviously she hurt him if she pinched him, but how bad was it?'

'It was very bad. I found him crying in his cot one day and Keeley was standing over him. Danny had a nasty big bruise on his arm and several down each leg. I started to watch him like a hawk after that. I couldn't let him out of my sight for a second when Keeley was in the house, even when Danny was asleep. It was really stressful, as I'm sure you can imagine.'

We'd looked after children of all ages in our time as foster carers, including babies and very young children, and I knew how taxing it was looking after such little ones in the best of circumstances. When the baby is sleeping it really should be a time for the parent or carer to get some rest too. Being on high alert at all times when Keeley was in the house must have been incredibly draining.

'It must have been very tough,' I said, searching for any words at all that might offer comfort. 'You must have been so upset.'

'Upset, yes, and anxious too. Honestly, Angela, if I went to the toilet I carried Danny's basket in with me, even if it meant he woke up. It was ridiculous, but I couldn't take the risk, could I? I couldn't trust Keeley at all.'

'I understand, and I'm really sorry to hear that.'

'It got worse, I'm afraid. One day we were going shopping and I put Danny in the car first, strapped in his baby seat in the front. I didn't realise it, but Keeley had already climbed into the car too. I think she must have hidden on the back seat, because I didn't see her as I strapped Danny in.'

My heart was pounding as Mandy began to tell this

story. I could already imagine several endings, none of them happy.

'I nipped back into the house and called all three girls to come and get in the car, and of course only my two appeared. When I got back to the car Danny was screaming blue murder. I must have left him for less than a minute, but Keeley had pinched his arm so hard he was bleeding, bless his little heart.'

Mandy was fighting back tears, but she went on.

'As I've said, I was so concerned about Keeley's behaviour I wrote a very long report and asked for it to be put on her file. I also made it known that I thought she should be in a single placement, so that this could absolutely not happen to anybody else.'

I thought about how Keeley had behaved towards Carl and Phillip, and the children in the neighbourhood. I have to admit my heart was always in my mouth whenever Keeley went out to play on the rec. More often than not she came home complaining about the other children's behaviour or claiming they had been nasty to her. It was the same at school. Keeley appeared to have a skin as thick as a rhino, because after repeatedly rubbing the other kids up the wrong way and causing arguments she would come out fighting every time, blaming everybody but herself when things went wrong. As Jonathan had said more than once, she was no angel.

'I'm really sorry,' I said to Mandy, 'and I'm very grateful you came today. I'm surprised you did, to be honest.'

'Well, if the truth be told I was interested to find out how you were coping. I was thinking, in the future, that maybe I'd go into specialist caring, when my kids are a lot older, of course. I miss fostering, and I'm really interested in how the mind works in a child like Keeley. That's what spurred me on to write such a long report.'

Before we parted company Mandy went on to confide in me that she had actually felt very low towards the end of Keeley's placement, which was another reason she was taking a break from fostering.

'I was worried I was getting depression,' she said. 'That really bothered me. Obviously, nobody wants to be depressed, but I was also concerned that if I ended up having to take anti-depressants I'd have to tell Social Services, and they might not let me foster anymore. I didn't feel much better after the last girl stayed with us, so in the end I thought it was better to make the decision myself to have a break and start again when the time is right.'

I told Mandy I understood how she felt. I'd been there myself once, feeling on the verge of depression. This was not because of fostering, but when bereavements in my family, many years earlier, had put me at a low ebb. I'd talked to the GP about dealing with stress, but taking anti-depressants was something I had wanted to avoid and thankfully did, for the same reason as Mandy.

I liked Mandy a lot and appreciated her honesty. In fact, even though we had only just met it felt as if I'd known her for a long time, and it was very useful and ultimately quite therapeutic for me to talk to somebody other than Jonathan who had an insight into Keeley's behaviour. I didn't think twice about sharing with her the fact I'd had low moments too, because I wanted to make her feel better and to know she was not alone. I also tried to offer some encouragement to help restore Mandy's faith in fostering, as I wanted us to part on a positive note.

'I've found a good way to engage with Keeley is through arts and crafts,' I told her. 'She really enjoys working with her hands and having one-to-one time. It seems to really help. Did you find that at all?'

'Yes,' Mandy said, adding quite bitterly: 'I wrote about that in the report too, but what a waste of time that was!'

'What were your experiences then? What worked?'

Mandy thought quite hard about this.

'We did finger painting and she loved that. It quickly progressed to whole hand painting and she made loads of pictures that we put on the walls in the kitchen and in her bedroom. I even feel bad about that though.'

'Why?'

'Well, one day she got paint on the curtains in her room because she didn't wash her hands properly as I'd asked her to. I lost my temper and went absolutely mad with her. My husband said I was way too hard, but it was very out of character, Angela. I'm normally very calm and understanding. I'm the type of person who mops up spills and gets on with it. With Keeley it was different. I wasn't myself in the end. It was definitely the right thing to end the placement.'

'It sounds like you made a good decision,' I said. 'I don't think you should feel guilty at all. You did your best, and I can see you are the sort of person who would always go the extra mile. I mean, look at you here today! Lots of people would have made excuses, but you're here.'

Mandy smiled.

'Thanks, Angela' she said. 'I'm really pleased I made the effort. It's been lovely to meet you, and I'm very glad you know about that report now. At least you have the specialist training, and you have your husband's support too. I guess that's why they've taken a chance in not putting Keeley in a single placement. I'm sure you can deal with her very well between you, despite having the boys too. It looks like you are doing a great job.'

'Thanks, and please don't worry about us, Mandy. We're doing all right and I'll be extra vigilant after today, so thanks again.'

The children had a wonderful afternoon without a single tiff, and when we finally said our goodbyes I'm happy to say that Keeley was smiling like an angel.

'You make sure you look after yourself, Angela,' Mandy said.

'I will,' I smiled confidently, because I wanted Mandy to go home feeling she had done all she could for Keeley, and for me.

When I look back now, however, I can see that Mandy was looking out for me as much as I was looking out for her. She didn't want me to go through anything like the trauma she had suffered and she was trying to protect me, because she knew exactly how tough it was to care for Keeley.

29

'Don't let her drag you down, Angela'

I called Sandy and relayed Mandy's news about the report, plus the information she'd given me about the effect Keeley's placement had on her personally. I was very calm as I spoke and I didn't show any anger or annoyance. Looking back, I was feeling worn out and really quite deflated. I didn't see the point in jumping up and down and screaming and shouting about this because what was done was done and, quite frankly, I didn't have the energy. The report was old news now, and it didn't really change anything, at least not for Jonathan and me. We asked ourselves, would we have refused to take Keeley in had we read this before? Probably not; she had nowhere else to go. Would we have changed how we cared for her? It's unlikely; we practised 'safe caring' as vigilantly as we possibly could in any case. All I asked of Sandy was that, if Keeley didn't go to live with her father, any subsequent carer be made aware of this report, a duplicate copy of which Mandy would supply if the original wasn't located by Social Services.

Sandy agreed to this. She listened very patiently as I spoke and she reassured me that she would do her best to find out what had gone wrong with the system. Some time later we discovered the report was actually in Keeley's file all along but had simply been buried among several years of notes and other documents, which didn't really surprise me. This was not the first time information had been inadvertently hidden or misplaced, and it was symptomatic of a very stretched system in which social workers were constantly overloaded with work.

'So, Angela, are you all ready for the holiday?' Sandy asked at the end of our phone call, no doubt trying to finish our conversation on a positive note.

'Not really. I've got loads to sort out. It's always a lot of hassle getting the shop staffed and taken care of, and Keeley's got her second visit with her dad to fit in, not to mention a therapy session . . .'

'It does sound like you have a lot on your plate, Angela, but it'll all be worth it in the end,' Sandy reassured. 'I'm sure you'll all have a lovely time.'

'I hope so. I really need a break. Bye, Sandy, I must dash now, got lots to do. Bye.'

My head was crammed full with mental notes. I needed to check the car insurance, pay some household bills, buy Keeley some flip-flops, pack factor 50 sunblock for Phillip, who had very sensitive skin, double check our accommodation bookings, and so on and so on. The list felt endless; I had a headache just thinking about how much I had to do before the holiday. Normally I would have completely agreed with Sandy's optimistic view that it would all be worth it in the end, but that's not how I felt. My mind kept wandering back to the stressful weekend in Wales, and I was starting to dread packing Keeley into the back of the car alongside Carl and Phillip. Would she behave herself? What if she aggravated Phillip again? I wouldn't be able to relax, and I was seriously wondering if it was worth going on holiday at all. After all, what was the point, if I'd feel frazzled and on edge the whole time?

The phone rang about half an hour after I'd ended my call with Sandy. I picked the receiver up reluctantly, thinking rather irritably, *Who's this now? As if I haven't got enough to do . . .*

'Angela, it's me again.'

'Oh, hello, Sandy. Did you forget something?'

'Not really, but I've been thinking. Would you and Jonathan like to talk to a counsellor too?'

'What for?'

'To help you deal with Keeley, perhaps unload a bit. I've been thinking about this for a while. The situation you're in with Keeley isn't ideal, having to cope with her on top of caring for the boys. I know it's not easy. We're still no closer to finding a more suitable placement, as the situation with her father is still uncertain. I know it's very tricky for you, not knowing how long Keeley may be with you . . .'

'In what way is the situation with her father uncertain?' I asked bluntly, as this seemed a much more urgent topic than whether Jonathan and I wanted to chat to a counsellor.

'Is there a problem with Keeley's dad? I thought it all sounded positive. That's the last I heard.'

'There's not a problem as such. It seems he's not averse to the idea of having Keeley live with him; in fact he's quite keen, from what I can gather. The issue is that of course it's very early days and there's a process to go through that will take time, which I'm well aware doesn't help you. In the meantime, I think you and Jonathan might benefit from some extra help.'

'Are you worried we're not coping, because honestly, Sandy, even though it's tough at times we are managing—'

'I know you are doing a very good job in the circumstances, Angela. However, there is such a thing as "transference" and I am wondering if you may be suffering from a touch of this.'

'Transference?' I stuttered, wondering what on earth Sandy was talking about. It sounded serious, if not a little sinister. 'What's that?'

Sandy explained that she'd heard about transference on a training course, and she told me in very simple terms that it meant a child like Keeley sets out to make their carer unhappy. Sandy said the youngster subconsciously thinks that if the person who is looking after them feels unhappy like they do, and shares their hurt, then somehow their own pain may be reduced.

'For example,' Sandy said, 'the way Keeley winds you up and gets you feeling cross and irritated is not about her trying to punish you gratuitously. Rather, it's possible she is trying to get you to feel how she is feeling. She wants to drag you down to her emotional state, so she has an ally, if you like.'

'I see,' I said, feeling quite shocked by this but also a little comforted. I had definitely not been feeling my usual upbeat self of late, and I could see that the holiday preparations were getting on top of me much more than they should have been.

'I think you may have a point, Sandy . . . I've never really analysed it, but this is ringing all sorts of bells in my head.'

I thought back to several incidents that had occurred recently, when I'd been much more short-tempered than I ought to have been. The time I said Keeley couldn't have a glass of milk at bedtime, after her mum's visit, loomed large in my mind. Keeley had been rude and had even insulted my mother, but it was completely unlike me to deny a child a drink like that, under any circumstances. Jonathan had also been uncharacteristically grumpy, shouting at Phillip about the mud in the hallway, I thought.

After hearing a little bit more about how the counselling would work I agreed that Jonathan and I would go along for a session together, to talk through how we were dealing with Keeley. Sandy reassured me that the session would be informal and was simply an opportunity to get things off our chest and find out more about transference and how to deal with it. Whatever we discussed would be confidential, and the fact we'd had counselling would not go against us as foster carers. One session might be all we wanted; it was up to us.

There didn't seem to be anything to lose and, very

impressively, we were swiftly offered a slot before our holiday, which tied in conveniently with Keeley's next therapy
visit.

Before that, Keeley also had another contact visit with her
dad, which she said she was really looking forward to. This
time a social worker collected her from our house, and
Keeley was ready well in advance and stood waiting in the
hallway, jumping with delight when her lift arrived. She was
all sweetness and light as she said goodbye to me and
headed to the waiting car, her favourite doll tucked sweetly
under her arm.

'Bye bye, Angela,' Keeley said in her prettiest voice. 'I'll
miss you when I'm at my dad's. So will Jinty, won't you?'

With that she lifted up one of Jinty's rag arms and gave
me a little wave.

'Oh, that's sweet of you,' I said, feeling quite touched.

'Will you miss me, Angela?' she called.

'Of course! See you later, sweetheart. Hope it goes well.'

The contact social worker smiled at us both and I stood
at the door waving them off. A feeling of wellbeing swept
over me. It meant a great deal to be treated this way by
Keeley, and I drank in the moment. I watched Keeley obediently buckling her seatbelt in the back of the car and
thought what an unexpected turn of events this was. She
looked as pretty as a picture too; her long hair was flowing
in shiny ringlets and she was positively beaming as she
looked me straight in the eye.

I grinned back, but moments later the smile froze on my

face. Keeley suddenly stretched out the corners of her mouth wide and stuck out her tongue very cheekily at me. Then, to my absolute horror, just as the car disappeared around the corner Keeley pushed her hand up to the window and stuck her middle finger up at me.

I went in the house and allowed myself a little cry. It was very upsetting to be treated like that, but once again I dug deep and made allowances for Keeley's behaviour. She is an abused child, I reminded myself sternly. *If Sandy is right, Keeley is just trying to make me feel rubbish about myself, so she is not alone in feeling that way about herself.* I was very glad I'd agreed to the counselling; I was starting to feel I would need all the help I could get to survive the holiday.

When Keeley returned from seeing her dad she was in an extremely annoying, belligerent mood.

'How was it?' I asked, having told myself to treat Keeley as I normally did, despite what she'd done earlier. My plan was to talk to her gently later, when she had settled back at our house and was hopefully in a responsive mood.

'How was what?'

'Seeing your dad.'

'What would you care?'

'I care very much.'

'You only care about how much longer you've got me here. You're worried I'll tell everyone what you're like!'

'I beg your pardon, Keeley. What are you talking about?'

'I know you don't care about me. I can tell, but I don't care. I'm going to live with my dad. He told me. SO THERE!'

Keeley pushed past me, went into the kitchen and helped herself to a chocolate biscuit.

'I'd rather you didn't eat that now,' I said.

'Why?' she said, taking a bite.

'Dinner will be ready soon, and that biscuit will spoil your meal. Plus you didn't ask me, and you know that you must ask before you help yourself to biscuits.'

'God I hate this house!' she announced, before finishing the biscuit in one bite. 'Can I ask you something, Angela?'

'Yes, of course.'

'Why are you such a boring person? And do I really have to come on holiday with you and the Invisible Man and those two dorks?'

'Keeley,' I said, taking a deep breath and thinking to myself, *Don't fall for it. Don't let her drag you down, Angela.* 'Your behaviour has upset me today. I was very sad about what you did from the window of the car, and I don't like the behaviour I'm seeing now. You're being rude and ungrateful when I know that inside you are a lovely girl. I was very proud of you when I saw you earlier today, before you went to your dad's. You looked lovely and you were very polite and a pleasure to be around when the contact worker picked you up. I think it would be so much better if you could be like that more often.'

'Why? To make your life easier?'

'No, Keeley, not to make my life easier. It would help *you*. You would be happier, I think. Nobody is happy when they are being rude and upsetting other people.'

'Well I am, and I'm very happy now I'm going to live

with my dad!' she shouted, and then she ran off to her room.

Once again I found myself stooped over my diary, writing a log. Before Jonathan and I went to our counselling session I looked back over all the notes I'd made on Keeley during her time with us, and I was shocked to see so many irritating incidents and reports of bad behaviour recorded. It had been one thing after another, and when Jonathan and I chatted about how we would handle our forthcoming meeting we found ourselves agreeing on two descriptions that we felt summed up caring for Keeley, which we would attempt to share with the counsellor.

'I know we've said it before, but I still say it's like being on a roller-coaster ride,' Jonathan said thoughtfully, 'but not a normal roller coaster; a very rocky one with lots of twists and turns and unexpected plunges into *darkness* and *despair . . .'*

'Very good,' I said, smiling, as Jonathan had finished his sentence with a slightly tongue in cheek flourish. 'Quite poetic actually, Jonathan! I'm impressed.'

'Are you taking the mickey, Angela?' he smirked. 'How would you describe it then?'

'I think I would say that the effect Keeley's behaviour has on me is like a dripping tap. Drip, drip, drip. I don't always notice it, but it's there; chipping away, wearing me down. One day, if I'm not careful, whoosh! It'll break down my defences completely and there'll be an almighty flood that washes me clean away and smashes me into the rocks!'

Jonathan laughed, but it was a bittersweet moment. We

may have gone deliberately over the top with our florid descriptions, desperate as we were for some light relief in our lives, but there was a lot of truth in what we said.

The counselling session turned out to be useful and enlightening. It took the form of a fairly relaxed and informal chat with a lady called Jackie, in which Jonathan and I shared many of the experiences we'd had with Keeley. The counsellor listened sensitively and carefully to us. Jackie didn't offer any practical advice and I knew not to expect any; I'd learned over the years, through the experiences of several children we'd looked after, that therapy is focused on talking, not action plans.

Jackie confirmed that she thought Sandy was right in suggesting we had experienced a 'touch of transference', as she put it, and she talked to us in general terms about being vigilant about our own state of mind, and continuing to talk to each other and to Sandy regularly.

'It's not uncommon for foster carers to suffer some degree of transference,' she said, 'and this isn't helped by the fact you have to keep your work confidential, as of course you can't communicate with friends or unload in the normal way that other people do about difficulties they have in their jobs.'

I agreed with this; I'm a great believer that 'a problem shared is a problem halved', but Jonathan and I had nobody to share our troubles with besides each other, plus our support social worker, who was obviously very involved herself in Keeley's case. I found it really helpful to talk to Jackie. Just having a new person listening and caring was very therapeutic, and I felt she understood and supported us. I felt more confident in our abilities, too, because Jackie said several times that we were doing all the right things with Keeley, and that our reactions were perfectly normal in the difficult circumstances.

The counsellor smiled when we told her the analogies we'd come up with involving the rocky roller coaster and the dripping tap, and she suggested one of her own after we told her about the recurring problems we'd had with Keeley sharing the bathroom with the boys, for example, and refusing to take regular showers.

'It's very irritating because even if I feel I've made progress and got through to her one day, the next we're always back to square one,' I lamented. 'The bathroom is a regular battleground.'

'Yes, it sounds like *Groundhog Day*,' Jackie replied, and we smiled wearily and agreed that it was a pity this was real life and not a film, or we might find that comparison very funny.

Jackie went on to provide us with some rather dense information about transference, which was slightly different to how Sandy had described it. Jackie explained that it wasn't as simple as Keeley trying to get us to feel just as bad as she did, to dilute her pain, so to speak. She said that transference was a bit more complicated than that, and that it also occurs when a person takes the perceptions and expectations he or she has of one person, often from childhood experience, and projects these onto another person.

'For example,' Jackie explained, 'a child who is lucky enough to come from a happy home may view their foster carer as an idealised version of their mother or father. They feel safe and protected when in care, as they transfer how they feel, or felt, about their natural parents onto their foster carers. However, the opposite may also be true. In Keeley's case, it's likely she was expecting to be treated badly by you and Jonathan, as she wasn't treated well at home. Potentially, she then transferred her expectations of a mother or father figure onto you and Jonathan, and then carried on behaving as she did at home, as she knew no different.'

'So are you saying this is subconscious, not deliberate?' I asked, trying to get my head around it all.

'Absolutely. Keeley's current behaviour is a reaction to her past, and she's heavily influenced by what happened to her as a younger child. Imagine she has one very definite blueprint of a mother figure in her head, based on her natural mother, and she simply can't shift from that. She sees you, Angela, in exactly the same way as she saw her natural mother in the past, when she was being emotionally and physically abused. She had to fight back then, and she was deeply unhappy. Now she's replaced you with her mother in her mind, so you are on the receiving end of her difficult behaviour, even though you don't deserve to be, and despite the fact you treat her very differently to how her mother did.'

This was all quite mind-blowing to me back then, and not easy to get my head around. As I've said before, Jonathan and I had done our fair share of being amateur psychologists over the years, but this was extremely interesting news to us. We found it fascinating, slightly alarming but also strangely reassuring. After all, I'd spent months telling myself that Keeley needed careful handling, and that it wasn't her fault she behaved the way she did. Until this point I was basing my reaction to Keeley on the little I knew about the emotional, physical and possible sexual abuse she had suffered in the past. My default position was simply to think 'she can't help it', but I had barely scratched the surface of understanding exactly why. Now I felt I had some professional psychology backing up how I was handling her, and this spurred me on.

Today, transference is more commonly known as secondary trauma, compassion fatigue or sometimes vicarious trauma. When it's talked about in fostering circles it now generally refers to the carers and how they start to take on the childrens' problems as their own and get ground down as a result, although Jackie's descriptions are still valid.

In hindsight I can confidently say that this had happened to Jonathan and I, to a degree, when caring for Keeley. We really weren't ourselves, the longer the placement went on. We'd lost some of our natural humour and had become quite careworn and unsettled; in other words, Keeley's discontent had certainly rubbed off on us. Seeing the counsellor helped us recognise that, and quite possibly stopped us from slipping further into total burnout.

30

'Let's all try to get along and enjoy the holiday'

My mum had volunteered to stay in our house while we were on holiday, and she was going to lend a hand to the assistant we had managing the shop. Despite living close by, Mum arrived with a large suitcase and a cool box of food she'd brought from her fridge, which she explained would otherwise have gone to waste.

'Well, I feel as if I'm on my holidays too!' she announced cheerfully, clearly enjoying the change of scene and the sense of purpose she felt. She'd been talking enthusiastically for several days now about some of the 'little jobs' she wanted to do in the shop while we were away, like revamping the window display and decluttering some of the storage areas. It was heartening to see her like this, as it was how I remembered her when she and my father ran the shop, and I was a little girl. Both my parents were extremely hard working and threw themselves into building up the florists into a very successful enterprise. I was very glad I'd had the chance to take the business on and continue the family tradition. My dad would have been very proud to see us all today, I thought, with the shop still thriving and my mum still involved and enjoying herself like this.

I looked at my mum with pride and admiration, but as I did so I caught Keeley giving her a sceptical, sideways glance. My pulse quickened a little, as I wondered what Keeley was going to say or do next. I really didn't want her to poke fun at my mum for arriving with her suitcase and the cool box, or being so excited about helping us out while we were on holiday. I'd seen Keeley giving sideways looks like this before, though, and they often preceded a sly comment, rude remark or cheeky dig.

'That's really funny!' Keeley giggled.

'What's funny?' I asked nervously.

'Your mum, of course, saying this is like going on her holidays! You're funny, Thelma! I'm going to miss you.'

Keeley said this with meaning, and I immediately felt ashamed of myself for doubting her. She was genuinely quite tickled by my mum's comment and was being very sweet and endearing. Mum, of course, lapped it up.

'What a lovely thing to say, Keeley. I'll miss you too. Ten whole days! Goodness me, you are very lucky to be having such a lovely long holiday.'

Keeley sat herself down beside my mum at the kitchen table, clasped her hands primly in front of her as if she had something serious to say, and looked Mum in the eye.

'I know,' she said. 'I've never had a proper holiday. My mum never has any money for holidays. She isn't like Angela. She hasn't got a shop or anything.'

I flicked my mum a knowing look, to remind her not to be drawn into a conversation about Keeley's mother; I certainly didn't want a reportable incident of any kind at this point in time.

'No, dear, oh well, dear,' my mum said, clearly now a little flummoxed.

'It's OK,' Keeley said. 'I don't mind talking about my mum. She's a really good mum. She's letting me go on holiday and she could have said no, couldn't she? And she told me she's happy about me seeing my dad again. I think that's good, because she *hates* my dad.'

'She hates your dad, does she?' I interrupted, as I didn't feel it was fair, or sensible, to leave my mother navigating this conversation on her own for any longer. This was the first I'd heard about how Tina may have felt about Keeley's dad, though, and I didn't want to close down the conversation completely. I would never do that, as these moments can be very important to a child in helping them work through issues from the past. Keeley seemed to be in the mood to talk, and so I stopped what I was doing and sat at the table with her and my mum, hoping to make it easier for her to carry on.

'Yes. She hates him. She used to tell me he was a pig. When we went to the zoo together, Mum pointed to a big fat pig and said it looked like my dad. He's nice, though, and he's not fat. It was just my mum being silly! Oh well! Angela, will we see any animals on holiday?'

'There's a small zoo at the theme park,' I said. 'I think

they have monkeys, plus rabbits and giant guinea pigs you can pet, and all sorts of reptiles.'

'Do they have pigs though?'

'I'm not sure.'

'Oh. It sounds good, though. I hope there's a gift shop.'

With that, Keeley gave me a smile and then skipped out of the kitchen, saying she was going to put some colouring books in her backpack for the car journey. 'I'm packing pens,' she said. 'I want to send Ellie a postcard.'

'Isn't she a funny little girl?' Mum said kindly, as Keeley disappeared up the stairs, 'such a sweet little thing.'

'Yes, she has her moments,' I grinned.

Obviously, my mum knew that Keeley had some serious issues from the past, but she was quite rightly judging Keeley as she was that day: a delightful, albeit idiosyncratic, eight-year-old girl. I took note. Mum hadn't been affected by Keeley's behaviour in the way I had, and she was displaying a normal, generous response to her. *That's how I need to be again*, I thought, and I found myself praying that Keeley's good mood would spread into the holiday.

As usual I jotted down some notes as soon as I had the chance. I had no idea if Keeley's chatter about the pig or her mother's supposed hatred of her dad had any relevance, but I took note of her comments nonetheless, because it wasn't up to me to decide what was and wasn't potentially important. Keeley had said very little about her father, and as he was now very much in the spotlight I thought I'd be as cautious as possible and jot down as much as I could whenever she mentioned him.

*

Sandy had explained to me a day or two earlier that assessments were now being carried out on Keeley's father, to see if he was suitable to take her in. This involved background checks and police checks to make sure he had no criminal record or other black marks against his name. Tina had been informed that her ex-partner was potentially going to have Keeley living with him, and that Joan was in charge of checking his suitability and his accommodation, as he would need to have a spare room that was suitable for Keeley. If everything was in order, Keeley would be allowed to go for weekend visits after the holiday, with a view to moving in in the near future. The full care order she was under would be changed, and contact with Tina would be reorganised to fit in with Keeley's new circumstances.

Keeley had been made aware that Social Services were looking into the possibility she could live with her dad, although exactly how much detail Joan had gone into I didn't know. This was not unusual; carers like us would only be kept informed of the details that were relevant to us, on a need to know basis. This mean that we'd be told the dates of Keeley's weekend visits with her father, and a potential moving out date, but probably little else. Our opinion about the move wasn't sought at all; what we thought of the plans wasn't relevant. Our job was simply to look after Keeley while she was in our care, and provide Social Services with any information we considered might be important to have placed on Keeley's file.

After Sandy had given me the latest update, Jonathan

had asked me how I felt about Keeley potentially moving in with her dad.

'On paper it couldn't be better, could it?' I said tentatively. 'After all, it's not sustainable having her here with the boys, and what could be better than going to her dad's, especially as he has no other children.'

'Exactly,' Jonathan replied. 'So why the hesitation in your voice?'

'I just don't know. I think I'm worried about him being on his own with Keeley. I know he's her dad, but it could be very tough for him. I know I couldn't do it on my own.'

Jonathan hugged me.

'It's typical of you to think of others,' he said. 'Lots of people would be critical of Keeley's dad for being off the scene for so long, but here you are worrying about him and his wellbeing, and not focusing on yourself at all.'

I smiled, grateful for the compliment.

'Don't worry about what you can't control, Angela. You are doing all you can for Keeley. Let's just try and give her and the boys a really good holiday. That's our job for now, and that's what we need to focus on.'

The long journey to the theme park, our first destination, was dreadful. After being extremely helpful with the packing, waving angelically to my mother and buckling herself into the back of the car as I'd asked her to, Keeley's mood soon changed. We were just a few miles from home when it happened, and hadn't even reached the motorway.

'Oi!' Phillip said. 'Don't do that, Keeley!'

'What?'

'You know what!'

'What?'

'DIGGING ME IN THE RIBS.'

'Never did. Liar!'

'Jesus Christ!'

'Phillip!' I implored. 'Don't use language like that. Keeley, what is going on?'

'Nothing.'

'Then why is Phillip complaining that you are digging him in the ribs?'

'Because Phillip is a wanker,' she said pointedly, over enunciating the word wanker.

'Right, Keeley, that is enough. I don't want to hear another word from you until I say so, do you understand?'

'How am I supposed to answer you, Angela, if I can't talk?'

'Keeley!' Jonathan snapped. 'For heaven's sake, please don't use bad language, don't be rude to Angela and please don't cause any trouble. Let's all try to get along and enjoy the holiday.'

She frowned and tut-tutted and stared out of the window, studiously ignoring Jonathan, while Phillip began to shake his head in disbelief.

'I said Jesus Christ and she said wanker and we both got the same telling off! How does that work?'

Carl started sniggering.

'*Let's all try to get along and enjoy the holiday*,' Jonathan repeated.

Phillip huffed and put his head in his hands while Carl began fumbling in his bag for a book, which was his way of disengaging from the conflict.

I detected a note of desperation in Jonathan's voice; we still had hours of driving ahead of us and this did not bode well. Jonathan and I looked at each other and I imagined a shared thought bubble appearing between us. The words 'groundhog day' loomed large inside the bubble; we'd seen it all before, with Keeley aggravating Phillip, and it was all happening again, as if on a repeat loop.

We were staying in a hotel near the theme park, and then carrying on to a mobile home on a campsite on the south coast. After we'd had about twenty minutes of peace and quiet in the car, Phillip asked me about the sleeping arrangements at the hotel.

'We have a family apartment,' I explained. 'Everybody has their own room, but all inside the same apartment.'

'Are there locks on the doors?' Phillip asked. 'Only I don't want *her* coming in, pestering the hell out of me.'

The next moment he let out an almighty shriek, which made me jump. Jonathan gripped the wheel tightly, exclaiming: 'What on earth!'

I turned round to see Keeley giving me a really sarcastic grin, and Phillip was clutching his side.

'What's happened now?' I asked.

Keeley mouthed something to me silently.

'Keeley, what are you doing?'

She made the same silent mouth movements while

Phillip said, 'The silly cow is jabbing me in the ribs again, Angela.'

'You are allowed to talk now, Keeley,' I said, remembering I'd told her to not say another word until I said so, 'so please tell me what is going on back there.'

'Nothing!' she yelled indignantly. 'If you hadn't stopped me talking none of this would have happened.'

'None of what?'

'Nothing!'

'I give up!' Phillip said, exasperated. 'I just give up. Can't Carl sit in the middle instead of me?'

Jonathan and I decided this was a good idea, and we pulled into the next motorway services so that everybody could go to the toilet, and then Carl would sit between Phillip and Keeley. This seemed like a sensible plan, but Keeley used the stop as an opportunity to wreak yet more havoc. She pointedly refused to buckle her seatbelt again once we were all back in the car, and when Jonathan refused to move until she had done so we ended up in a very frustrating stalemate situation.

'Keeley, I can't drive the car until you have your seatbelt on.'

'See if I care.'

'Well I think you will care, when we are still sitting here instead of being in our hotel, having fun.'

'I don't. I never wanted to come on holiday with you anyway. I told you that, didn't I? I'd rather be at my dad's.'

'Can't you just take her to her dad's?' Phillip said. 'That would do us all a favour.'

'Shut it, wanker. You're just jealous because I'm going to live with my dad and you're not.'

Phillip unbuckled his seatbelt, flung open the car door and stomped out onto the forecourt of the motorway services. I saw him take a deep breath and clench his fists. He looked fit to punch something, or somebody. Jonathan got out and went to talk to him, while I tried another tactic.

'Look, Keeley, I know you don't really mean to upset anyone, but that is what you're doing. I don't want to get cross with you. I don't want to shout or tell you off or anything else. I would much rather we all got along and enjoyed the holiday, as Jonathan said. Please can you stop upsetting Phillip, because you are ruining things for everyone.'

'You're weird, Angela, do you know that?'

'Why are you saying that?'

'Because most people would smack me and tell me I was being a little bitch, but you are being all nice to me. I don't get it. What are you up to? Are you messing with me?'

'Most people wouldn't smack you or call you a name like that, Keeley. It's not the right way for anyone to behave, is it?'

'My mum knew what was what! She wouldn't have put up with this! She'd have smacked my bare arse! So would my granddad. But you're useless!'

I could scarcely believe my ears. Keeley was telling me off for not physically or verbally abusing her. That was what she had grown up with, and that was what she expected of me, as her carer. It was all very upsetting and confusing. I thought about the whole transference business, and realised this was probably what was going on here. Keeley was projecting her extremely low expectations of care onto me, and when I wasn't playing ball she was upping her game, to try to get me to fit into the blueprint she had in her head of a mother figure. I didn't really know what to do next; it was a mind game too far.

Thankfully, Jonathan returned to the car and intervened. He called Phillip over to hear his plan.

'I've got a good idea,' he said. 'How about, if we can all get along on this car journey, I'll treat everyone to some extra pocket money for the holiday?'

It was shameless bribery but we were desperate and I didn't blame him at all; in fact, I was relieved he said this. Each summer Social Services gave us an extra allowance, which could go towards a holiday away or for activities during the holidays. The amount of money involved didn't come close to covering our costs, but it was welcome, all the same, and we always found a way of passing it on as directly as we could to the children. Jonathan and I had already agreed between us that we were going to give the extra money to the kids, for their spending money. This was the time to do it, and it worked, thank God. Hardly surprisingly, all three kids readily agreed to Jonathan's deal. Carl said a very polite thank you and sounded very grateful while Keeley and Phillip huffily accepted the bargain, while also making it clear they still weren't happy.

'I hate this seatbelt,' Keeley grumbled as we had another attempt at setting off. 'That's what caused the trouble. It was too tight, that's how I came to knock into Phillip before.'

'So you admit you did hit me?'

'No, I didn't say that, idiot!'

'THAT IS ENOUGH!' Jonathan said. 'Keeley, buckle yourself in, please, and let's get going.'

'No.'

'Then we can't go anywhere.'

'Good. I don't want to go on holiday with you losers!'

'For the love of God . . .' Jonathan said, gripping the steering wheel hard.

'What do you propose then, Keeley? Shall I turn the car around?'

'What would you do that for?'

'What do you think?'

'To get rid of me?'

'I don't want to get rid of you!'

'All right then, I'll put my seatbelt on.'

'Good. Let's go.'

Phillip groaned, but thankfully the rest of the journey went by without another row. The atmosphere was tense, but at least the peace was kept. That was about the best I could hope for, in the circumstances.

31

'Help! You need to pull over, right now'

'This is boring,' Keeley said.

We were standing in a long queue for a water ride, and the waiting time was about half an hour.

'It'll be worth it,' I said. 'I've been on a ride exactly like this before. It's really good fun.'

'It better be.'

I tried to ignore this. Jonathan and I had agreed that we would start the day with this ride, which everybody could do together, and then we would split up into different groups as the day went on, depending on which rides people wanted to go on. Keeley wasn't tall enough for several of the big attractions, and Carl wasn't keen on the fastest and scariest rides, so we'd just have to work out what was best for everyone as we went along.

'I don't want to wait any longer,' Keeley whinged. 'Can't we leave the boys here and do something else, Angela?'

'No. We're here now. Let's do this ride and then we can decide what to do next.'

The sun was beating down and Keeley then began to complain about the heat.

'You'll soon cool down when we're on the ride,' Jonathan said.

'How? It's all outside.'

'Because you have to get out of the boat and swim the last bit, and the water's quite chilly. Freezing cold, actually. You did bring your swimsuit, didn't you?'

Carl laughed, immediately realising Jonathan was making this up, but Keeley wasn't so quick to cotton on.

'I'm not swimming in that shitty water!' she shouted.

'Keeley! Language, please,' Jonathan said. 'I'm only joking.'

Carl laughed again, but I could see he was looking embarrassed too, as the people in front of us in the queue turned around.

'Call that a joke, do you, Jonathan?' Keeley said cheekily.

'Look, Keeley,' I soothed. 'You can't use bad language like that. Please stop trying to annoy people. You have to have a bit of patience in a theme park, but it'll all be worth it.'

She huffed and went to stand next to Phillip, who was quietly minding his own business. He'd brought his iPod with him, which was his pride and joy as he'd received it as a gift from his mother, and he had his earphones in and was listening to music.

'What are you listening to?' Keeley asked, jabbing her finger into his arm to get his attention.

Phillip frowned, took out one earphone and said, 'What?'

'What are you listening to?'

'Music.'

He put the earphone back in and turned away from Keeley.

'Shall we have a look at the map?' I suggested, trying to distract her.

'OK,' she said. 'I want to go on the shooting range and to the zoo.'

'Shooting range?'

'Yes. Look, I saw it on the way in. You get to fire a rifle. Bang, bang, BANG!'

Jonathan winced. 'Sounds a bit violent!' he said.

'We're in a theme park,' she mocked. 'I'm not going to really kill anyone. You just have to hit the tin cans.'

I wasn't sure how suitable this was for an eight-year-old girl, and I thought back to the time she became very animated at the mocked-up sword fight we saw in Wales, when she had chanted 'KILL, KILL, KILL' from the audience. I kept my thoughts to myself, though. Having Keeley start a row in this queue was really not something I wanted.

'What do you want to go on, Angela?' she asked.

'Well, I fancy the swing boat, the carousel and perhaps we could see what's on in that 3D cinema show.'

'Yippee!' Keeley said, giving me an exaggerated smile. 'I want to go on exactly the same things as you, Angela, so we can leave the boys, can't we?'

'I like the 3D cinema too,' Jonathan said, which Keeley ignored.

'I wonder if they'll be showing the *Invisible Man* . . . ?' Jonathan then winked at me.

'Or *Groundhog Day*?' I quipped, out of Keeley's earshot.

The water ride was good fun in the end, but the rest of the day turned into what felt like a tightrope walk for Jonathan and me. We found ourselves watching everything we said, wary that if we veered off course in any way then we may have a heavy price to pay, as Keeley seemed constantly on the verge of kicking off and causing trouble.

We reluctantly let her have a go at shooting after she nagged us relentlessly, and said the day would be ruined if she couldn't do it.

'Done this before, little lady?' the Stetson-clad stallholder asked.

'No, but I know what I'm doing.'

'Right, hit three cans and you get a prize.'

'Get out of my way or I'll blow your balls off!' she replied.

The stallholder was over six foot tall and looked as hard as nails. His mouth fell open but no words came out, and then he jokingly pinned himself as far out of Keeley's firing range as possible. It's comical in hindsight, but at the time I wanted the ground to swallow me up.

'Sorry,' I said to the man. 'Keeley, what have I told you about watching your language?'

'Shut BANG up BANG shut BANG up,' she muttered, as she took her turn, hitting three cans right on target and toppling an entire display.

She chose a large purple and yellow dinosaur as her prize, which Jonathan ended up lugging around for the rest of the day. By the time we turned in for the night I felt completely shattered.

Jonathan and I snatched a bit of time alone together once all three children were in their beds, and we reflected on the day. We'd had some fun moments and some touching ones too. We both agreed that Keeley was adorable in the children's petting area in the zoo, for instance, where she sat transfixed for ages, stroking the rabbits and guinea pigs before admiring the lizards and terrapins in the reptile house.

'This is amazing,' she'd said, wide-eyed. 'It would be good to live in a zoo, wouldn't it? You wouldn't have to go to school or follow any rules. You could sleep when you wanted to and just wee in the corner without going to the toilet!'

'Yes, and you wouldn't need a shower!' Carl teased.

We had all laughed conspiratorially, and even Phillip saw the funny side. Enjoying moments like that made all the effort Jonathan and I were putting in worth it; smiling faces were our reward.

The second leg of our trip started very successfully. Keeley loved the mobile home and put her new dinosaur on her pillow next to Jinty. We decided to hire bikes to use around the site and the local area, and Keeley, who turned out to be a confident cyclist, was very excited when we set out for the first time.

'Where are we going?'

'Not sure, just exploring the campsite,' I told her.

'Ooh, an adventure!'

'Exactly!'

'Fasten your helmet on and we'll get going.'

'Do I have to?'

'Yes,' I said, 'we all have to wear a helmet.'

I was stealing myself for an argument, but Keeley dutifully clipped her helmet on. 'Ready!' she called.

The boys led the way and we had a very pleasant ride around the site and down a cycle track that took us to a local lake. It was idyllic, and we stopped for ice creams and sat by the lake for a while, where the boys and Jonathan skipped stones and Keeley hunted for bugs.

'There you go,' I heard her say, after she'd found some crickets. 'That's better.'

'What are you doing, love?' I asked.

'Burying the crickets, because they are dead.'

'How did they die?'

'I don't know. Just died.'

I'd seen Keeley catching live crickets, and I think she must have crushed them, hopefully by accident.

'Have you found anything else?'

'Yes. A ladybird. Dead too.'

With that she lifted her right foot and then slammed it down onto a rock beside her.

'What was that?' I asked, jumping up from my seat on another rock nearby.

'Ants. Naughty ants. You can go in the insect grave too.'

I distracted Keeley with talk of what we would do later that day, having decided there was nothing to be gained from tackling her about this rather disturbing game now. Instead, I made a note of this little episode in my diary later.

We went on to have a really lovely break, going on lots more bike rides, swimming in the campsite pool, playing table tennis, visiting some local attractions and having some good barbecues in the evenings, sitting around outside our mobile home and meeting a few other holidaymakers. However, there were four other incidents that marred the holiday.

The first happened after Keeley developed an irritating cough. It didn't shift for a couple of days, and so in the end I bought her some cough medicine in the local chemist, which I gave to her straight afterwards when we all sat in a cafe over the road. Keeley took the two spoonfuls of medicine off me without a fuss, but then she held it in her mouth, unable to swallow it.

'Just gulp it down,' one of the boys said, 'that's always the best way.'

She shook her head and looked around with her cheeks puffed out, as if searching for a place to spit it out.

I was about to tell her she should just drink it quickly and not spit it out, when an awful thought invaded my head. On a training course once, I was told to be very mindful of forcing children who had been abused to swallow anything they didn't want to. Some had been forced to drink alcohol, nasty concoctions of drinks and medicines or even chemicals by their abusers. Others, who had been sexually abused, had memories and fears that made them freak out whenever unpleasant liquids were put in their mouth.

Keeley then went as white as a sheet, made a dash for the door and spat the green liquid all over the steps of the cafe. I chased after her and cleaned her and the steps up as best I could with a fistful of paper napkins.

'Are you all right?'

Keeley looked straight through me, and she didn't say another word for quite some time.

'You can talk to me whenever you want, about whatever you want,' I said protectively.

'Thanks,' she said, but we never discussed this scene again, and I noted the details in my log with a heavy heart.

The next incident was caused by sheer bad luck. On our last day we all went for a long bike ride, and the boys raced on ahead. Keeley tried to keep up with them and pushed forwards too, turning a corner moments before Jonathan and I, who were bringing up the rear. We caught up with the boys very shortly afterwards, spotting them whizzing along on a straight stretch of the path beyond a fork in the cycle track. Keeley, however, was nowhere to be seen, and we immediately realised she must have taken the other side of the fork by mistake.

'Wait a minute, boys!' I called, as Jonathan did a U-turn and pedalled off to catch up with Keeley.

He found her sobbing her heart out on the side of the track.

'Keeley!' he called. 'We're all back this way! Are you all right?'

She couldn't speak she was so upset. Tears were crashing down her cheeks and she was coughing and spluttering as she gasped for breath. Jonathan pushed the two bikes back, asking Keeley to hold on tight to her bike, so she felt safe again, but didn't have to hold his hand.

'What happened?' Carl asked. 'Did you fall off?'

Keeley blanked him.

'She just went the wrong way,' Jonathan said. 'Easily done.'

Phillip snorted a little unkindly, which prompted Keeley to give him an evil stare.

'I'll get you,' she said.

Thankfully, Keeley cheered up quite quickly, and we rounded off the holiday with a visit to a pretty local village, where the three kids spent their pocket money. Keeley bought a postcard for Ellie and some colouring books and fancy pens, and the boys got a T-shirt each, and some fudge, which they both loved and shared around.

Jonathan and I gave each other a satisfied smile as we prepared to drive away from the campsite on the last morning of our holiday. We'd had some heart-in-the-mouth moments, which didn't surprise us, but we felt we'd done what we'd set out to do. The children had all had a really good break. We'd explored new parts of the country, had some laughs and enjoyed plenty of fresh air, exercise and good food.

'Well done,' he said to me, giving me a kiss and a hug, and not realising the kids were watching.

'Urgh!' Keeley said. 'You're disgusting!'

Everybody laughed.

'Sorry!' I shrugged. 'Now, come on, everybody in the car. Keeley, do you think you could sit in the middle seat?'

'Why?'

'Because it's the narrowest and you are the smallest. We seem to have a few more belongings than when we set out, and we're a bit tight for space.'

'No. I want to sit by the window.'

'Please, Keeley,' I implored. 'It would be very helpful. It's no big deal, is it?'

'No fucking way!' she shouted, and then ran off towards the centre of the holiday park.

Jonathan and I watched her for as long as we could before we worried we'd lose sight of her. She stopped about fifty metres away, turned around and put up her middle finger.

'Wankers!' she shouted. 'You're all wankers, and you're a cunt!'

This reaction was so extreme I couldn't help thinking that Keeley might have suffered an unpleasant experience in a car in the past, or perhaps she simply had an issue being in such close proximity to the two boys, given that her grandfather may have sexually abused her. Jonathan and I had already been talking about getting a seven-seater car, and now we both agreed this should be a priority. It would make life so much easier for everybody and we would also be able to take my mum with us on trips, which would be a bonus.

I assumed Keeley's last foul-mouthed insult was thrown at me and I blanched. At that moment a young family appeared from down the side of one of the other mobile homes, and the parents looked at Keeley and then directly at me. I don't mind admitting I was so shocked and embarrassed that, in the heat of the moment, I tried to pretend Keeley wasn't with us.

'Honestly!' I muttered, giving a forlorn look designed to say, 'Who on earth is that girl, behaving like that?'

The family shuffled on, and I watched as Keeley sat down cross-legged on the side of the path, as if she were staging a sit-in protest. Jonathan eventually talked her round, unfortunately resorting to yet more bribery after first telling her off for her bad language and display of temper.

'I'm upset you have behaved like this, Keeley,' he said calmly but forcefully. 'It's not nice to see you like this, all miserable and being rude. I much prefer the happy Keeley we've seen on this holiday, don't you?'

She said nothing.

'I tell you what, if you sit in the middle seat of the car now, I will let you choose the music we have on,' he said. 'I know the middle seat is a bit cramped, but somebody has to sit there, or how would we go on holiday?'

She nodded silently, walked to the car and buckled herself into the middle seat. Then she demanded that Jonathan play her favourite songs from Beyoncé, Jamelia and Busted. Phillip plugged himself into his iPod again, and Carl shut his eyes, leaned on a rolled up sweatshirt that he placed against the window, and tried to go to sleep. Despite the tense atmosphere, we drove on peacefully for most of the rest of the trip. I don't think anybody felt like speaking; the boys had looked quite stunned at Keeley's latest outburst, and they both stayed very quiet and didn't make a single comment on the music, which we knew was not to their taste at all.

On the very last leg of our journey, Keeley complained she was bored and then started nudging Phillip and asking him to turn his iPod down.

'I can hear it through your earphones,' she complained.

'Then you must have bionic ears,' he said loudly, 'the volume's on low.'

'I can hear it!' she wailed. 'It's so annoying! Your music is so shit as well.'

Phillip then did something he really shouldn't have. He turned the volume up as loud as possible, which was like a red rag to a bull.

Keeley was enraged and tried to grab Phillip's iPod off him.

'Get off, you nutter!' he said.

'Stop it,' I said, turning in my seat. 'Please stop it! It's very distracting to Jonathan and we're on the motorway . . .'

My plea was ignored and drowned out by the ongoing argument.

'Worried I'll break it?' she said, snatching the iPod with both hands, which wrenched the earplugs from Phillip's ears.

'Give it to me!'

'Your mum gave you this, didn't she?'

'JUST GIVE IT TO ME!'

'Your mum hates you! You have to stay with Angela because your mum hates you! All your mum does is buy you rubbish presents. My dad isn't like that!'

'KEELEY!' I shouted. 'Stop it this minute!'

'Fuck you all, wankers. I'm going to live with my dad! I'm going to live with my dad!'

With that Keeley threw the iPod in Phillip's face, and he retaliated by landing a very hard punch square on her nose. She shrieked hysterically, and then blood dripped down onto her T-shirt. I cried, 'Oh my God!' in shock and even Carl started to panic, wailing, 'Stop the car, Jonathan! She's bleeding! Help! You need to pull over, right now.'

This very unfortunate event marked the beginning of the end of Keeley's placement with us. She was left with a black eye and a sore nose that day, but I felt strongly that we had all had a lucky escape – Keeley included.

It's a great pity she got hurt, but at least some good did come from the situation. We had reached crisis point and, though we didn't know it at that moment, at last life was going to improve for everybody.

When we got home I immediately phoned Sandy to report exactly what had happened. She listened carefully, taking notes, and telling me she would place this on Keeley's file and inform Joan and Phillip's social worker straight away. Then she said, 'Angela, I have some very timely news.'

'What is it?'

'The assessments on Keeley's dad have all been carried out and everything is in order, and proving very straightforward. There is no reason Keeley can't go and live with him, if she wants to. We just have a few formalities to complete in terms of the paperwork, that's all. It could be sorted out in a matter of weeks. All we really need to do is make sure Keeley is happy and arrange some weekend visits so they can make sure they both want to go ahead.'

I breathed a deep sigh of relief.

'I know Keeley does want to live with her dad,' I said, 'and I know she'll tell her social worker the same. She has talked about her dad a lot, and I am sure this is what she wants. This is terrific news, Sandy. I can't tell you how happy I am for her, and for the boys.'

'And I'm happy for you, Angela,' Sandy said.

'Me?'

'Yes, you and Jonathan. You have been very patient with Keeley. Without you she would have certainly ended up in a special unit; there is still no single placement available anywhere in the vicinity. I'm very glad that you can now focus on the boys again, without all the added stress you've had to deal with. Thank you for everything you have done. You have been patience personified. Keeley is a lucky girl.'

I was very pleased, and extremely relieved, to hear Sandy say this. I'd been dreading calling her to tell her about the punch, for fear of what she might think of me and Jonathan. We had had to stop at KFC for a bag of ice on the way home, and Keeley had sat with it pressed to her nose for the remainder of the car journey.

All the way home I thought what a dreadful mess we were all in, and what a failure I felt as a foster carer.

'What will Social Services say, do you think?' I'd hissed to Jonathan when we stopped at the services. 'I mean, what foster carers take the children on holiday and have one of them punching seven bells out of the other? And how many eight-year-old girls are punched on the nose like that?'

'Angela, you and I both know that this is not our fault and it is no reflection of our capabilities as foster carers. Granted, it is not a good situation to be in and I would certainly rather not be in it, but what have we done wrong? Nothing. Absolutely nothing. We've been telling Social Services for ages that Keeley needs to be looked after as the only child in a placement, and we've persevered against the odds. We've bent over backwards trying to give all the kids the best holiday we possibly could, but we are not magicians. We're honest, hard-working foster carers, trying our very best in extremely difficult circumstances.'

Jonathan spoke with passion and authority, and I looked at him with admiration. I knew he was right, deep down, but I didn't allow myself to fully believe his wise words until I spoke to Sandy, and heard her offering support and praise too.

It took just over a month for Keeley to move in with her dad. She went to him for three weekend visits beforehand, all organised by a social worker who arranged for Keeley to be picked up and returned to us by car. It was a blessed relief when she was out of the house, because her behaviour had become even more unbearable when she was with us.

Sorting out the paperwork before handing it back to Social Services, I was reminded of a catalogue of incidents we coped with in those latter weeks. Among my notes were the following entries:

> Keeley spat on Phillip's cutlery at the dinner table . . .
> Keeley called the lads dickheads and bastards . . .
> Took Keeley to apologise to the neighbours for
> pulling up their flowers . . . Keeley punched a boy in
> the stomach at break time . . . Called up to school
> again; Keeley put another girl's PE kit down the toilet
> . . . Keeley stuck two fingers up at my mother . . .
> Found large lumps of Keeley's hair blocking up the
> washbasin . . . Keeley told me I was a sad old woman
> and she could not wait to get away from me . . .
> Keeley chalked on the back seat of the car . . . Keeley
> cut holes in some of her dresses.

As I read them I thought about some of the good things that had happened too, most of which I'd also noted down, to show the positive progress she was making. Keeley had learned how to make fairy cakes, which she really enjoyed, and she decorated them beautifully with icing and edible silver baubles. She told me I was kind for teaching her to bake, and one morning she got up early and made me breakfast, to say thank you. She knew she wasn't allowed to use the kettle or any other appliances unless I was in the kitchen to supervise her, so she made me a large glass of cold milk and a jam sandwich on thick white that was plastered with butter. I was on a diet, as I often was, and this was not my ideal breakfast, but Keeley looked so thrilled with herself for making it for me that I ate and drank the lot. Seeing her smile when I did so was priceless. She didn't smile nearly as much as she should have done, so I cherished those happy moments, and I will never forget them.

Unfortunately, the hours immediately before and after seeing her dad were particular trouble spots at our house. Keeley became cocky and boastful in advance of each visit, often rubbing Phillip's nose in the fact she was seeing her father and was due to move in with him, while he was 'stuck in foster care, like a sad loser'. Afterwards, she delighted in telling me how everything was so much better at her dad's house. 'He's got a bigger telly. My dad's a better cook than you, Angela! He makes nice chips. My dad is funny. My dad could beat up any other dad in the world! My dad has loads of coke and crisps for me to have!'

However, when Keeley spent time with her friend Ellie, she never failed to behave impeccably. The two girls sang and looked like little angels when they took part in the musical theatre show they had rehearsed hard for, and Ellie's mum, Hazel, put her hand on mine as we sat beside each other, clapping and waving as the final curtain dropped.

'Angela, I don't know how you do it,' she said. 'I would be

in pieces doing your job. How are you going to cope, saying goodbye to Keeley?'

Hazel, like every other person in my life bar Jonathan and the social workers, was in the dark about the finer details of our life as foster carers. All she knew was that I often had children coming and going, and that Keeley was due to move in with her dad and change to a school near his home very soon. The bruising on Keeley's face after the punch had healed very quickly, though Hazel had seen her when she still had a trace of a black eye.

'Oh dear, what happened?' she had asked.

'In the wars on holiday,' I'd said vaguely, while thinking to myself: *Hazel, you really would not believe your ears if I told you the full story.*

I told her that I would miss Keeley, of course, but that I was happy to see her go, as she was moving in with her father, which was the truth. 'I can only be happy for the kids when they are returned to their family,' I said. 'It's all about them, not me. I get my reward from seeing their life improve.' Incidentally, I made a point of asking after Jake regularly, and I had no further worries that Keeley may have pinched him or harmed him in any way on the day she visited their house and he was out of sorts. Hazel always reported that he loved having the girls fussing over him, which of course I was very relieved about. You can never jump to conclusions as a foster carer, and this was a good reminder of this rule. Instead you must approach each day with an open mind and never, ever make judgements that are based on opinion rather than fact.

*

I helped Keeley pack her belongings before her move, and she told me she couldn't wait to leave.

'It would have been good if it was just me and you, Angela,' she said wistfully, 'but the boys spoilt everything. Boys! I hate boys.'

'I hope you're very happy living with your dad,' I said.

'Thanks, Angela. I know I will be. He loves me. He told me.'

My heart swelled. I'd suspected it for a long time, but now I felt certain I had worked out what really made Keeley tick. It wasn't spite and aggression, and she didn't want to make other people angry or upset. She just wanted to be loved, but she simply didn't know how to go about it. Her mother hadn't shown her the love she should have done, and the results were catastrophic for Keeley.

'I'm very pleased for you, Keeley,' I said. 'I really hope it all works out.'

'It will. He's really cool, like you!'

I thought I'd misheard for a moment, and then Keeley reached in her bag and gave me a very neat and detailed picture she had drawn on a blank page in one of her colouring books. It showed the two of us together, holding hands, and she had written on the top:

To Angela, thank you for being the kindest person in the world, and thank you for having me.
Hugs and kisses and lots of love, Keeley XXX

Epilogue

Keeley refused to say a proper goodbye to Jonathan or the boys and, after waving her off for the last time outside our house, I didn't hear anything about her for more than ten years. Then, out of the blue, a social worker I knew very well mentioned to me that she had heard on the grapevine that Keeley had finally spoken to the police about her grandfather, Eric, accusing him of raping her from the age of four to six.

My heart bled for Keeley. She'd had an unbelievably rough start in life, and it was no wonder she was such a disturbed little girl. The social worker told me that Keeley still lived in the region, but that she had no details about her life now, or the outcome of her case.

I hoped to goodness that Keeley got the justice she deserved, but I resigned myself to the fact I might never know what became of her. Most of the foster children we are still in touch with left our care as teenagers, but with Keeley being just eight years old when she moved out the contact had been long since lost, despite the fact Jonathan and I had told Keeley's father that we were happy to stay in touch if he or she wanted to.

Then last year we found out more, after Jonathan and I unexpectedly bumped into Keeley at a pub on the outskirts of town, where we were attending a family birthday party. Keeley was sitting at a table outside along with her mum and a man we didn't know. I spotted Tina first, as she'd hardly changed a bit. She was still platinum blonde and was wearing bright clothing and talking very loudly on a mobile phone.

'Oh, hello!' I said, glancing first at Tina and then looking directly at Keeley, who still had a mane of black curls and looked very beautiful, dressed in pretty clothes and wearing immaculate make-up. I was taken aback for a moment; had we not walked right in front of their table I'm not sure I would have made myself known like this at all.

'Angela?' Keeley said slowly, her eyes widening.

'Yes, and do you remember Jonathan?'

He smiled and said hello, and Keeley stood up, gasped and put her hands over her mouth.

'Oh my God! I was such a little madam when I lived with you! Oh my God!'

She looked at her mum, but Tina indicated that she couldn't end her call and stepped away from the table, cackling at something she'd heard on the phone.

The man got to his feet, and Keeley politely introduced him.

'Dad, I lived with Angela and Jonathan for a bit before you moved back.'

'Frankie,' he said, bobbing his head and offering his hand. 'Pleased to meet you. Thanks for all you did.'

I was surprised to see that Keeley's dad was very slightly built and could not have been more than about five foot four or five. In my mind's eye he was a big, strapping man, and I realised later why this was the case. I remembered Keeley writing about him in her literacy book at school, and describing him as very tall, muscular and strong. I could see where Keeley got her looks from now, though: Frankie appeared to be of Spanish or Italian descent with thick, black hair, and Keeley's deep brown eyes were perfect copies of his.

'Very pleased to meet you, Frankie,' I smiled. 'It's a long time ago now. You must be, what, nineteen, Keeley? How have you been?'

'Nineteen, yes. You've got a good memory! I'm very good, thanks, Angela. Still living with Dad. Had a few boy-friends but it always goes wrong! Mum lives round the corner; she's all right, I guess. You know what she's like. Life's good for me though. I'm at college now. I started a bit late with one thing and another, but I'm doing art and drama and loving it. How about you?'

I told her that we were still fostering, which she was amazed at.

'I thought I'd have put you off,' she joked.

'No,' I said, 'not at all. It's really lovely to see you.'

'It's lovely to see you too. What happened to the two boys? Poor lads, I think I terrorised them!'

'Both doing well, both in touch. Carl's happily married to a local girl, Phillip's moved away, working for a construction firm. We have reunions from time to time, if you ever fancy joining us.'

'Are you sure I'd be welcome?'

'Keeley, you would be most welcome. We've never forgotten you.'

'I'm not surprised to hear that,' her dad quipped, and she slapped him on the back and started to laugh.

'He loves me really, don't you, Dad?'

'I do, as a matter of fact, Keeley. You're the best daughter anyone could wish for.' With that he gave her a big cuddle and she hugged him back lovingly.

I wrote down our phone number and handed it to Keeley. In return she gave me her email address so I could let her know about the next reunion, and then we said our goodbyes. One day I hope she will take us up on our invitation, and that we can catch up properly.

Jonathan and I were so pleased to have bumped into her. This was a tiny snapshot into Keeley's life, but it was a very positive and reassuring one. It was clear that she was loved by her father, and it was heart-warming to see her enjoying what she had craved for so many years. Love was all Keeley needed, and all she every really wanted was to be loved. I hope she finds a lot more love in her life ahead.

Other stories from foster mum Angela Hart ...

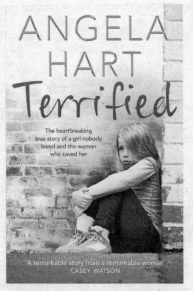

Terrified

The heartbreaking true story of a girl nobody loved and the woman who saved her

Available now in paperback and ebook

Vicky stared through the windscreen, her eyeballs glazed like marbles. She was sitting completely rigid in her seat, frozen with fear.

I took a deep breath and then asked Vicky, as gently as possible, if she was all right. 'I'm here, right beside you, Vicky. Can you hear me? I'm here and I can help you. Take a deep breath, love. That's what I've just done. Just breathe and try to calm yourself down. You're with me, Angela, and you're safe.'

Vicky seemed all self-assurance and swagger when she came to live with Angela and Jonathan as a temporary foster placement. As Vicky's mask of bravado began to slip, she was overtaken with episodes of complete terror. Will the trust and love Angela and her husband Jonathan provide enable Vicky to finally overcome her shocking past?

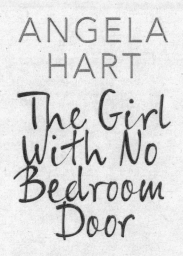

ANGELA
HART

The Girl
With No
Bedroom
Door

'I hope Angela Hart inspires many others to foster'
TOREY HAYDEN

A true short story

Available now in ebook

Fourteen-year-old Louise has been sleeping rough after running away from her previous foster home. Unloved and unwashed, she arrives at foster carer Angela Hart's door stripped of all self-esteem. Can Angela's love and care help Louise blossom into a confident and happy young woman?